ANCIENT GREEK LAWS

In this comprehensive and accessible sourcebook, Dr Arnaoutoglou presents a collection of ancient Greek laws, which are situated in their legal and historical contexts and are elucidated with relevant selections from Greek literature and epigraphical testimonies. A wide area of legislative activity in major and minor Greek city-states, ranging from Delphoi and Athens in mainland Greece, to Gortyn in Crete, Olbia in S. Russia and Aegean cities including Ephesos, Samos and Thasos, is covered. Dr Arnaoutoglou divides legislation into three main areas:

- the household – marriage, divorce, inheritance, adoption, sexual offences and personal status
- the marketplace – trade, finance, sale, coinage and leases
- the state – constitution, legislative process, public duties, colonies, building activities, naval forces, penal regulations, religion, politics and interstate affairs

Dr Arnaoutoglou explores the significance of legislation in ancient Greece, the differences and similarities between ancient Greek legislation and legislators and their modern counterparts and also provides fresh translations of the legal documents themselves.

Dr Ilias Arnaoutoglou graduated from the School of Law, Aristotelian University of Thessalonike, Greece and completed a PhD in Classics at the University of Glasgow. He is currently Assistant Editor for the *Lexicon of Greek Personal Names*.

ANCIENT GREEK LAWS

A Sourcebook

Ilias Arnaoutoglou

London and New York

First published 1998
by Routledge
11 New Fetter Lane, London EC4P 4EE

Transferred to Digital Printing 2003

Simultaneously published in the USA and Canada
by Routledge
29 West 35th Street, New York, NY 10001

Typeset in Garamond 3 by Keystroke, Jacaranda Lodge,
Wolverhampton

British Library Cataloguing in Publication Data
A catalogue record for this book is available from the British Library

Library of Congress Cataloging in Publication Data
A catalog record for this book has been requested

ISBN 0–415–14984–3 (hbk)
0–415–14985–1 (pbk)

CONTENTS

CONTENTS

CONTENTS

CONTENTS

Building

Naval affairs

Inter-*polis* relations

Religion and *polis*

PREFACE

The study of ancient Greek laws seems to have flourished in the last decade or so in Britain. Athenian law has taken the lion's share in this revival, due partly to the increased interest in oratory. Consequently works of reference tend to concentrate on Athenian law and legal system.[1] In spite of this interest, there is no collection of legal sources of the Greek *poleis* (the Athenian *polis* included) though only some texts have appeared in collections about the history of the Greek *poleis*.[2] The need for a sourcebook on ancient Greek laws is illustrated by the almost century-old *Recueil des Inscriptions Juridiques Grecques*, which remains, despite its age, a remarkably complete survey of Greek laws. Its structure (laws and decrees, contracts, court decisions) covers the whole spectrum of legal life. A revision of the magisterial work of B. Haussoullier, R. Dareste and Th. Reinach lies beyond the scope of the present work. This collection aims to open the normative world of the ancient Greek *poleis* to students (undergraduate and postgraduate) of ancient history and at the same time to present a concise picture of legislation in ancient Greek *poleis*, with all its shortcomings from the viewpoint of a modern reader.

The book is divided into three chapters each dealing with statutes regulating relations generated in different parts of a Greek *polis*.

---

1 The most recent contribution is that of Todd (1993).
2 See *Nomima* and the posthumously published collection of R. Koerner, *Inschriftliche Gesetzestexte der frühen griechischen Polis*, Köln 1993 (Akten der Gesellschaft für griechische und hellenistische Rechtsgeschichte 9) for archaic Greece; M-L for classical Greece; for Hellenistic Greece, L. Moretti (ed.) (1967–76) *Iscrizioni storiche ellenistiche*, 2 vols, Florence, M.M. Austin (1981) *The Hellenistic world from Alexander to the Roman conquest. A selection of ancient sources in translation*, Cambridge, and R. Bagnall and P. Derow (1981) *Greek historical documents: the Hellenistic period* (Sources for Biblical study 16).

The first chapter includes laws pertaining to relations created and regulated in the context of the household (*oikos*), such as inheritance, divorce, marriage, adoption, sexual offences, status of the person. The second part covers laws concerning the interaction of individuals in the marketplace (*agora*), regulatory frames and restrictions imposed on their activity (trade, coinage, sale). The third chapter accounts for the relationships among citizens as members of the community, of the *polis*. This chapter is the longest because the range of the legislative intervention of the *polis* was quite large. Different subjects such as awarding public honours to war dead, safeguarding of the constitution (*politeia*), legislating process, cleanliness of public spaces, judicial procedures, action against behaviour undermining social stability (male prostitution, theft, *hybris*), colonization, property and debts are included.

The spatial division into *oikos*, *agora* and *polis* is problematic and wholly practical. The fluidity and the overlap of concepts like *oikos*, *agora* and *polis* can be illustrated in the following cases. A slave was sold and bought in the market, therefore one would assume that he or she should be treated as an object, part of the *agora*. At the same time, slaves were a part of the *oikos* into which they were bought, and they had some rights (see *oikeis* in Gortyn no. 16). Another example presented here is the law for the protection of olive trees; besides a superficial economic relevance, there are other cultural and religious factors involved. Olive oil (and olive trees) were essential for the performance of certain rituals in the *gymnasion* and the *palaistra*. The reference to texts of similar themes such as tyranny can inform about development of institutional responses in the course of time and space.

One of the criteria of selection is that the text should be a decision of a *polis* (or of some other state formation like *koina*, *amphiktyonies*, confederations,[3] Epirot and Macedonian kingdoms). Decisions of civic subdivisions such as demes, *phratries*, or cult or professional associations are not presented here. The decision should sanction a rule of impersonal character and regulate an aspect of human activity; on the basis of the above definition honorary decrees are excluded. This decision should be accompanied by an enforcement clause, of civil or religious character. The distinction developed in Athens

---

3 For the laws of the Boiotian League see P. Roesch (1982) *Études Béotiennes*, 262, Paris. For other federal states see J.A.O. Larsen (1968) *Greek federal states: their institutions and history*, Oxford.

between decrees as decisions of the assembly of the citizens after consideration in the Council and laws as decisions of the assembly after deliberation at the committee of officials called *nomothetai* (legislators) and at the Council in the late 5th century and early 4th century BC may not be as fruitful as it seems. First of all, we do not know to what extent, if at all, this distinction existed in other Greek *poleis*. In some cases decrees may well contain rules similar to those included in laws and therefore I have chosen to include some decrees into the collection (decree from Zelea no. 92), and a ruling (*diagramma*) of the Macedonian kings (no. 111). Decisions of *polis* for leasing public property are included because they set out rules for the administration of property, irrespective of the individual lessee.

Both epigraphical and literary evidence are used in this collection and both might pose problems for the student. Literary evidence usually favours the elite of the *polis* because lawcourts were one of the arenas of the competition of members of the elite for offices. Lawcourt speeches, then, preserve to a large extent the ideology, interests, values and ambitions of these individuals. However, the speeches are equally problematic since their transmission is not free of error (or misunderstanding or corruption).[4] The epigraphical record does not necessarily include all the laws of any *polis*. At the same time, epigraphical evidence is biased in the sense that it preserves material thought worth inscribing in a piecemeal way, usually obeying criteria other than the full publication of the laws, such as monumental impressiveness and conferral of divine protection. In archaic times especially, it was thought that inscribing a law on a stone would make the law enjoy the same respect as the rules of customary law.[5] Moreover, in some cases and for most *poleis* outside Athens, inscriptions are our only source of information. I have decided to translate reasonably safe restorations, leaving aside bigger gaps marked as [. . .] . I tried to translate as accurately as possible without ignoring style.[6]

---

4 I used quite freely references to Plato's *Laws*. This does not mean that these regulations were applied; they are a source for comparative study, since in some cases they reflect Athenian legal practices.

5 For a discussion of the criteria for inscribing a law see R. Thomas, 'Written in stone? Liberty, equality, orality, and the codification of law' in Foxhall and Lewis (1996: 9–32).

6 Further information on bibliography and general and specific problems of ancient Greek laws can be found in: lemmata in *L'Année Philologique*, *Bulletin Épigraphique* (BE) published annually in the *Revue des Études Grecques* (REG);

Categories of material for which there are already particular collections, such as sacral legislation[7] and interstate agreements have not been systematically included.[8] Evidence from papyri have not been covered since there is already a collection of texts with juristic interest[9] as well as a collection of all the legal pronouncements of the Ptolemies,[10] admittedly without English translation. However, I have decided to include three interstate agreements which pertain to the attribution of equal rights to citizens of another *polis* (*isopoliteia* no. 104), to the unification of two *poleis* (*sympoliteia* no. 105) and to bilateral judicial agreements (*symbola* no. 106). The reason for the inclusion of these texts is that they do not only affect existing rights and duties of citizens but they also regulate crucial aspects of the citizens' activity outside their original *polis*.

Ancient Greek *poleis* were not only political but also religious communities. The religious aspect of the *polis* is too predominant to be ignored. Therefore I decided to include four texts illustrating this side of the *polis*' normative activity; one concerns arranging sacrifices (no. 108), one deals with the sale of priesthood of a deity by the *polis* (no. 107) and two regulate funerals and mourning (nos. 109, 110). Something has to be said at this point about the two texts preserving the public imprecations from Teos (known also as *dirae Teiae*). Public imprecations were not unknown in other Greek *poleis*; in certain cases laws contained such clauses next to 'secular' penalties. The structure of these texts resembles closely that of other laws; their difference (and interest) lies in the sanction imposed. It is not a fine, exile, confiscation or death penalty but the invocation of divine powers to punish the offender.

new epigraphical material and lemmata in *SEG*, review of inscriptions regarding sacral laws published in *Kernos*, periodical reviews of bibliography in *Revue d'Histoire du Droit Français et Étranger (RHD)*, *IURA*, *Archiv für Papyrusforschung (AfP)*; the bibliographies of (i) G.M. Calhoun and C. Delamere (1927) *A working bibliography of Greek law*, Cambridge, Mass.; (ii) G. Sautel (1963) *Introduction bibliographique à l'histoire du droit et à l'ethnologie juridique: A/7 Grèce*, Brussels (Centre d'Histoire et d'Ethnologie Juridiques) and (iii) the *Annual Bibliography* of the Centre de Documentation des Droits Antiques, Paris; the essay of S. Todd and P. Millett (1990) 'Law, society and Athens' in *Nomos*, 1–18.

7 For which see the three volumes of F. Sokolowski, *Lois sacrées des cités grecques, Lois sacrées des cités grecques. Supplément*, and *Lois sacrées d'Asie Mineure*.

8 See the collection of documents in *Staatsvertrage*.

9 See L. Mitteis and U. Wilcken (eds) (1912) *Grundzuge und Chrestomathie der Papyruskunde*, 2 vols, Leipzig.

10 See M.-Th. Lenger (ed.) (1990) *Corpus des Ordonnances des Ptolémées*, 2nd edn, Brussels.

The chronological range of material spans a period from the end of the 6th century BC (some Gortynian texts) to the Roman conquest. However, I included a decree issued well into the Roman period (no. 49) in order to demonstrate that the imposition of the Roman political and legal order did not mean the annihilation of the Greek *polis*, as some scholars have suggested. The new political organization certainly restrained the political status of the *polis*, but *poleis* retained substantial autonomy.

I deliberately preferred not to give prominence to Athenian material in favour of less known, mainly epigraphical, material from other Greek *poleis*. The Athenian material is easily accessible in various collections; in the *IG* series there are already three editions of inscriptions from Athens and one should add to that the inscriptions published in *The Athenian Agora* series and the volumes of *Hesperia*. There is one more reason for not giving prominent position to texts from Athens. Most scholars agree that Athens was an atypical *polis* in terms of size, population and institutional development. A case for the institutions of a 'typical' *polis* may emerge from this collection of legal texts. This does not mean, however, that all or even most of the *poleis* are represented. Information about legal institutions outside Athens depends wholly on the survival of inscriptions and on undertaking organized excavations. Discussions about ancient Greek law are dominated by the Athenian example, perhaps rightly so since it is widely documented both in inscriptions and in literature. In some cases I chose to provide Athenian texts side by side with texts from other *poleis* in thematic units such as cleanliness, coinage, constitution, inheritance, marriage, sexual offences, etc. The purpose of this arrangement is to illustrate the differences and similarities among the legislation of different *poleis*.

Each text is preceded by a brief introduction, where the context of the law and the source is explained. Footnotes are used for clarifying particular points of the text and comments; when terms appear in more than one text (marked with an asterisk) they are explained in the glossary, which can be found at the end of the book. The translated text is followed by a paragraph (**relevant texts**) where texts with a similar theme from different *poleis* (such as contracts, agreements, court decisions) are cited. Reference to parallel cases is not meant to be exhaustive but is illustrative of the existing material. The last paragraph of each entry (**further reading**) contains the most recent bibliography (English and international); I tried to collect references mainly from the 1980s and 1990s (to the end of 1996) without neglecting earlier contributions of paramount importance.

In cases where several texts refer to the same topic there will be a single paragraph on **relevant texts** and **further reading**, the reason being to avoid unnecessary repetition of references and relevant texts.

I am indebted to several people who read (and some re-read) sections of the sourcebook; in particular to S.C. Todd, P. Cartledge, O. van Nijf, D. Yiatromanolakis, R.C.H. Catling, P.M. Fraser, M. Hatzopoulos and, above all, to Professor D.M. MacDowell, who encouraged me and helped in many ways in the undertaking of this work.

ABBREVIATIONS

Abbreviations for classical authors follow the conventions of *LSJ*. Journals are abbreviated following the conventions of *L'Année Philologique* and epigraphical collections according to *Guide de l'épigraphiste*.

Ancient Macedonia II = 'Ancient Macedonia II. Papers read at the second international symposium held in Thessalonike' (19–24 August 1973) Thessalonike 1977 (Institute for Balkan Studies 155).

BGU = *Ägyptische Urkunden aus den königlichen (staatlichen) Museen zu Berlin, Griechische Urkunden*, 1895– , Berlin.

Choix = J. Pouilloux (ed.) *Choix d'inscriptions grecques*, 1960, Paris.

CID = G. Rougemont (ed.) *Corpus des Inscriptions de Delphes. Lois sacrées et règlements religieux*, 1977, Paris.

CIRB = V.V. Struve *et al.* (eds) *Corpus Inscriptionum Regni Bosporani*, 1965, Moscow.

Delphinion = A. Rehm (ed.) *Das Delphinion in Milet*, 1914, Berlin.

Epigraphica = R. Bogaert (ed.) *Epigraphica. Texts on bankers, banking and credit in the Greek world*, 1976, Leiden (Studia Minora).

FD = Th. Homolle *et al.*, *Fouilles de Delphes*, 1909– , Paris.

FXanthos = P. Demargne *et al.*, *Fouilles de Xanthos*, 1958, Paris.

Gofas, *Meletai* = D. Gofas, *Meletai archaiou ellenikou dikaiou ton synallagon*, 1993, Athens (Bibliotheke tes en Athenais Archaiologikes Etairias 133).

IAdramyt = J. Stauber (ed.) *Die Bucht von Adramytteion*, 2 vols, 1996, Bonn (IK 50–1).

IC = M. Guarducci (ed.) *Inscriptiones Creticae*, 4 vols, 1935–50, Roma.

ICos = M. Segre (ed.) *Iscrizioni di Cos*, 1993, Roma.

ID = A. Plassart *et al.* (eds) *Inscriptions de Delos*, 7 vols, 1926–72, Paris.

IEph = R. Merkelbach *et al.* (eds) *Die Inschriften von Ephesos*, 7 vols, 1979–81, Bonn (IK 11–17).

IErythrai = H. Engelmann and R. Merkelbach (eds) *Die Inschriften von Erythrai und Klazomenai*, 2 vols, 1973, Bonn (IK 1–2).

IG = *Inscriptiones Graecae*, 1873– , Berlin.

IGB = G. Mihailov (ed.) *Inscriptiones Graecae in Bulgaria repertae*, 5 vols, 1958–70, Sofia.

IIasos = W. Blümel (ed.) *Die Inschriften von Iasos*, 2 vols, 1985, Bonn (IK 28).

IIlion = P. Frisch (ed.) *Die Inschriften von Ilion*, 1975, Bonn (IK 3).

IIznik = S. Sahin (ed.) *Katalog der antiken Inschriften des Museums von Iznik (Nikaia)*, 2 vols, 1987, Bonn (IK 9–10).

IKalchedon = F.K. Dorner and S. Sahin (eds) *Die Inschriften von Kalchedon*, 1980, Bonn (IK 20).

IKyme = H. Engelmann (ed.) *Die Inschriften von Kyme*, 1976, Bonn (IK 5).

ILabraunda = J. Crampa (ed.) *Labraunda. Swedish excavations and researches. The Greek inscriptions*, 2 vols, 1969–72, Lund.

ILamps = P. Frisch (ed.) *Die Inschriften von Lampsakos*, 1978, Bonn (IK 6).

ILindos = Chr. Blinkenberg (ed.) *Lindos II. Inscriptions*, 2 vols, 1941, Copenhagen.

IMM = O. Kern (ed.) *Die Inschriften von Magnesia am Maeander*, 1900, Berlin.

IMyl = W. Blumel (ed.) *Die Inschriften von Mylasa*, 2 vols, 1987, Bonn (IK 34–5).

IOSPE = B. Latyshev (ed.) *Inscriptiones antiquae Orae Septentrionalis Ponti Euxini graecae et latinae*, 3 vols, 1885–1901, Saint Petersburg.

IPArk = G. Thür and H. Taeuber (1993) *Inschriften der griechischen Poleis I. Arkadien* (IPArk), Wien (Sitzungsberichte der österreichische Akademie der Wissenschaften, Philol-Hist. Klasse 607).

IPriene = F. Hiller von Gaertringen (ed.) *Inschriften von Priene*, 1906, Berlin.

ISamothrace = P.M. Fraser (ed.) *Samothrace. The inscriptions on stone*, 1960, New York.

ISestos = J. Krauss (ed.) *Die Inschriften von Sestos und des thrakisches Chersones*, 1980, Bonn (IK 19).

La loi gymnasiarchique = Ph. Gauthier and M.B. Hatzopoulos (1993) *La loi gymnasiarchique de Beroia*, Athens (Meletemata 16).

L'émprunt = L. Migeotte (1984) (ed.) *L'émprunt public dans les cités grecques. Recueil des documents et analyse critique*, Paris.

LSAG = L.H. Jeffery, *The local scripts of archaic Greece. A study of the origin of the Greek alphabet and its development from the eighth to the fifth centuries BC*, 2nd edn, with a supplement by A.W. Johnston, 1990, London.

LSAM = F. Sokolowski (ed.) *Lois sacrées de l'Asie Mineure*, 1955, Paris.

LSCG = F. Sokolowski (ed.) *Lois sacrées des cités grecques*, 1969, Paris.

LSCG Suppl. = F. Sokolowski (ed.) *Lois sacrées des cités grecques. Supplément*, 1962, Paris.

M–L² = R. Meiggs and D. Lewis (eds) *A selection of Greek historical inscriptions*, 1989, 2nd edn, Oxford.

Nomima = H. van Effenterre and F. Ruze (eds) *Nomima. Recueil d'inscriptions politiques et juridiques de l'archaisme grec*, 2 vols, 1994, Roma (Collection de l'École Française de Rome 188).

Nomos = P.C. Millett, P.A. Cartledge and S.C. Todd (eds) *Nomos. Essays in Athenian law, politics and society*, 1990, Cambridge.

Nouveau Choix = Institut Fernand-Courby, *Nouveau choix d'inscriptions grecques*, 1971, Paris.

OGIS = W. Dittenberger (ed.) *Orientis Graeci Inscriptiones Selectae*, 2 vols, 1903–5, Leipzig.

Paton–Hicks = W.R. Paton and E.L. Hicks (eds) *The inscriptions of Cos*, 1891, Oxford.

PHal = *Dikaiomata: Auszuge aus alexandrinischen Gesetzen und Verordnungen in einem Papyrus des Philologischen Seminars der Universitat Halle mit einem Anhang weiterer Papyri derselben Sammlung*, 1913, Berlin.

RIJG = R. Dareste, B. Haussoullier, Th. Reinach (eds) *Recueil des inscriptions juridiques greques*, 2 vols, 1894–1904, Paris.

Ruschenbusch = E. Ruschenbusch, *Solonos Nomoi. Die Fragmente des solonischen Gesetzeswerkes mit einer Text- und Überlieferungsgeschichte*, 1966, Wiesbaden (Historia Einzelschriften 9).

Schwyzer = E. Schwyzer (ed.) *Dialectorum Graecarum exempla epigraphica potiora*, 1923, 3rd edn, Leipzig.

SEG = *Supplementum Epigraphicum Graecum*, vols 1–42, Amsterdam.

SGDI = H. Collitz and F. Bechtel (eds) *Sammlung der griechischen Dialekt-Inschriften*, 5 vols, 1884–1915, Leipzig.

Staatsvertrage = H. Bengtson and H. Schmitt (eds) *Die Staatsvertrage des Altertums*, 2 vols, 1962–9, München.

Syll³ = W. Dittenberger (ed.) *Sylloge Inscriptionum Graecarum*, 4 vols, 3rd edn, 1915–24, Leipzig.

Symposion 1971 = H.J. Wolff (ed.) *Symposion 1971. Vortrage zur griechischen und hellenistischen Rechtsgeschichte*, 1975, Köln (Akten der Gesellschaft für griechische und hellenistische Rechtsgeschichte – 1).

Symposion 1974 = A. Biscardi (ed.) *Symposion 1974. Vortrage zur griechischen und hellenistischen Rechtsgeschichte,* 1979, Köln (Akten der Gesellschaft für griechische und hellenistische Rechtsgeschichte – 2).

Symposion 1977 = J. Modrzejewski and D. Liebs (eds) *Symposion 1977. Vortrage zur griechischen und hellenistischen Rechtsgeschichte,* 1982, Köln (Akten der Gesellschaft für griechische und hellenistische Rechtsgeschichte – 3).

Symposion 1979 = P. Dimakis (ed.) *Symposion 1979. Vortrage zur griechischen und hellenistischen Rechtsgeschichte,* 1982, Köln (Akten der Gesellschaft für griechische und hellenistische Rechtsgeschichte – 4).

Symposion 1982 = F.J. Fernandez Nieto (ed.) *Symposion 1982. Vortrage zur griechischen und hellenistischen Rechtsgeschichte,* 1989, Köln (Akten der Gesellschaft für griechische und hellenistische Rechtsgeschichte – 5).

Symposion 1985 = G. Thür (ed.) *Symposion 1985. Vortrage zur griechischen und hellenistischen Rechtsgeschichte,* 1989, Köln (Akten der Gesellschaft für griechische und hellenistische Rechtsgeschichte – 6).

Symposion 1988 = G. Nenci and G. Thür (eds) *Symposion 1988. Vortrage zur griechischen und hellenistischen Rechtsgeschichte,* 1990, Köln (Akten der Gesellschaft für griechische und hellenistische Rechtsgeschichte – 7).

Symposion 1990 = M. Gagarin (ed.) *Symposion 1990. Vortrage zur griechischen und hellenistischen Rechtsgeschichte,* 1991, Köln (Akten der Gesellschaft für griechische und hellenistische Rechtsgeschichte – 8).

Symposion 1993 = G. Thür (ed.) *Symposion 1993. Vortrage zur griechischen und hellenistischen Rechtsgeschichte,* 1994, Köln (Akten der Gesellschaft für griechische und hellenistische Rechtsgeschichte – 10).

Tod = M.N. Tod (ed.) *A selection of Greek historical inscriptions,* 2 vols, 1933–48, Oxford.

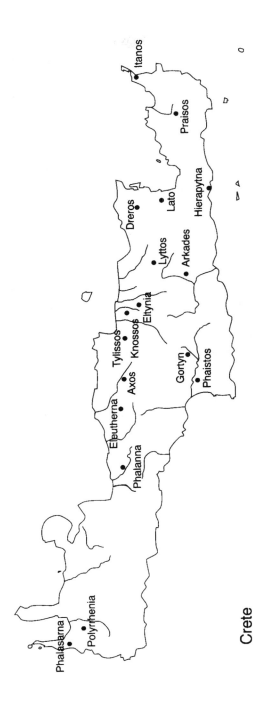

Crete

Mainland Greece

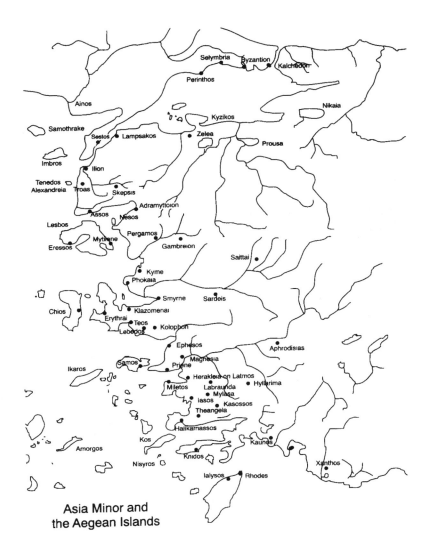

Asia Minor and
the Aegean Islands

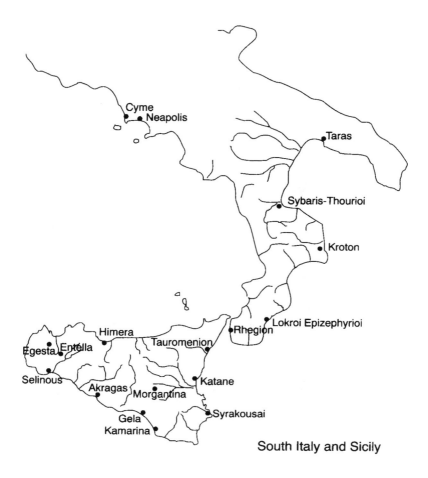

South Italy and Sicily

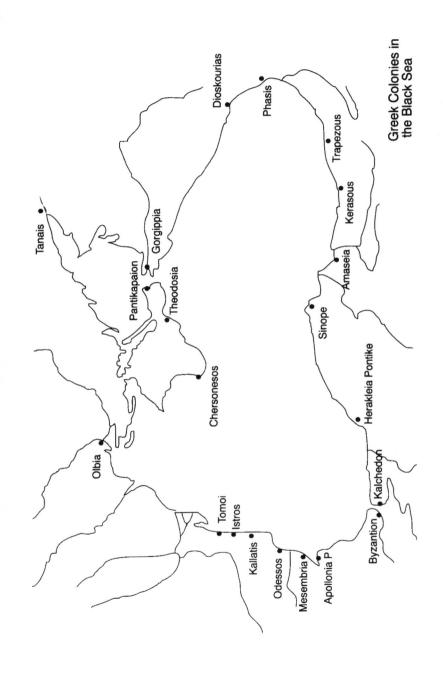

Greek Colonies in
the Black Sea

Tanais

Gorgippia

Dioskourias

Phasis

Pantikapaion

Theodosia

Trapezous

Kerasous

Chersonesos

Amaseia

Sinope

Olbia

Herakleia Pontike

Tomoi
Istros

Kallatis

Odessos

Mesembria

Apollonia P

Kalchedon

Byzantion

1

OIKOS

INHERITANCE

1 Athens, Law on wills

{Demosthenes} xlvi (Against Stephanos II) 14
early 6th century BC

The law on wills is mentioned in the context of a long-standing dispute between Appollondoros[1] and Phormion over the administration of the paternal property of the former. Appollodoros, having lost a suit against Phormion (see Dem. xxxvi), prosecuted Stephanos, a witness for Phormion in the first trial, for false testimony. At this point Appollodoros claims that his father had never drafted a valid testament and cites the law on the requirements for a valid will.

Anyone, apart from those who had been adopted when Solon (*c.* 594 BC) entered upon his office, and had thereby become unable either to renounce or to claim an inheritance,[2] shall have the right to dispose of his own property by will as he wishes, if he has no legitimate, male children, unless his mind is impaired by lunacy or old age or drugs or disease, or unless he is under the influence of a woman or under constraint or has been deprived of his liberty.

---

1 For Appollondoros' career and personality see J. Trevett (1990) *Appollodoros, the son of Pasion*, Oxford.
2 The restriction was necessary since adopted children could not dispose of property of their adopter.

Relevant texts

Athens: law on testaments, Hyp. iii 17, [Dem.] xliv 68, Is. ii 13, iii 68, iv 14, 16 and vi 9, Isocr. xix 49–50; Solonian origin and purpose of the law on testaments, Dem. xx 102, Plu. *Solon* 21. 13; prohibition of the adopted to dispose of property of the adopter, [Dem.] xliv 67–8; testament of Pasion, [Dem.] xlv 28; other wills, Dem. lii 10, 20–3, And. iv 15, Lys. frg. 24; validity of wills when sons do not survive their majority, [Dem.] xlvi 24; requirements for validity of a will, Pl. *Laws* 923e–924a and Plu. *Mor.* 265e; opposition of oligarchies to making of wills, Aristot. *Pol.* 1309a 20; limitation of the involvement of people's courts in inheritance cases during the oligarchic interval of 404/3 BC, *AthPol* 35.2; collection of testaments from other regions, *RIJG* ii 23 and **Lykaonia (Asia Minor)**: *SEG* xlii 1256 (Imperial era); for the nature of the alleged testament of Xouthias from **Tegea** see the commentary in *IPArk* 1 (*c.* 450 BC); wills of philosophers, D.L. v 11–16 (Aristotle); x 16 (Epikouros); **Sparta**: introduction of testaments, Plu. *Agis* 5; **Epiz. Lokroi (S. Italy)**: testaments on tablets, *Nomima* II 55–8 (5th century BC).

Further reading

The meaning of the provision as establishing the freedom to dispose of property, E. Ruschenbusch (1962) 'Diatithesthai ta heautou. Ein Beitrag zum sogennanten Testamentsgesetz des Solon', *ZSS.RA* 79, 307–11; M. Cataudella (1972) 'Intorno alla legge solonica sul testamento', *Iura* 23, 50–66; A. Biscardi (1979) 'Osservazioni critiche sulla terminologia "diathekai-diatithesthai"', *Symposion 1979*, 23–35; *episkeptein* denoting a unilateral act arranging family and sacral affairs, F. Sanmarti Boncompte (1954) 'Episkeptein como acto de ultima voluntad', *RIDA* 1, 259–68 and (1956) 'Episkeptein y diatithesthai', *Studi in onore di U.E. Paoli*, 629–42; L. Gernet (1955) 'La notion du testament' in *Droit et société dans la Grèce ancienne*, 121–49, Paris; W.E. Thompson (1981) 'Athenian attitudes towards wills', *Prudentia* 13, 13–23; comprehensive summary of law on testaments in Athens, Harrison (1968: 149–55) and Karabelias (1992); **Sparta**: MacDowell (1986: 99–110).

2 Athens, Law on intestate succession

Demosthenes xliii (Against Makartatos) 51   *?6th century BC*

In a prolonged dispute about the inheritance of Hagnias, the plaintiff argues that his wife has a better entitlement to the inheritance than the person to whom the property has been awarded. The law stipulates the order of succession; male relatives have precedence over female and the nearest over the remotest.

If anyone dies without making a will, if he leaves daughters his property will go with them; if not, the following shall be entitled to his property: brothers by the same father and legitimate sons of brothers shall take the share of their father. If there are not any brothers or sons of brothers . . .,[3] their descendants likewise shall inherit. The male (relatives) and their male descendants are to take precedence, both if they are of the same parentage and if they are of remoter kinship. And if there are no relatives on the father's side to the degree of children of cousins, those relatives on the deceased's maternal side will inherit likewise. And if there is no relative, within the degree mentioned on either side, the nearest of kin on the father's side shall inherit. No illegitimate child of either sex shall have sacred or secular rights of kinship from the year of the archon Eukleides (403/2 BC).

3 Gortyn (Crete), Intestate succession

IC iv 72 col. IV 23–col. VI 46   *c. 480–460 BC*

Rules of succession in Gortyn were different from those in Athens. Children, grandchildren, great-grandchildren, brothers and their descendants, sisters and their descendants, *epiballontes** and finally *klaros** are designated as heirs. It is prohibited to sell, pledge or promise property to be inherited. Certain parts of the inheritance are kept for sons (paternal houses) and daughters (maternal houses). Children who, on the occasion of their wedding, chose to receive property are not entitled to have a share in the inheritance. A procedure for the division of the property is set out, according to which in case of disagreement among heirs the property should be auctioned and the proceeds should be shared.

---

3 In this point there is a gap in the text; Karabelias (1982: 57) suggested that Is. xi 1–2, where it is said that the sisters from the same father and their children and paternal cousins were called to inherit if there was not any son of the deceased, may provide the missing part.

The father has authority over his chidren and the division of his property and the mother over her property; while they are alive, there is no need to divide it; but if any of the sons is fined, he shall take his portion (of the property) according to the law. And if the father dies, his sons shall inherit the houses in the town and anything within them, if no *oikeus** lives in them, those sheep and cattle, which do not belong to *oikeis*. All the remaining property shall be divided fairly and the sons, whatever their number, will take two portions each and the daughters, whatever their number, will get one portion each. When the mother dies her property shall be divided in the same manner as the paternal. If she does not have any property but a house, the daughters shall inherit it, according to the law. If the father, while living, wants to give property to his daughter, on the occasion of her wedding, let him give according to the law and not more. The daughter to whom her father has donated property or promised to do so, shall keep that property but she shall not take any more from the paternal property. A woman who does not have any property either from donation by her father or by her brother or from pledge or from inheritance at the time when Kyllos[4] and his colleagues from Aithale were *kosmoi**, such a woman shall take her portion, but there will not be any legal remedy for beneficiaries before the archonship of Kyllos. When a man or a woman dies, his or her property will belong to their children or grandchildren or great-grandchildren. If there are not any, the property shall belong to the brothers of the deceased and their children or their grandchildren. If there are not any of them, their property will belong to their sisters and their children or their grandchildren. If there are not any of them, the property will belong to the *epiballontes*. If there are not any of them, the property will belong to those who constitute the *klaros*. And if some of the *epiballontes* want to divide the property and some others do not, a judge will decide that the property will belong to those who wish to divide the property until they divide it. And if anyone damages or steals or removes anything after the issue of the decision, he shall pay ten staters and double the value of the object removed. Regarding the animals, produce, clothes, jewellery and furniture, if they are not to be divided, the judge shall on oath give a decision taking into account the submitted claims. But if the heirs do not agree about the division, they shall auction the property. Having it sold to the highest bidder, the heirs shall take each his share. The division should take place in the presence of three or more adult free witnesses. Property given to daughters should follow the same procedure. While a father is alive, his sons are not allowed to sell or to pledge anything from the paternal property. The son himself can dispose of anything he has obtained or inherited. A father is not permitted to dispose of the property of his children, whatever they themselves obtained or inherited. Neither the husband nor the son is permitted to

---

4 The person and the date of his archonship is unknown.

alienate or to promise the property of wife or mother. If anyone buys or takes on mortgage or accepts a promise, on a different understanding from that required by the law, the property shall belong to the mother and to the wife, and the person who sold, pledged or promised it shall pay to the buyer, the person who accepted the pledge or the promise double the amount and any other incurred damages. Apart from earlier cases, no legal remedy shall be available. If the defendant claims that the property does not belong to a mother or a wife, the action shall be brought before the judge responsible for each case, according to the law. And if the mother dies and leaves children, their father will manage the maternal property; he is not permitted to sell or to mortgage anything, unless his children, having reached their majority, consent. If anyone buys or takes on a mortgage, the property will belong to the children but the person who sold or mortgaged it shall pay to the buyer or to the person who accepted the mortgage, double the amount and any incurred damages. If the husband marries again, the maternal property will belong to the children.

Relevant texts

Athens: reference to the law on intestate succession, Is. vii 20, xi 1–2; **Lokris (Central Greece)**: *Nomima* I, 44 (below, no. 94); mention of an inheritance law, **Gorgippia (S. Russia)**: *SEG* xli 614 (AD 16).

Further reading

The whole dispute over Hagnias' estate is discussed by W. Thompson (1976) *De Hagniae hereditate. An Athenian inheritance case*, Leyden (Mnemosyne Supplement 44); discussion of evidence on intestate succession in Athens, J.C. Miles (1950) 'The Attic law of intestate succession', *Hermathena* 75, 69–77 and Karabelias (1982), with a discussion of the terms *anchisteia, syggeneia* and 'children of cousins'; summary discussion, Harrison (1968: 130–48); succession by ascendants in Lokris, A. Biscardi (1985) 'La successione legittima degli ascedenti nel diritto ereditario panellenico: Uno spunto epigrafico del VI o V secolo A.C.', *Symposion 1985*, 7–13; **Gortyn**: detailed examination of the order to inherit, E. Karabelias (1986) 'Modalités successorales *ab intestato* à Gortyne', *Festschrift für A. Kränzlein. Beiträge zur antiken Rechtsgeschichte*, 29–41, Graz; Sealey (1990: 74–80); *epiballontes* as heirs, S. Avramovic (1990) 'Die Epiballontes als Erben im Gesetz von Gortyn', *ZSS.RA* 107, 363–70. A. Maffi (1994) 'Regole matrimoniali e successorie nell'iscrizione de

Tegea sul rientro degli esuli' in H.-J. Gehrke (ed.) *Rechtskodifizierung und soziale Normen im interkulturellen Vergleich*, 113–33, Tübingen (ScriptOralia 66).

4 Athens, Law on protection of orphans and heiresses

Demosthenes xliii (Against Makartatos) 75   ?6th century BC

The speaker claiming the estate of Hagnias brings as proof of his claim his continued interest in keeping the *oikos* of Hagnias 'alive', in contrast to the neglect shown by the defendants. The speaker also contrasts the interest of the *polis* as a whole for orphans and heiresses with the neglect of his opponents. In particular, he mentions that he named his sons after his wife's relatives and that his daughter married into the family. To make his point even clearer, he uses the law referring to the protection of orphans and heiresses. However, it is unclear to a modern reader how this law can support the argument advanced.

The (eponymous) archon shall take responsibility for the orphans and for the heiresses and for *oikoi* about to become extinct and for widows remaining in the houses of their dead husbands, claiming that they are pregnant. It is his duty to look after them and ensure that nobody humiliates them. And if anyone humiliates them or does anything unlawful to them, the archon shall have the power to impose a fine according to the fixed limit.[5] If the archon thinks that the offender deserves a more severe penalty, he shall summon the offender, give him five days' notice, and bring him to court writing down the penalty he thinks the offender deserves. And if the offender is convicted, the court shall decide what he ought to suffer or pay.

Relevant texts

Athens: public suit for maltreatment (*graphe kakoseos*), *AthPol.* 56.6; maltreatment of orphans, Aisch. i 158; procedure available against anyone who wronged orphans, Dem. xxxvii 45; denouncement (*eisaggelia*) for maltreatment of orphans, Is. xi 6; maltreatment of sole heiress, [Dem.] xliii 54 (below, no. 5); rules about heiresses

---

5 The fixed limit for fines imposed by magistrates on their own authority and without a court's decision was probably fifty drachmas.

attributed to Solon, Plu. *Solon* 20.2–4; legitimacy of children, Dem. xlvi 18 (below, no. 12); decree of Theozotides providing for the war-orphans, *SEG* xxviii 46 (403/2 BC); law of *hybris*, Dem. xxi 47 (below, no. 60); **Gortyn (Crete)**: paternity claims, *IC* iv 72 col. III 45–col. IV 23 (below, no. 18); **Thasos**: provisions for orphans, *LSCG Suppl.* 64 (below, no. 78); **Aiolis (Asia Minor)**: mention of orphans, *SEG* xxxiv 1238 (*c.* 200 BC); guardians of orphans (*orphanophylakes*) in Athens, X. *Poroi* 2.7; in **Naupaktos (Aitolia)**, *IG* ix² (2) 624g and 643; in **Beroia (Makedonia)**, *La loi gymnasiarchique* (below, no. 98); *orphanodikastai* in *Gortyn*, *IC* iv 72 col. xii 6–17; *orphanistai* in **Selymbria (Thrace)**, *BCH* 36 (1912), p. 551; *orphobotai* in **Morgantina (Sicily)** *SEG* xxxix 1008 (3rd century BC); *orphanophylakes* as officials in religious associations, **Gorgippia (S. Russia)**, *CIRB* 1129, 1130, 1162 (2nd century AD); alleged legislation of Charondas, D.S. xii 15.1.

Further reading

Maltreatment of orphans, MacDowell (1978: 94); relation of this law to the law on *hybris*, Fisher (1992: 54); war-orphans, W. den Boer (1979) *Private morality in Greece and Rome. Some historical aspects*, 37–61, Leiden (Mnemosyne Suppl. 57); I. Weiler (1988) 'Witwen und Waisen im griechischen Altertum. Bemerkungen zur sozialen Stellung und Integration' in H. Kloft (ed.) *Sozialmassnahmen und Fursorge. Zur Eigenart antiker Sozialpolitik*, 15–33, Graz (Grazer Beiträge. Supplementband III).

5 Athens, Law about heiresses

Demosthenes xliii (Against Makartatos) 54   *?6th century BC*

This law, according to the plaintiff, illustrates the obligations incumbent on the relatives when there is a heiress in the family. The nearest male relative was obliged either to marry her, or to give her in marriage providing a dowry set by law. If there were more than one male relative, the expense was to be shared between them. If there were more than one heiress, each kinsman had to marry or to give to marriage one of them.

Concerning the heiresses belonging to the class of *thetes**, if the next of kin of these heiresses does not wish to marry her, let him give her in marriage providing a dowry of five hundred drachmas if he belongs to the class of *pentakosiomedimnoi**, three hundred drachmas if he belongs to the class of *hippeis**, a hundred and fifty drachmas if he belongs to the class of *zeugitai**, in addition to her own property. And if there are more than one next of kin of the same degree, each of them shall contribute his due share. And if there is more than one heiress, it shall not be necessary for one kinsman to give more than one in marriage, but the next kinsman in each case must give her in marriage or marry her himself. And if the nearest of kin does not marry her or give her in marriage, the archon shall force him either to marry her himself or to give her in marriage. If the (eponymous) archon does not force him to do so, he shall owe a thousand sacred drachmas to Hera. Anyone wishing to denounce any person disobeying this law, may do so to the archon.

6 Gortyn (Crete), Heiress (Patroiokos)

IC iv 72 col. VII 15–col. IX 21   *c. 480–460 BC*

A woman with no father or paternal brother inheriting property was an heiress (*patroiokos* in Gortyn, *epikleros* in Athens). The Gortynian regulation seems to be more detailed than the Athenian and to pay greater attention to the administration of property and its possible side-effects. While in Athens attention is paid to the obligation to marry the heiress, in Gortyn there are provisions for almost all eventualities, such as difference of status and age, non-existence of relatives, willingness to marry, the process of *aphairesis* (taking away a married woman who has become an heiress from her husband).

The heiress shall marry the oldest brother of her father. If there are more heiresses and brothers of the father, each heiress shall marry the next oldest brother. And if there are not any paternal brothers but only their sons, she shall marry the son of the oldest brother. If there are more heiresses and sons of brothers, each heiress shall marry the son of the next oldest brother. An *epiballon** shall have only one heiress and not more. In case the person required to marry the heiress or the heiress herself is too young, if there is a house, it shall belong to her and half the revenue from any source will belong to the person required to marry the heiress. If the person required to marry a heiress does not wish to do so, although both are of age to marry, because he is an *apodromos**, all the property and any revenue shall belong to her until he marries her. And if the adult *epiballon* does not wish to marry the heiress, while she is of age and willing to marry him, the *kadestai** shall bring a suit and the judge shall decide that the man is required to marry the heiress within two months. But if he does not marry her, as it is written, she, keeping all her property, shall marry the next *epiballon* in order, if there is any. If there is no *epiballon*, she shall marry anyone from the tribe she likes and who asks her. If the heiress, being of an age to marry, does not want to marry the *epiballon* or he is too young and she does not want to wait, she will keep the house in the town and its contents, if there are any, and from the rest she will keep half and she will be able to marry anyone from the tribe she likes and who asks her. But she shall give to the *epiballon* she did not marry the appropriate portion from her property. And if there are no *epiballontes*, according to the law, the heiress shall keep all her property and shall have the right to marry anyone she likes, from the tribe. If nobody from the tribe wants to marry her, the *kadestai* of the heiress shall proclaim to the tribe 'Does no one want to marry her?' and if anyone wishes to marry her, he shall do so within thirty days from the announcement; if not, she is allowed to marry anyone she can. If a woman becomes an heiress after being given to marriage by her father or brother, if she does not wish to remain married, although her husband so desires, and she has children from him, she can marry anyone from the tribe keeping the appropriate portion of the property according to the laws.[6] But if she does not have any children, she can marry the *epiballon* keeping all her property, if there is any, otherwise she should follow the existing provisions. If the husband of an heiress dies and leaves her with children, she may marry anyone from the tribe she wishes but without compulsion. But if there are no children, she shall marry the *epiballon*, according to the laws. If the person who has the duty to marry an heiress is abroad and she is of an age to marry, she shall marry the next in order, according to the laws. A woman is considered an heiress when she does not have a father or a paternal brother. The relatives from the paternal line shall be responsible for the administration of the property and the heiress shall receive half of the produce as long as she is a minor. But if she is not of age to marry and there is no *epiballon*, she shall manage her own property and the produce and she shall remain with her mother until she is of age to marry. If she has no mother, she is to be brought up by her maternal relatives. If anyone marries the heiress contrary to the existing rules, the *epiballontes* shall inform the *kosmos**. If a debtor dies and leaves an heiress, then she, personally or through her paternal or maternal relatives, can sell or mortgage property up to the amount owed and the sale and the mortgage shall be valid. But if anyone sells in any other way or mortgages her property, the property shall remain in her ownership, and the person who sold or mortgaged, if he is defeated in court, shall pay double the amount to the person who bought or accepted the mortgage and the simple value of any incurred damages. This provision will be valid for cases after the introduction of the law; for cases which occurred earlier there will be no legal remedy. And if a plaintiff claims that the property does not belong to the sole heiress, the judge will decide, having sworn an oath; and if the

6 In this case the provision about divorce was applying. See *IC* iv 72 col. II 45–col. III 1 (below, no. 15).

plaintiff wins his case, action should be brought where it is prescribed, according to the law.

Relevant texts

Patrouchos in **Sparta**: Hdt. vi 57.4–5; epikleros in **Athens**: AthPol. 56.7, 58.3, Plu. Solon 20.2–3, Pl. Laws 923c–925a; epikleros while her father is still alive, IG ii² 1165 (early 3rd century BC); mention of a patroiochos in **Dodone (Epeiros)**: SEG xxxii 1647 (5th–4th century BC); poleis in **Chalkidike (Makedonia)**, Aristot. Pol. 1274b 23; **Phokis (Central Greece)**, Aristot. Pol. 1304a 4; **Thourioi (S. Italy)**, D.S. xii 18.3–4; mention of epiklaros in **Thera (Cyclades)**, IG xii (3) 330 (3rd/2nd century BC), BE 1991, 426; reference to epiklaroi in **Aiolis (Asia Minor)**, SEG xxxiv 1238 (c. 200 BC); taking away the wife from the husband (aphairesis), Dem. xli 4 and Men. Epitr. 657–9, 714–15; **Gortyn**: rules on administering the property of an heiress, IC iv 72 col. XII 6–19; fragmentary regulation concerning heiress, IC iv 44 (beginning 5th century BC).

Further reading

Athens: Solonian legislation on heiresses: E. Ruschenbusch (1988) 'Bemerkungen zum Erbtochterrecht in der solonischen Gesetzen', Symposion 1988, 15–20; I. Karnezis (1972) He epikleros. Symbole eis ten hermeneian ton attikon rhetoron kai eis ten meleten tou idiotikou biou ton Athenon, 173–84, Athens; Harrison (1968: 132–8); Sparta: E. Karabelias (1982) 'L'épiclerat à Sparte', Studi in onore di A. Biscardi II, 469–80 and MacDowell (1986: 96); evidence from New and Latin comedy, E. Karabelias (1971) 'L'épiclerat dans la comedie nouvelle et dans les sources latines', Symposion 1971, 215–54 and D.M. MacDowell (1982) 'Love versus the law: An essay on Menander's Aspis', G & R 29, 42–52; function of the epikleros at law, Schaps (1979: 39–42); heiress as a common theme in ancient Greek laws, R. Sealey (1994) The justice of the Greeks, 15–21 and 83–7, Ann Arbor, and in the Hellenistic era, E. Karabelias (1977) 'La situation successorale de la fille unique du défunt dans la koine juridique hellénistique', Symposion 1977, 223–34; possibility to divorce (aphairesis) a woman who has become epikleros, A. Maffi (1988) 'E' esistita l'aferesi dell'epikleros?', Symposion 1988, 21–36 and L. Lepri-Sorge (1988) 'Per una riprova storica dell'aphairesis tes epiklerou', Symposion 1988, 37–39; epikleros and marriage between relatives as part of a strategy of exchanges and alliances, G. Sissa (1990)

'Epigamia. Se marier entre proches à Athènes' in J. Andreau and H. Bruhns (eds) *Parenté et stratégies familiales dans l'antiquité romaine*, 199–223 (Actes de la table ronde des 2–4 octobre 1986, Paris), Rome (Collection de l'École Française de Rome 129); for an anthropological approach, J. Goody (1990) *The Oriental, the Ancient and the Primitive. Systems of marriage and the family in the pre-industrial societies of Eurasia*, 386–97 and 429–64, Cambridge (Studies in Literacy, Family, Culture and the State); Gortyn: E. Karabelias (1980) *Recherches sur la condition juridique et sociale de la fille unique dans le monde grec ancien excepté Athènes*, Paris; Sealey (1990: 63–9); on the meaning of col. viii 20–30, A. Maffi (1987) 'Le mariage de la patroôque "donnée" dans le code de Gortyne', *RHD* 65, 505–25; E. Ruschenbusch (1991) 'Die verheiratete Frau als Erbtochter im Recht von Gortyn', *ZSS.RA* 108, 287–9; S. Link (1994) 'Die Ehefrau als Erbtochter im Recht von Gortyn', *ZSS.RA* 111, 414–20; meaning of *kadestas*, cross-cousin marriages and sole heiress, Morris (1990); linguistic study of the provision on sole heiress and the terms *kadestai* and *epiballontes*, M. Bile (1993) 'La patroiokos des lois de Gortyne', *Symposion 1993*, 45–51 and the response by S. Avramovic; retroactivity and the rights of women in the code, M. Gagarin (1993) 'The economic status of women in the Gortyn code: Retroactivity and change', *Symposion 1993*, 61–71 and the reply by A. Maffi; Athens: *aphairesis*, V.J. Rosivach (1984) 'Aphairesis and apoleipsis: a study of the sources', *RIDA* 31, 193–230.

7 Gortyn (Crete), Property settlement in case of death of one of the spouses

IC iv 72 col. III 17–36   *c. 480–460 BC*

In a patrimonial system like that of Gortyn in which the spouses' properties remained separate entities, the death of one spouse was the cause of disputes. This provision makes clear that the wife shall keep under any circumstances what she has brought plus whatever she was given by her husband. In the case of her death, her spouse will return her property, with her trousseau and any produce, to her relatives.

If the husband dies leaving children, his wife can remarry keeping her property and anything else her husband has given to her in the presence of three adult witnesses, according to the law; and if she takes anything belonging to the children, she shall be liable to prosecution. If the husband dies childless, she shall keep her property, half of her trousseau and she shall take her portion from the family produce, together with the *epiballontes** and

11

anything else her husband had given to her according to the law; but if she takes anything more, she shall be liable to prosecution. If the wife dies without children, her husband shall return her property to her *epiballontes*, together with half of her trousseau and half of the produce, if it comes from her property.

Relevant texts

Athens: woman's property after her death without children, Is. iii 36 and Dem. xl 14, 50; husband's property after his death without children, Is. iii 8–9, 78 and viii 8.

Further reading

Summary, Sealey (1990: 74–80) and Metzger (1973: 86–9); **Athens**: dowry after the death of one of the spouses, Dimakis (1959: 208–84); wives as owners of their dowry, P.D. Dimakis (1974) 'À propos du droit de propriété de la femme mariée sur les biens dotaux d'après le droit grec ancien', *Symposion 1974*, 227–43; character of the dowry contract, A. Biscardi (1988) 'Sulla cosiddetta consensualita del contratto dotale in diritto attico', *Symposion 1988*, 3–13.

8 Athens, Law on challenging the award of an inheritance

Demosthenes xliii (Against Makartatos) 16   *?6th century BC*

When a citizen died without any natural male heirs, any adopted son by testament or other relative had to apply to the eponymous archon to adjudge the property; the same procedure was followed if the deceased was survived by a daughter. This law sets out, not in a great detail, the technicalities of the whole process.

If anyone challenges the adjudication of an inheritance or of an heiress, he has to summon the beneficiary of the adjudication before the (eponymous) archon as in other suits. The challenger shall pay the deposit. And if the challenger wins the case without having summoned the beneficiary, the adjudication shall be void. And if the beneficiary is not alive, his successor at law shall be summoned in the same manner, provided that the legal period to do so has not elapsed.[7] And the beneficiary shall have to prove on what terms the property was adjudicated to him.

---

7 The legal period to challenge the adjudication of an inheritance or of an heiress was five years.

Relevant texts

Athens: process of *epidikasia*, [Dem.] xlvi 22; testamentary adoption, [Dem.] xlvi 14 (above, no. 1); heiress, Dem. xliii 54 (above, no. 5).

Further reading

Athens: formalities of the procedure, E. Karabelias (1974) 'Contribution à l'étude de l'epidikasie attique', *Symposion 1974*, 201–25; summary, Harrison (1968: 158–62), MacDowell (1978: 102–3) and Todd (1993: 228–9).

9 Gortyn (Crete), Liability for debts of a deceased

IC iv 72 col. IX 24–43   *c. 480–460 BC*

The provision provides a limit of one year for any suit connected with debts resulting from pledges and securities provided by the deceased. The testimony of witnesses is decisive for the judge. If the object of litigation is related to a previous suit, then the official recorder and the judge are summoned to testify.

If anyone, who has provided a guarantee or lost a suit or owes money given as security or was involved in fraud or has made a formal promise, dies or if anyone else in a similar relationship to him dies, any suit against him should be filed within a year; and the judge will decide on the basis of the statements by the witnesses; if the suit relates to a previous case won by the plaintiff, the judge and the *mnemon** shall testify, if they are alive and have not lost their civic rights, as well as the *epiballontes;** but in case of a pledge given to secure debt and of defrauding and of formal promise, the *epiballontes* are to testify. At the end of the testimonies, the judge shall decide, having sworn an oath himself as well as the witnesses, that the plaintiff will win the simple amount. If a son provides security, while his father is alive, the son and his property shall be liable.

Relevant texts

Gortyn: liability of heirs for debts, *IC* vi 72 col. XI 31–45; revoking of an adoption, *Nomima II* 39 (before 500 BC).

Further reading

Metzger (1973: 106–12); provision establishes a procedural law, Maffi (1983: 121–70); **Athens**: Harrison (1968: 124).

10 Gortyn (Crete), Donation

IC iv 72 col. X 14–24   *c. 480–460 BC*

The Gortynian legislation provided for donations to a limit of a hundred staters. Any donation over this threshold while there are debts would be void. This regulation was introduced to prevent defrauding by debtors. Donation of land, although not unknown earlier, had become widespread during Hellenistic times as well as in a religious context.

A son is allowed to give to his mother or a husband to his wife a hundred staters or less but not more. If he gives more, the *epiballontes** can keep the excess amount if they wish and give the amount. If anyone gives while he owes money or has a fine to pay or is involved in litigation, the donation shall be void, if the remaining property is not sufficient to pay for the debt.

Relevant texts

Gortyn: rules pertaining to donations, *IC* iv 72 col. XII 1–5; among spouses, *IC* iv 72 col. III 20–2; donation of land by Makedonian kings: **Kassandreia (Makedonia)**, *SEG* xxxviii 619 (285/4 BC); *Syll*³ 332 (305–297 BC); **Gambreion (Mysia – Asia Minor)** *Syll*³ 302 (326/5 BC); **Athens**: grant of land by the *polis*, Lys. vii (*On the olive stump*) 4; **Thessalonike (Makedonia)**: donation of a vineyard to a cult group, *IG* x (2) 259 (1st century AD); donations from wealthy citizens: **Kerkyra**, *IG* ix (1) 694 (2nd century BC); **Kyme (Aiolis – Asia Minor)**, *SEG* xxxiii 1041 (end 2nd century BC); **Xanthos (Lycia – Asia Minor)**, *SEG* xxx 1535 (AD 152).

Further reading

Summary, A. Kränzlein (1963) *Eigentum und Besitz im griechischen Recht des fünften und vierten Jahrhunderts v. Chr.*, 91–3, Berlin; donations of land by Hellenistic kings, B. Funck (1978) 'Landschekungen hellenistischer Könige', *Klio* 60, 45–55, and R.A. Billows (1995) *Kings and colonists. Aspects of Macedonian imperialism*, 111–45, Leiden.

11   Gortyn (Crete), Adoption

IC iv 72 col. X 34–col. XI 23   *c. 480–460 BC*

Adoption was widespread in antiquity and especially in Athens, where a dying man could adopt in order to avoid the extinction of his *oikos*. However, in Gortyn adoption does not seem to play such a prominent role, although the adoptee has similar duties to those of his Athenian counterpart. Adoption as well as the renunciation of the adoptee was held in public. The adoptee had the same duties as natural sons (especially religious-ritual) but not the same rights of inheritance; the adoptee was entitled to half of a son's portion of the property. However, the position of adopted children remained precarious in the family structure; if an adoptee died childless, his property passed to the relatives of the adopter.

A man can adopt from whatever source he wishes. The declaration of adoption shall be done in the marketplace (*agora*) when the citizens are assembled, from the tribune (*bema*) from which proclamations are made. The adopter shall give to his *etaireia** a sacrificial victim and a measure of wine. If the adopted inherits all the property of the adopter and there are no legitimate children, he shall fulfil all the obligations of the adopter to gods and humans alike and he shall receive the property according to the prescribed manner for legitimate children. If he does not wish to fulfil these obligations, the property shall belong to the *epiballontes**. If the adopter has legitimate children, the adopted shall inherit property on the same terms as the sons, in the same way as daughters receive from their brothers;[8] if there are no sons but there are daughters, the adopted child shall receive an equal portion with theirs; in such case, he shall not be obliged to perform the duties of the adopter and to receive the property left by the adopter; the adopted shall not have any further rights. If the adopted dies without legitimate children, the property will belong to the *epiballontes* of the adopter. The adopter can, if he wishes, renounce the adopted in the marketplace (*agora*) from the tribune where proclamations are made, in the presence of the citizen body. The adopter shall deposit ten staters with the court and the magistrate responsible for foreigners shall give this amount to the renounced. No woman or minor shall have the right to adopt. These rules shall be valid from the moment they were written. As for earlier cases, in which someone has property from adoption or from the adopter, there shall be no legal remedy.

---

8 The participation of the adopted child in inheritance together with other natural children is vague. One can explain it in relation to the general provision on inheritance (*IC* iv 72 col. IV 39–43), according to which male children received two portions and female one portion.

Relevant texts

Athens: testamentary adoption, [Dem.] xlvi 14 (above, no. 1); an adopted child cannot adopt, Dem. xliv 23–4; an only son cannot be given in adoption, Is. ii 10, 21; women and children cannot adopt, Is. vii 25 and x 10; adoptions attested in tombstones: **Rhodes**, *SEG* xxvii 470 (2nd–1st century BC); **Aphrodisias (Caria – Asia Minor)**, *SEG* xxvii 717 (early 3rd century AD); **Kos**: *ASAA* 41/2 (1967) 187ff.; **Gortyn**: fragmentary rule on adoption, *IC* iv 21 (*c.* 550 BC).

Further reading

Athens: legal requirements, procedures, relation to intestate succession and heiress, L. Rubinstein (1993) *Adoption in IV. century Athens*, Copenhagen (with a list of adoptions on pp. 117–25); epigraphical evidence on adoption in Hellenistic and Roman Athens does not suggest any decline in adoptions, L. Rubinstein *et al.* (1991) 'Adoption in Hellenistic and Roman Athens', *ClassMed* 42, 139–51; testamentary adoption, Karabelias (1992); overview, Harrison (1968: 82–96), Todd (1993: 221–5); adoption as strategy for dealing with problems after the death of the adopter, A. Maffi (1990) 'Adozione e strategie successorie a Gortina e ad Atene', *Symposion 1990*, 205–32 and the response by S. Avramovic; **Rhodes**: G. Poma (1972) 'Ricerche sull'adozione nel mondo rodio (III sec. a.C. – III sec. d.C.)', *Epigraphica* 34, 169–305; adoption of women, E. Stavrianopoulou (1993) 'Die Frauenadoption auf Rhodos', *Tyche* 8, 177–88.

MARRIAGE – DIVORCE

12 Athens, Law on betrothal – marriage

{Demosthenes} xlvi (Against Stephanos II) 18

mid 5th century BC

In arguing his case for false witness against Stephanos, Appollodoros discusses the question of who is legally responsible for giving a woman in marriage. The whole question touches upon the legitimacy of the offspring. The answer is provided by the following law.

If a woman is betrothed for lawful marriage by her father or by her brother from the same father or by her grandfather on her father's side, her children shall be legitimate. If there are no such relatives and the woman is an heiress, her guardian shall marry her, but if she is not an heiress, whomever the guardian entrusts her to shall be her guardian.

Relevant texts

Athens: prohibition in concluding marriage with foreigners, [Dem.] lix 16, 52 (below, nos. 13, 14); ceremonial formalities, Hyp. i 3–7; boundary stones (*horoi*) for estates given as dowry in Athens and in the Cyclades, Finley (1951: 44–52 and 156–63, nos. 132–56); register of dowries: **Mykonos (Cyclades)**, *Syll³* 1215 (4th–3rd century BC); **Tenos (Cyclades)**, *IG* xii 5 (2) 872 and 873 (4th/3rd centuries BC); dowries and hypothecation in Roman **Egypt**: *OGIS* 669 (AD 68); providing dowries to poor girls: **Xanthos (Lycia – Asia Minor)**, *SEG* xxx 1535 (AD 152).

Further reading

On the genuineness of the Athenian law, I. Karnezis (1976) 'The law of engue in [Dem.] xlvi 18, 20, 22', *Apollinaris* 49, 278–85; on betrothal and marriage, H.J. Wolff (1944) 'Marriage law and family organization in ancient Athens. A study on the interaction of public and private law in the Greek city', *Traditio* 2, 43–95 [= 'Eherecht und Familienverfassung in Athen' in *Beitrage zur Rechtsgeschichte*, 155–242, 1961]; for a discussion of a wide range of evidence on the structural elements of marriage [giving away (*ekdosis*), procreation, transfer of tutelage (*kyrieia*), dowry], J. Modrzejewski (1979) 'La structure juridique du mariage grec', *Symposion 1979*, 39–71 now in *Statut personnel et liens de famille dans les droits de l'Antiquité* V, 1993, Leyden; vocabulary of *engue*, Sealey (1990: 25–6); survey of questions, Harrison (1968: 1–60), R. Just (1989) *Women in Athenian law and life*, 40–75, London, and Todd (1993: 210–16); detailed analysis of the epigraphic records from Tenos, R. Etienne (1990) *Tènos II. Tènos et les Cyclades du milieu du IVᵉ siècle av. J.-C. au milieu du IIIᵉ siècle ap. J.-C.*, 52–84, Paris (Bibliothèque des Écoles Françaises d'Athènes et de Rome 263bis).

13 Athens, Law prohibiting *epigamia* with Athenian women

{Demosthenes} lix (Against Neaira) 16　　　**end 5th century BC**

Both the following two laws concern violation of the exclusive right of citizens to intermarry. Husbands and guardians are punished if they give a foreign woman in marriage as an Athenian or if they live as husband with an Athenian woman; the woman is not punished. The central theme here is the prevention of usurping citizenship but not the conditions or requirements to marry.

And if a foreign man lives as husband with an Athenian woman in any way or manner whatsoever, he may be prosecuted before the *thesmothetai** by any Athenian wishing and entitled to do so. If he is found guilty, he and his property shall be sold and one-third of the money shall be given to the prosecutor. The same rule applies to a foreign woman who lives with an Athenian as his wife. And an Athenian convicted of living as husband with a foreign woman, shall be fined a thousand drachmas.

14   Athens, Law prohibiting *epigamia* with Athenian male citizen

{Demosthenes} lix (Against Neaira) 52   *end 5th century BC*

And if anyone gives a foreign woman in marriage to an Athenian citizen, as being his relative, he shall lose his civic rights and his property shall be confiscated and one-third will belong to the successful prosecutor. And those entitled may prosecute before the *thesmothetai**, as in the case of usurpation of citizenship.

Relevant texts

Athens: Law of Perikles on citizenship (451/0 BC), *AthPol.* 26.4, Plu. *Perikles* 37.3; punishment of an illegitimate infiltrating a *phratry*, *FGrH* 342 F 4; scrutiny of members of a *phratry*, *IG* ii² 1237 (396/5 BC); decrees enforcing the Periklean legislation, *FGrH* 77 F2 and Athen. 577b–c; similar regulations in other cities: Aristot. *Pol.* 1275b; **Byzantion (Thrace)**: [Aristot.] *Oecon.* 1346a; **Argos (Peloponnese)**: policy of mixed marriages, Plu. *Mor.* 245f. (if genuine); rules concerning recognition of marriages with foreign women: **Thasos**, *IG* xii Suppl. 264 (below, no. 77); **Phalanna (Thessaly)**: *IG* ix (2) 1228 (3rd century BC); grant of right to marry into the host community (*epigamia*), **Aitolia**: *Staatsvertrage* III 480 (*c.* 263 BC), **Messene (Messenia – Peloponnese)**: *Staatsvertrage* III 495 (*c.* 240 BC); **Hierapytna (Crete)**: *Staatsvertrage* III 512 (*c.* 220 BC); **Teos (Ionia – Asia Minor)**: *SEG* xxix 1149.16 (3rd–2nd century BC); **Gonnoi (Thessaly)**: *AE* 1911, p. 134, no. 70 (Hellenistic); **Olynthos (Chalkidike)**: X. *HG* v 2.19 (early 4th century BC); *epigamia* in **Athens**: Dem. xviii 187, Aristot. *Pol.* 1280b, Lys. xxxiv 3; sale of rights of citizenship: **Ephesos (Ionia – Asia Minor)**, *IEph* 2001 (*c.* 297 BC); **Thasos**, *IG* xii Suppl. 355 (early 3rd century BC); mixed marriages attested in tombstones, e.g. **Attica**: *IG* ii² 7883 etc., **Rhodes**: *NS* 19; *ILindos* 51 cl, 26–7, 88; *ASAA* 41–2 (1963–4) 183–4, no. 26; **Kos**: Paton-Hicks no. 10; **Miletos (Ionia – Asia Minor)**: *Delphinion* 46, 1.6 etc.; legislation of **Charondas**, D.S. xii 18.1.

Further reading

Athens: Harrison (1968: 29); survey of other *poleis*, A.P. Christophilopoulos (1954) *O met'allodapes gamos kata to archaion hellenikon kai hellenistikon dikaion*, Athens (Pragmateiai Akademias Athenon 17. 2) now in *Dikaion kai istoria. Mikra meletemata*, 68–85, 1973, Athens; Cl. Vial (1992) 'Mariages mixtes et statut des enfants. Trois examples en Égée orientale' in R. Lonis (ed.) *L' étranger dans le monde antique* II, 287–96, Nancy (Actes du deuxième colloque sur l'étranger, Nancy 19–21 septembre 1991); critical examination of Aristotle's account based on epigraphical evidence, J.-M. Hannick (1976) 'Droit de cité et mariages mixtes dans la Grèce classique. À propos de quelques textes d'Aristote (*Pol.* 1275b, 1278a, 1319b)', *AC* 45, 133–48; **Athens**: citizenship, C. Patterson (1981) *Pericles' citizenship law of 451/0 BC*, New York; scrutiny in a *phratry*: C.W. Hedrick (1990) *The decrees of Demotionidai*, Atlanta, and Lambert (1993: 161–89); motives of Periklean legislation, A.L. Boegehold, 'Perikles' citizenship law of 451/0 BC' in Boegehold and Scafuro (eds) (1994: 57–66); critique of the current conceptualization of citizenship, P.B. Manville 'Toward a new paradigm of Athenian citizenship' in Boegehold and Scafuro (eds) (1994: 21–33); illegitimacy, Harrison (1968: 24–8, 61–8); A. Maffi (1985) 'Matrimonio, concubinato e filiazione illegittima nell'Atene degli oratori', *Symposion 1985*, 177–214.

15 Gortyn (Crete), Property settlement in divorce

IC iv 72 *col. II 46–col. III 1*   *c. 480–460 BC*

This provision regulates the division of property in case of divorce; women are allowed to keep their property and part of the produce from it together with half of their trousseau. Responsibility of the husband for the divorce is confined to a fine of five staters. The same principle governs the divorce of household slaves (*oikeis*).

If a husband and wife divorce, the wife shall keep the property which she brought with her, and half of the produce, if it comes from her property, and half of her trousseau, whatever it is, and, if the man is responsible for the divorce, he shall pay a sum of five staters; if the man claims that he is not responsible, the judge shall decide on oath.

16 Gortyn (Crete), Divorce of *oikeis*

IC iv 72 col. III 40–4   *c. 480–460 BC*

If a woman-*oikeus** separates from her husband, in life or due to the husband's death, she shall keep her property; if she keeps anything more, she shall be liable to prosecution.

Relevant texts

Athens: return of dowry in case of divorce, Is. ii 9 and iii 35–6, [Dem.] lix 52; **Gortyn**: rule on swearing an oath in divorce cases, *IC iv 72 col. XI 46–55.

Further reading

Overview, Dimakis (1959: 228–45); **Athens**: Harrison (1968: 45–60) and MacDowell (1978: 88); fresh discussion of modes and grounds for divorce, L. Cohn-Haft (1995) 'Divorce in classical Athens', *JHS* 115, 1–14; Gortyn: Willetts (1967: 28–9).

17 Gortyn (Crete), Appropriation of marital property

IC iv 72 col. III 1–16   *c. 480–460 BC*

It is not unusual in divorce cases that allegations of appropriation of property belonging to the other spouse surface. The Gortynian regulation, unique, so far, among the legislations of Greek *poleis*, provides that sworn oath on this would be enough proof that the wife has not taken anything from her husband's property.

And if the wife keeps anything else belonging to her husband, she shall pay five staters and whatever she took away; and she shall restore anything she kept. If she denies that she kept anything more, she shall swear by Artemis in the Amyklaion[9] in front of the statue of Archeress, that she has not kept

---

9 In Gortyn, like in Sparta, the hero Amyklos was worshipped in a temple called Amyklaion. The hero was probably depicted as a warrior.

anything more; and if anyone deprives her of anything, once she has sworn the oath, he shall have to pay five staters and return anything he carried away; and if a stranger helped her in carrying off property belonging to her husband, he shall pay ten staters and double the value of anything the judge swears that the stranger helped to be carried away.

Relevant texts

Similar regulation about *oikeis**, *IC* iv 72 col. III 1–16.

Further reading

Comparative study of the Gortynian provision and Egyptian evidence, E. Seidl (1975) 'Zur Vorgeschichte der actio rerum amotarum', *ZSS.RA* 92, 234–8.

18 Gortyn (Crete), Paternity and illegitimacy
IC iv 72 col. III 45–col. IV 23   *c. 480–460 BC*

The following provision regulates the guardianship of a child in case her parents are divorced. The mother has to ask for the recognition of the child by her ex-husband and after a rejection either to expose it or to rear it. The same regulation pertains to household slaves; the only difference was that instead of the child being brought up in the father's house, it was brought up in his father's master's house. Unlawful exposure of the child is punished with a fine.

If a woman gives birth to an infant, while she is divorced, the child is to be brought to her ex-husband's house in the presence of three witnesses. And if her ex-husband does not accept it, the mother has the right either to bring it up herself or to expose it; the *kadestai** and the witnesses will testify under oath that she brought the infant. If a woman-*oikeus** gives birth, while she is divorced, the infant shall be brought to her ex-husband's master in the presence of two witnesses; if her ex-husband does not recognize it, the child will be under the guardianship of the master of his mother. If she remarries her ex-husband, before the end of a year, the baby will fall under the guardianship of the man's master. The witnesses and the person who brought the child will testify under oath. If a woman exposes her infant, before he is brought before his mother's husband according to the law, the mother shall pay, if she is convicted, fifty staters, if the child is born free, and twenty-five staters, if he is born a slave.[10] If the ex-husband does not

10 The status of the newborn is decided according to the provisions in *IC* iv 72 col. VII 1–10 (below, no. 26).

have a home, where the woman can bring the infant, or if she does not see him, she is to go unpunished, if she exposes the child. If an unmarried woman-*oikeus* is pregnant and gives birth, the child will be under the guardianship of her father's master; if her father is not alive, the infant will fall under the guardianship of her brother's master.

Relevant texts

Athens: possible disputes on paternity, Dem. xliii 75 (above, no. 4); recognition of a child, Is. iii 30, Dem. xxxix 22; proposed ban on exposure, Aristot. *Pol.* 1335b; **Sparta**: decision on exposing infants, Plu. *Lyk.* 16.1–2.

Further reading

Survey, Harrison (1968: 68–70), E. Cantarella (1988) *Pandora's daughters. The role & status of women in Greek & Roman antiquity*, 43–4 and especially n.18 (Engl. translation), London; **Sparta**: exposure, MacDowell (1986: 52–4); **Athens**: paternity, J. Rudhardt (1962) 'La reconnaissance de la paternité: sa nature et sa portée dans la société athénienne. Sur un discours de Démosthène', *MH* 19, 39–64; infanticide and exposure from an anthropological point of view, P. Brule (1992) 'Infanticide et abandon d'enfants. Pratiques grecques et comparaisons anthropologiques', *DHA* 18.2, 53–90; D. Ogden (1996) *Greek bastardy in the classical and hellenistic periods*, Oxford.

SEXUAL OFFENCES

19 Athens, Law on adultery

{Demosthenes} lix (Against Neaira) 87   *?5th century BC*

In his speech against Neaira, Apollodoros claims that since Neaira committed adultery, her husband, Stephanos, should have repudiated her. The law does not define a penalty for the adulterer, who could have been killed with impunity, but determines the consequences that the adulteress shall suffer (divorce and exclusion from public cultic activity).

And he who catches the adulterer, shall not be allowed to continue living with his wife; if he does, he shall be deprived of his civic rights. And the woman who committed adultery shall not be allowed to attend public sacrifices; if she does, she may suffer any penalty, except death, with impunity.

20 Gortyn (Crete), Adultery

IC iv 72 col. II 20–45   *c. 480–460 BC*

In marked contrast to Athens where a woman was repudiated, adultery in Gortyn did not have any legal consequence for the woman involved. That social sanctions were imposed is probable. As with rape and seduction, the status of the victim and the place where adultery has been committed determine the fine to be paid.

If anyone is caught committing adultery with a free woman in the house of her father or her brother or her husband, he shall pay a hundred staters; and if anywhere else, fifty staters; whoever commits adultery with the wife of an *apetairos**, he shall pay ten staters; and if a slave commits adultery with a free woman, he shall pay double this amount; and if a slave with the wife of a slave, he shall pay five staters; the person who apprehended them shall announce in the presence of three witnesses to the *kadestai** of the person apprehended that the adulterer will be released in five days after the payment of ransom; in the case of a slave, the person who apprehended him shall announce this to the slave's master in the presence of two witnesses; if the ransom is not paid, the people who apprehended the adulterer will have the right to treat him as they like; if the adulterer claims that he was apprehended by subterfuge, if the penalty is fifty or more staters, the person who apprehended him, together with four others, shall swear an oath, each claiming that they caught him committing adultery and not by subterfuge; if the person who caught the adulterer is an *apetairos*, he shall swear the oath together with two more people and if he is an *oikeus*, he shall swear the oath together with his master and one other person.

Relevant texts

Killing the adulterer: **Athens**, Lys. i, Dem. xxiii 53; humiliating practices on adulterers, Ar. *Clouds* 1083–4; allegation of adultery, Hyp. i; other cities, X. *Hiero* iii 3–4; a different account of procedure at **Gortyn**, Ael. *VH* xii 12; **Athens**: law, [Dem.] lix 87 (above, no.19); punishment for adultery: **Lokroi Epizephyrioi (S. Italy)**, Ael. *VH* xiii 24; **Lepreon (Peloponnese)**, Aristot. frg. 611.42 (Rose); **Tenedos**, Aristot. frg. 611.24 (Rose).

Further reading

Summary, Metzger (1973: 30–2); Sealey (1990: 69–74); Todd (1993: 276–9); U.E. Paoli (1950) 'Il reato di adulterio (moicheia) in diritto attico', *SDHI* 16, 123–82 (now in *Altri studi di diritto greco e romano*, 251–307, 1976); collection of laws of adultery in Athens and dates, K. Kapparis (1995) 'When were the Athenian adultery laws introduced?', *RIDA* 42, 97–122; law of adultery, E. Cantarella (1990) 'Moicheia. Reconsidering a problem', *Symposion 1990*, 289–96 and the response by L. Foxhall, and Cohen (1991: 98–132); adultery and social control, Cohen (1991: 133–70); reiteration of the thesis that adultery was regarded as a more important crime than rape, Carey (1995); on humiliating punishments for adulterers, P. Schmitt-Pantel (1972) *L'âne, l'adultère et la cité: Le charivari*, Paris, C. Carey (1993) 'Return of the radish or just when you thought it was safe to go back into the kitchen', *LCM* 18.4, 53–5, and K. Kapparis (1996) 'Humiliating the adulterer: the law and the practice in classical Athens', *RIDA* 43, 63–77; **Sparta**: MacDowell (1986: 87); Gortyn: the fines mentioned did not exclude killing the adulterer, U.E. Paoli (1955) 'La legislazione sull'adulterio nel diritto di Gortine', *Studi in onore di G. Funaioli*, 306–16 (= *Altri studi di diritto greco e romano*, 509–18, 1976).

21   Gortyn (Crete), Rape and seduction

IC iv 72 col. II 2–20   *c. 480–460 BC*

This section provides an exhaustive catalogue of penalties for cases of rape. All the penalties imposed are fines and they are increased according to the status of the injured party. The brief provision on seduction imposes a severe penalty only when the free woman is under the authority of a guardian.

If anyone rapes a free man or woman, he shall pay a hundred staters; and if the victim is an *apetairos**, ten staters; and if a slave rapes a free man or woman, he shall pay double the amount; if a free man rapes an *oikeus**, man or woman, he shall pay five drachmas; if an *oikeus* rapes another *oikeus*, man or woman, he shall pay five staters. Whoever rapes a house slave-girl, he shall pay two staters; if he rapes an already seduced girl, he shall pay, if it took place during the day, one obol*, and if it took place during the night, two obols; and the slave woman will testify under oath. If anyone seduces a free woman, while she is under the tutelage of a *kadestas**, he shall pay ten staters, if there is any witness to testify.

24

Relevant texts

Athens: fines for rape, Lys. i 32, Pl. *Laws* 874e and Plu. *Solon* 23; similar provision in the treaty between **Delphoi** and **Pellana** (**Central Greece**), F. Salviat and Cl. Vatin (1971) *Inscriptions de la Grèce centrale*, 63–75, Paris; **Keos** (**Cyclades**): prohibition on women walking alone, due possibly to fear of rape, *SEG* xxxix 868 (300–250 BC).

Further reading

Gortyn, Metzger (1973: 26–9); survey of regulations, S. Cole (1984) 'Greek sanctions against sexual assault', *CPh* 79, 97–113; no sanction of rape in Greek myths but only seduction and/or abduction, M.R. Lefkowitz 'Seduction and rape in Greek myth' in Laiou (1993: 17–37); manipulation by Lysias of the evidence regarding rape in Athens, E.M. Harris (1990) 'Did the Athenians regard seduction as a worse crime than rape?', *CQ* 40, 117–36; limited role of the concept of consent in cases of rape and adultery, D. Cohen, 'Consent and sexual relations in classical Athens' in Laiou (1993: 5–16); Gortyn: *IC* iv 72 col. II 16–20 concerns attempted rape, L. Gernet (1955) 'Observations sur la loi de Gortyne' in *Droit et société dans la Grèce ancienne*, 51–9, Paris; attempted seduction, M. Gagarin (1984) 'The testimony of witnesses in the Gortyn laws', *GRBS* 25, 345–9 (where previous bibliography is mentioned); seduction with the guardian's connivance, A. Maffi (1984) 'Le "leggi sulle donne" IC. 4, 72. 16–20, Plut., Sol. 23. 1–2', *Sodalis. scritti in onore di A. Guarino* IV, 1553–67; relation between rape and adultery, Carey (1995); function of witnesses in cases of seduction, M. Gagarin (1985) 'The function of witnesses at Gortyn', *Symposion 1985*, 29–54; comparative account, S. Deacy and K.F. Pierce (1997) (eds) *Rape in Antiquity. Sexual violence in the Greek and Roman worlds*, 1–42, London.

22 Delphoi (Central Greece), Law against maltreatment of parents

RPh (1943) pp. 62–3   *end 4th century BC*

One of the duties of children towards their parents was to treat them with due respect. Some *poleis* institutionalized this moral obligation, while in Athens maltreatment of parents could disqualify a citizen from public office. Unfortunately, this fragmentary law from Delphoi does not provide more details about the requirements of the obligation, but it provides an illustration of the importance of the moral duty.

God. It was decided by the *polis* in a plenary assembly with three hundred and fifty three votes, to inscribe the law concerning parents; Melanopos, Philutas, Herakleios, Theudoridas, Hagetor were councillors; whoever does not provide for his father and mother, when denounced in the Council, shall be convicted by the Council and shall be incarcerated till [. . .]

Relevant texts

Athens: public suit for maltreatment of parents (*graphe kakoseos*), *AthPol* 56.6; questions during scrutiny for appointment in office, *AthPol* 55.3, X. *Mem.* ii 2.13; process for prosecution against maltreatment, Dem. xxiv 105 (below, no. 84); conduct constituting maltreatment, Lys. xiii 9, Is. viii 32; release of children from the obligation to provide for their parents, Aisch. i 13, Plu. *Solon* 22; allegation of maltreatment, Lys. xxxi 20–3.

Further reading

Athens: Harrison (1968: 77–8), MacDowell (1978: 92); wide survey on treatment of elderly in ancient Greece and Rome, M.I. Finley (1981) 'The elderly in classical antiquity', *G & R* 28, 156–71; parental affection and sentiments, M.-Th. Charlier and G. Raepsaet (1971) 'Étude d'un comportement social: Les relations entre parents et enfants dans la société athénienne à l'époque classique', *AC* 40, 574–88.

PERSONAL STATUS

23 Gortyn (Crete), Regulation about freedmen

IC iv 78   *5th century BC*

Slaves could have been freed by manumission; once freed they were not treated as full citizens but as resident foreigners (called *metics* in Athens). This law guarantees the right of freedmen to settle in a particular location and not to be seized and ransomed.

Gods. The Gortynians have decreed: Freedmen shall have the right to establish themselves in Latosion[11] under the same conditions as other people and nobody is permitted to enslave or to seize them for ransoming later. If anyone enslaves a freedman, the archon responsible for the foreigners shall release the freedman; and if a freedman is seized for ransoming, each of those responsible shall pay a hundred staters to the *titai** and shall pay double the amount of property they took. And if the *titai* do not act according to the law, they shall pay to the *polis* double the amount owed by each of the accused.

Relevant texts

Athens: conditions imposed on freedmen, Pl. *Laws* 915a–c; naturalization of an ex-slave, Dem. xxxvi 47, xlvi 15, and lix 2, 29; manumission of slaves who fought at Arginusae (406 BC), Ar. *Frogs* 693–4 and *FGrHist* 323a F 25; acts of manumission (sacral and secular), *RIJG* ii 30 pp. 233–318 (5th century BC–3rd century AD); to which add **Bouthrotos (Epeiros)**: *SEG* xxxviii 468–9 (3rd century BC); **Beroia (Makedonia)**: *SEG* xlii 609–14 (3rd century AD); **Athens**: *IG* ii² 1553–72, *SEG* xvii 36, xxv 178 (*c.* 320 BC); manumission record, **Larisa (Thessaly)**: *SEG* xxxv 599 (first half of 1st century BC); **Phigaleia (Arkadia – Peloponnese)**: *IPArk* 27 (370–325 BC); dedication of *phialai* by freedmen mentioned in a letter of Demetrios II to Beroians (249 BC): *SEG* xliii 379; **Olympia (Elis – Peloponnese)**: manumission, *Nomima II* 27 (before 450 BC).

Further reading

Gortyn: Metzger (1973: 22–6) and *Nomima* I, 16; manumission transforming a person without rights to an individual with certain rights, M.I. Finley (1980) *Ancient slavery and modern ideology*, 96–8, London; date and mode of manumission acts from Central Greece, K.-D. Albrecht (1978) *Rechtsprobleme in den Freilassungen der Böotier, Phoker, Dorier, Öst- und Westlokrer*, Paderborn; criticism at some points of Albrecht's interpretation, A. Kränzlein (1979) 'Bemerkungen zu den griechischen Freilassungsinschriften', *Symposion 1979*, 239–47; evidence about frequency of manumissions, social status of manumittors in Delphes, D. Mulliez (1992) 'Les actes d'affranchissement delphiques', *Cahier Glotz* 3, 31–44; Athens: Harrison (1968: 181–6);

---

11 A locality near Gortyn, possibly associated with a temple of Leto. See as well: *Nomima* I, 15 (end 6th century BC).

A. Bielman (1994) *Retour à la liberté. Libération et sauvetage des prison-niers en Grèce ancienne: recueil d'inscriptions honorant des sauveteurs et analyse critique*, Lausanne (Études Épigraphiques 1); survey, Y. Garlan (1988) *Slavery in ancient Greece*, 73–84 (Engl. translation), London.

24 Gortyn (Crete), Payment of ransom

IC iv 72 *col. VI 46–56*   *c. 480–460 BC*

Slavery, wars and piracy made any traveller vulnerable to enslave-ment. The ransoming of fellow-citizens by the wealthier citizens was considered almost a civic duty and agreements between *poleis* provided for such cases. The Gortynian provision is an attempt to regulate the procedure of ransoming rather than to sanction it.

If anyone, having an obligation to another person who is in another city, frees him at this person's request, he shall have authority over the freed person until the latter pays back the ransom. But if they do not agree over the amount of money or the freed person does not admit that he asked to be freed, the judge shall decide taking into account the pleas.

Relevant texts

Athens: failure to repay ransom, [Dem.] liii 11; honouring individuals for buying prisoners and enslaved citizens: **Aigiale (Amorgos – Cyclades)**, *IG* xii (7) 386 (early 3rd century BC), **Arkesine (Amorgos – Cyclades)**, Tod ii 152 (357/6 BC), *Athens*, *Syll*[3] 263 (336/5 BC), *IG* ii[2] 399 (320/19 BC); clauses banning the enslavement of citizens of one *polis* in another, agreement of **Miletos with Knossos, Gortyn and Phaistos (Crete)**: *Staatsvertrage* III 482 (after 260 BC); prohibition of ransoming, **Lyttos (Crete)**: *Staatsvertrage* III 511 (c. 220 BC).

Further reading

Metzger (1973: 50–3); study of the terminology, B. Bravo (1980) 'Sulân. Représailles et justice privée contre des étrangers dans les cités grecques', *ASNP* 10.3, 675–987; ransoming, W.K. Pritchett (1991) *The Greek state at war*, vol. 5, 245–97, Berkeley, Los Angeles; discussion of the Milesian–Cretan agreements, P. Brule (1978) *La piraterie cretoise hellénistique*, 6–12, Paris (Centre de recherches d'histoire ancienne 27).

25 · Gortyn (Crete), Law on illegal seizure

IC iv 72 col.1 1–col. II 2   *c. 480–460 BC*

Slavery was a feature of ancient Greek societies and a commodity. Rules about ownership and disputes were necessary. The beginning of the Gortynian code concerns the regulation of illegal seizures and prohibits any seizure of persons before the end of a trial. It also establishes the principle that in doubt the seized person should be considered free.

Gods. If anyone intends to initiate a trial about a free man or a slave, he may not seize him before the trial. If he does so and he is a free man, the judge shall fine him ten staters and if the opponent is a slave, five staters, and he shall order him to release the seized person within three days. If he does not release him, if he is a free man, the judge shall fine him one stater and if he is a slave, one drachma per each day, until he releases the improperly held person The judge shall decide about the time to be allotted for freeing the man, after having sworn an oath. If the defendant denies that he has seized him and there is no testimony of a witness, the judge shall decide after having sworn an oath. And if anyone claims that the constrained person is a free man and others that he is a slave, the decision shall be in favour of those who testify that he is a free man. If individuals litigate about slaves, each claiming that the slave belongs to him, if there is a witness' account, the judge shall decide according to the testimony. But if there are testimonies for both views or for none, the judge shall decide after having sworn an oath. If the holder of the body is defeated, he shall release the free man within five days and he shall hand over the slave to his master. But if he does not release him or hand over the slave, the defeated litigant shall pay, if the constrained is a free man, fifty staters and one stater for each day until he releases him, and if he is holding a slave, ten staters and a drachma per day until he returns him to his master. A year after the issue of the decision against the offender, the person constrained can receive three times the amounts prescribed or less, but not more; the judge shall decide about the precise time of execution of the clause. If a slave, about whom a suit was lost, takes refuge in a temple, the defeated litigant shall summon the winner and shall point out, in the presence of two adult witnesses, the slave in the temple where he took refuge, either in person or by proxy. But if he does not summon or point out (where the slave has taken refuge), he shall pay everything provided in the law and if he does not hand over the slave even after a year, he shall pay in addition single penalties. If the illegal holder dies during the trial, his heirs shall pay the single penalty. If a *kosmos** or anyone else seizes a slave belonging to a *kosmos*, the trial shall take place at the end of the *kosmos'* term in office; and if he is defeated, he shall pay from the time of the seizure, according to the laws. But anyone who apprehends a debtor or a person under pledge to redeem his offence shall not be punished.

Relevant texts

Athens: treatment of those illegally enslaving citizens, *AthPol* 52.1, Isoc. xv 90; case of a certain Menon enslaving a boy, Dein. i 23; **Lokroi Epizephyrioi** (S. Italy), Plb. xii 16; **Gortyn**: grant of asylum to anyone illegally seized, *IC* iv 72 col. XI 24–5.

Further reading

Meaning of the regulation, Maffi (1983: 3–99); M. Gagarin (1988) 'The first law of the Gortyn code', *GRBS* 29, 335–43, and M. Gagarin (1995) 'The first law of the Gortyn code revisited', *GRBS* 36, 7–15; **Athens**: MacDowell (1978: 80) and Todd (1993: 186–7).

26 Gortyn (Crete), Mixed marriages and status of offspring

IC iv 72 col. VII 1–10   *c. 480–460 BC*

While in Athens the status of an individual depended on the status of both his parents, the status of children according to the Gortynian laws depended on the matrilocal character of the marital union of their parents.

If a slave marries a free woman and goes to live with her, their children shall be free. If a free woman marries a slave and goes to live with him, their children shall be slaves. If free and slave children are born from the same mother, when the mother dies, her property will belong to the free children. But if she does not have any free children, her property will belong to the *epiballontes**

Relevant texts

Athens: prohibition of marrying non-Athenians, [Dem.] lix 16, 52 (above, nos. 13, 14 and the references).

Further reading

On intermarriage between slaves and citizens in Argos reported by Plu. *Mor.* 245F, R.F. Willetts (1959) 'The servile interregnum at Argos', *Hermes* 87, 495–506; **Athens**: Harrison (1968: 61–70).

27 Gortyn (Crete), Law about the responsibility of slaves

IC iv 47   *5th century BC*

This regulation determines the responsibility for damages in the case of a slave being given as pledge for debt, in litigation and when the slave dies. The slaves bear no responsibility if they were following instructions of their new masters. If they were acting on their own initiative, their original master would be responsible. If slaves are wronged, they could go to court and share the imposed fine with their masters. The new master bears any responsibility for the fate of the slave given as security.

And if a slave, man or woman, given as security commits an offence, if he was ordered to do so by the person who accepted him as security, that person shall be liable, but if the slave commits an offence on his own initiative, his old master shall be liable and the person who accepted him as security shall have no liability. And if the old master loses his suit, he shall give to the person who accepted the pledge whatever that person wishes. And if anyone else wrongs the slave given as pledge, if both the slave given as pledge and the person who accepted him go to court and win the case, they shall share the fine. And if one of them does not wish to go to court and the other wishes to do so, in case the prosecution wins, he shall keep the fine. And if the slave given as pledge disappears, the person who accepted him as a pledge shall testify under oath that he is not responsible himself or jointly with someone else or that he knew. And if the person given as a pledge dies, the creditor shall demonstrate the above in the presence of two witnesses. And if the person who accepted the pledge does not give the oath as prescribed or does not establish his claim, he shall pay the simple value. And if the person who accepted the pledge is accused of not handing over or concealing the person given as pledge, if he loses the case, he shall pay double the simple fine. And if the person given as pledge took refuge in a temple, it should be made clear (where he took refuge).

Relevant texts

Athens: provision for damages caused by slaves, Pl. *Laws* 936 c8–d4.

Further reading

Gortyn: Metzger (1973: 101–5); **Athens**: Harrison (1968: 171–6).

28 Gortyn (Crete), Regulation concerning liability of persons given as security for debts

IC iv 41 V   *5th century BC*

The law regulates liability in cases of a person given as security for debts. This implies that it was possible for anyone to give himself or a slave as a pledge, in contrast to what was the rule in Athens, where such self-pledging was banned by Solon in the late 6th century.

[. . .] and if he does not swear the oath, he shall pay the simple value. And if any slave given as security works on the land of another or carries off another's property after being ordered by the person who accepted him as security, he shall be left unpunished. And if the person who accepted the slave claims that it did not happen on his instructions, the judge shall decide having sworn an oath, if no witness testifies. If the person given as security wrongs any other person, he himself shall be punished; and if he has nothing to pay with, the winner of the case and the person who accepted him as security (shall pay).

Relevant texts

Athens: Solonian prohibition of giving a person as security for debts, *AthPol.* 6.1, 9.

Further reading

Meaning of *katakeimenos* (person given as security for debts), Metzger (1973: 46–8); Maffi (1983: 90–4); Gagarin (1985: 35–7); for the Solonian prohibition in Athens, Rhodes (1981: 125–6).

29 Gortyn (Crete), Regulation about slaves

IC iv 41 IV   *5th century BC*

The regulation concerns the status of a fugitive household slave. Once escaped he could not be sold after a year. If he belonged to a serving magistrate, he could not be sold as long as his master remained in office.

A fugitive *oikeus** cannot be sold when he is in a temple or for a year after his escape. And if the fugitive *oikeus* belongs to a *kosmos**, he cannot be sold as long as his master stays in office or for a year after his escape. And whoever

32

sells a fugitive *oikeus* before the deadline, he shall be condemned; for the limitation of time the judge shall decide after having sworn an oath.

Further reading

Metzger (1973: 70–1).

30 Gortyn (Crete), Regulation about taking pledges?

IC iv 41 VII   *5th century BC*

[. . .] the person who brings to or takes money from a temple or [. . .] The purchaser of a slave shall pay damages to those who have a claim on the objects, according to the laws in each case, and the slave himself shall belong to the claimants of the objects, if the purchaser does not cancel the purchase within thirty days. But if within ten days they agree not to cancel the agreement but to provide security [. . .]

Relevant texts

Legislation of **Charondas** on violence, Herondas, *Mime* II 48ff.

31 Gortyn (Crete), Law about people giving themselves as pledge

IC iv 41 VI   *5th century BC*

The fragment provides the right to a person who has given himself as pledge for debts to appear in court, with or without the consent of their creditor, and claim damages. In case they decide to go to court unilaterally, they shall have to repay their debt first.

[. . .] not more. And if anyone wrongs the individual who has pledged himself, his creditor shall go to court and claim the same damages as for a free man, and whatever he obtains he shall share with the pledged person. And if the creditor does not wish to go to court, the pledged person can go to court after having paid his debt. And if he [. . .]

Further reading

Metzger (1973: 48–50).

32 Eltynia (Crete), Regulation concerning children

IC i *p. 91, no. 2*   *?5th century BC*

We know very little about statutes regulating violence among
individuals; this regulation penalizes injuries caused in clashes
between youngsters or brawls that erupted during common
activities.

[. . .] and if he injures with the hand, he shall pay five drachmas; and if
blood runs from his nose [. . .] to the Eltynians; and if anyone initiates
fighting he shall pay ten drachmas however he started [. . .] days in which
he has to pronounce but not later; the *kosmos** shall exact the fine on behalf
of the *polis* [. . .] and if anyone strikes a blow in self-defence, he shall not be
prosecuted [. . .] to exact the fine from those who cause injury; and if a man
strikes a minor not to [. . .] or in an *andreion** or in an *agela** or in a
*symposion** or in a *choros* or in a [. . .] and if a person belonging to an *agela*
humiliates or seizes a minor, if [. . .] the *kosmos* shall decide having sworn an
oath, about the city? [. . .] injures, he shall pay five drachmas according to
the nature of the injury; and if [. . .] or injures, shall pay five drachmas each
time he assaults another [. . .] he shall give five drachmas; and if the victim
[. . .]

Relevant texts

Similar regulations in a fragmentary agreement between **Athens
and Troizen (Peloponnese)**: *IG* ii² 46 (after 400 BC); **Lato (Crete)**:
IC i p. 124, no. 6 (2nd century BC); fights among boys in **Sparta**: X.
LP 4.6; **Athens**: accusation for assault, Dem. xlvii 45, 64 and liv,
Isoc. xx 19.

Further reading

Athens: action for injury (*dike aikeias*), MacDowell (1978: 123) and
Todd (1993: 269); *aikeia* and *hybris*, Cohen (1995: 119–42); rights of
children, Harrison (1968: 78–81); **Sparta**: MacDowell (1986: 66–8).

2

AGORA

33 Athens, Law prohibiting the digging up of olive trees

Demosthenes xliii (Against Makartatos) 71

mid 4th century BC

It may seem irrelevant to a modern reader to invoke a law about olive trees in an inheritance dispute. However, a court hearing in classical Athens was more a contest than an effort to find the truth. In this context, vilification of the opponent was not only acceptable but was expected. The speech concerns Hagnias' estate; the plaintiff argues that the defendant neglected his duties towards the *oikos* of the deceased. One of the manifestations of this neglect, if not disregard and disrespect, was the uprooting and the cutting down of olive trees and the sale of the wood for a considerable profit.

Anyone digging up an olive tree at Athens, unless it is for a sacred purpose of the Athenian people or in its demes or for one's own use to a limit of two olive trees per year or for the needs of a deceased person,[1] shall owe a hundred drachmas for each olive tree to the treasury and one tenth of this shall belong to the Goddess. And he shall owe a hundred drachmas for each olive tree to the individual who prosecutes. And the indictments about these matters shall be brought to the archons according to their remit.[2] And the prosecutor shall pay the court fee for his part. And when a person is convicted, the magistrates, before whom the case was brought, shall report

---

1 The Athenians used to offer libations on certain occasions for the dead. After the funeral they used to leave a jar of olive oil on the tomb. See *LSCG* 97 (below, no. 109).

2 The vague phrasing makes any answer to the question as to the identity of these magistrates difficult. It may be possible to see two offences in this provision; one

in writing to the revenue-collectors (*praktores*) about the amount due to the public treasury and to the treasurers of the Goddess about the amount due to the Goddess. And if they do not report, they shall owe this amount themselves.

Relevant texts

Dreros (Crete): obligation of the young to plant an olive tree as a symbol of integration into the society of the *polis*, *Nomima* I, 48, 156–64 (=*IC* I ix 1) (end 6th century BC); **Athens**: import of olive oil in time of shortage: *IG* ii^2 903.5–10 (176/5 BC); Hadrian's law on olive trees and olive oil, *IG* ii^2 1100 (AD 124); accusation of destroying protective fence of an olive tree: Lys. vii; prohibition to cut trees, *AthPol* 60.2, *IG* ii^2 1177.17–21 (mid 4th century BC), *IG* ii^2 1362 (end 4th century BC); **Kos**: *LSCG* 150 A and B (end 5th century BC); **Korope (Thessaly)**: *LSCG* 84 (*c.* 100 BC); **Paros (Cyclades)**: *LSCG* 111 (end 5th century BC); **Gortyn (Crete)**: *LSCG* 148 (3rd century BC); **Andania (Arkadia – Peloponnese)**: *LSCG* 65 (1st century BC); leasing out land for cultivation of olive trees: **Gazoros (Makedonia)**, *SEG* xxiv 614 (below, no. 49).

Further reading

Discussion of olive production in Attica: R. Sallares (1991) *The ecology of the ancient Greek world*, 304–9, London; brief discussion on protecting trees in sacred groves, B. Jordan and J. Perlin (1984) 'On the protection of sacred groves', *Studies presented to St. Dow on his eightieth birthday*, 153–9, Durham, N. Carolina (Greek, Roman and Byzantine Monographs 10); legal procedure of *phasis*, D.M. MacDowell (1990) 'The Athenian procedure of phasis', *Symposion* 1990, 187–98; trade in olive oil, Velissaropoulou (1980: 195–7).

may concern violation of the law and the other offence may have been impiety, since the olive trees were consecrated to the goddess Athena. In this respect, one may think of the *thesmothetai** and the eponymous archon, the former as responsible for civil suits and the latter as the magistrate hearing cases of impiety (*asebeia*).

COLLECTIVITIES

34 Athens, Law on associations

Digest xlvii 22.4   *?6th century BC*

In the commentary of Gaius, a Roman jurist of the second century AD, on the legislation of the Twelve Tablets, the following law on associations, believed to be Solonian, survives. This commentary was reproduced by the compilers of the *Digest*, the sixth-century compilation of the work of Roman jurists. It provides that the groups mentioned will be free to take whatever decision they wish, provided that it does not contravene public statutes.

If the inhabitants of a deme, or members of a *phratry*, or members of groups aiming to hold religious feasts (*orgeones*), or sailors, or members of groups dining together or providing for their burial (*homotaphoi*), or members of religious clubs (*thiasotai*), or individuals engaged in some enterprise for plunder (*epi leian*) or trade (*eis emporian*), whatever they agree between themselves will be valid unless forbidden by public statutes.

Relevant texts

Athens: different kinds of associations and their nature, Aristot. *EN* 1160a 8–14, 19 and *EE* 1241b 25; monarchy and associations, Isoc. *Nikokles* 54; *orgeones*, Is. ii 14; *IG* ii^2 1252 (end 4th century BC) etc.; *thiasotai*, *IG* ii^2 1273 (281/0 BC) etc.; **Megara**: *orgeones*, *IG* vii 33 (1st century BC).

Further reading

Collection and discussion of epigraphical material from the Greek world, F. Poland (1909) *Geschichte des griechischen Vereinswesen*, Leipzig; Solonian origin, R. Wieacker (1971) 'Solon und die XII Tafeln', *Studi in onore di E. Volterra* III, 757–84; *orgeones*, W.S. Ferguson (1944) 'The Attic orgeones', *HThR* 37, 61–120, and (1949) 'Orgeonika', *Hesperia* Suppl. 8, 130–63; *thiasotai* as parts of *phratries*, Lambert (1993); demes, Whitehead (1986); sailors, Velissaropoulou (1980).

35 Gortyn (Crete), Liability among partners

IC iv 72 col. IX 43–53   *c. 480–460 BC*

In Gortyn disputes among partners were resolved largely on the basis
of the witnesses' testimonies. The number of witnesses required to
testify depended on the disputed amount. When there were no
witnesses, the judge was bound to decide in favour of the plaintiff.

If anyone has formed a partnership for a venture and does not pay back his
partners, in case of a dispute for a hundred staters if there are three adult
witnesses or two witnesses for a case down to ten staters or one witness in a
case of less than ten staters, the judge shall decide according to the
testimonies. But if there are no testimonies, in case the contracting party
appear, whichever way the plaintiff demands either to deny after swearing
an oath or [. . .]

Relevant texts

Athens: lawsuits about partnerships (*koinonikai dikai*), *AthPol* 52.2;
expected (but not delivered) support from co-associates in litigation,
[Lys.] viii; friendship in partnerships, Aristot. *EN* 1160a.

Further reading

Gortyn: Metzger (1973: 77–80); **Athens**: Harrison (1968: 242),
Rhodes (1981: 586).

TRADE

36 Thasos, Law on wine trade

IG xii Suppl. 347   *c. 425–412 BC*

This law aims at (i) protecting the production and the distribution of
Thasian wine by setting a time limit after which sale of the
production is allowed and (ii) avoiding dilution of the product and
subsequent loss of prestige and markets. At the same time it aims to
help the collection of the duty owed to the *polis*. Import of foreign
wine is prohibited, date and range of trading areas are clearly defined,
as well as the responsibilities of the magistrates.

I. Nobody is allowed to buy the fruits of the vine on the spot, for mustum or wine, before the first of the month Plynterion;[3] anyone selling against this provision shall owe an amount equal, stater for stater, to the price paid, of which half will be given to the *polis* and the other half to the prosecutor. Prosecution shall be brought according to the procedure for violence. When anyone buys wine in wine-jars, the sale will be valid if the wine-jars are sealed.[4]

II. [. . .] fines and pledges shall be the same; if nobody provides a security, let the magistrates appointed for the mainland[5] prosecute; if they win, the entire penalty will belong to the *polis*; if these magistrates, although informed, do not prosecute, they shall be liable to pay double the penalty; and anyone wishing to prosecute can do so, according to the above, and have half the imposed penalty and the *demiourgoi** shall prosecute the magistrates according to the above; no Thasian ship is to import foreign wine within the area delimited by Athos and Pacheia;[6] if anyone does, he shall pay the same penalty as in the case of diluting wine and the helmsman shall be liable to the same penalty; the prosecution and the securities shall be as above. Nobody is allowed to sell wine by cup from amphoras or casks or jars; prosecution, securities and penalties against anyone selling in this way will be as in the case of diluting wine.

37 Delphoi (Central Greece), Law prohibiting the export of wine

CID I 3   *mid 5th century BC*

While the Thasians tried to protect their market on wine, Delphoi tried to secure wine brought for religious purposes to the sanctuary from being resold. It is interesting to see in this law the interplay between religious sanctions and 'political' penalties imposed on the offenders.

---

3 Roughly early June.
4 The reason for sealing was to safeguard the interests of the *polis*, since the seals would have shown the exact quantity of wine, on which the duty had to be calculated. Moreover, it designated the passing of responsibility to the buyer for everything happening afterwards.
5 Pouilloux (1954: 389) thinks that these magistrates were introduced during the reorganization of the Thasian *polis* in order to reorganize the mainland opposite Thasos (perhaps the collection of revenue).
6 That is, the area from the peninsula of Athos in Chalkidike to the cape Pacheia, outside the ancient city of Ainos, modern Enez in Turkey.

It is not permitted to bring new wine outside the stadium; and if anyone does so, he must appease the god by libation and an expiatory sacrifice; and he shall pay five drachmas, half of which will belong to the denouncer.

Relevant texts

Thasos: law on the wine trade, *SEG* xviii 347 and xxxvi 790 (*c*. 480 BC); prohibition of the consumption of wine: **Eleutherna (Crete)**, *SEG* xli 739 (6th century BC); **Eretria (Euboia)**: delimited area of Eretrian commerce, *IG* xii (9) 1273–4 and *SEG* xli 715; prohibition on harvesting unripe fruits: **Egypt**, *BGU* vii (*Gnomon* of *Idios Logos*) 104; **Athens**, Pl. *Laws* 844 d8–e5; **Byzantion (Thrace)**: monopoly of currency exchange, [Aristot.] *Oec.* 1346b 3; **Keos (Cyclades)**: law on ruddle (*miltos*), Tod ii 162 (before 350 BC).

Further reading

Pouilloux (1954: 45 and 130–1); maritime zones and law on wine as protecting exports, Velissaropoulou (1980: 191–4 and 136–9); review of the evidence on Thasian wine, Fr. Salviat (1986) 'Le vin de Thasos: amphores, vin et sources écrites' in J.-Y. Empereur and Y. Garlan (eds) *Recherches sur les amphores grecques*, 145–96 (*BCH* Suppl 13).

38 Erythrai (Ionia – Asia Minor), Law regulating the wool trade

IErythrai 15   *c. 360–330 BC*

The fragmentary state of the inscription does not allow us to ascertain details of this law. However, it is clear that it concerns the conditions for trading, in wool (especially honest trading, prohibition on sale in rain, always weighing the quantity of wool for sale) and measures for policing the marketplace. The wool of the area was renowned throughout the ancient world (Pliny *HN* 119).

[. . .] and the traders shall weigh the wool they sell and they shall weigh it without deceit; if anyone does not comply, he shall pay twenty drachmas for each [. . .] ; the *agoranomos** shall exact the fine; sales shall last till noon. When it rains, wool should not be brought[7] (to the market?) and [. . .] they

---

7 The reason for this prohibition lies in the fact that wet wool weighs more when dry, and of the obligations of the traders being fairness.

shall not sell wool of a year-old sheep; if they do, the *agoranomos* shall fine them two drachmas per day. The trader or the retailer is not allowed to sell wool or the gratings from fleece, from any other source but their own; whoever sells wool from another flock shall be deprived of the wool and shall be fined twenty drachmas and the *prytaneis** will put in auction everything that it was for sale or [. . .]

Relevant texts

Tax on wool: **Kos**, *Syll*[3] 1000 (2nd century BC); groups of wool workers, **Saittai (Lydia – Asia Minor)**: *SEG* xxxiii 1017 (AD 156); honest trading: **Athens**, Hyp. iv 14; Dem. xx 9; prices for goods set by the *agoranomoi*: **Athens**, *BCH* 118 (1994) 51–68 (1st century BC); Theophrastos, *Laws* frg. 20.

Further reading

A. Wilhelm (1909) 'Inschriften aus Erythrai und Chios', *JÖAI* 12, 126–50 (= *Kleine Schriften* II.I, 348–72, Leipzig, 1984).

39 Kyparissia (Peloponnese), Law on import and export duties

SEG xi 1026   *4th–3rd century BC*

As the title implies, the law concerns the duties imposed on the import of goods to, or export from the territory of Kyparissia, on the west coast of the Peloponnese. The duty imposed was one-fiftieth of the value of the imported or exported goods, on the basis of a declaration submitted by the trader. The penalties for non-registration were ten times the amount of the tax.

God. If anyone imports anything in the territory of the Kyparissians, when he discharges his merchandise, he shall be registered with the *pentekostologoi** and pay one-fiftieth of the value of the goods before he buys or sells anything; if he does not, he shall pay tenfold this amount. Anyone who exports by sea, shall be registered with the *pentekostologoi* and pay the one-fiftieth as deposit when the *pentekostologoi* demand, but not before. If he does not pay this as demanded, he shall pay ten times that amount as the law requires. And if any other official imposes a lesser penalty, the *pentekostologos* will redress the difference according to the law.

Relevant texts

Customs laws: **Ephesos (Ionia – Asia Minor)**, *SEG* xxxix 1180 (AD 62); **Kaunos (Caria – Asia Minor)**, *SEG* xiv 639 (1st century AD); **Myra (Lykia – Asia Minor)**, *SEG* xxxv 1439 (2nd century AD); duty free status (*ateleia*): **Herakleia on Latmos (Caria – Asia Minor)**, *SEG* xxxvii 859 (*c*. 196 BC); **Aitolia**, *IG* ix 1² (1) 174 (*c*. 240 BC); *pentekoste* tax: **Delos (Cyclades)**, *ID* 509 (below, no. 40); **Keos (Cyclades)**, Tod ii 162 (before 350 BC); **Halikarnassos (Caria – Asia Minor)**, *Epigraphica* I, 26 (3rd century BC); **Anaktorion (Akarnania)**, *Choix* 29 (?216 BC).

Further reading

Customs and excise, Velissaropoulou (1980: 205–15); customs law of Kaunos, Velissaropoulou (1980: 223–8).

40   Delos (Cyclades), Law regulating the charcoal trade

ID 509   *end 3rd century BC*

The administration of the island controlled the import of grain and of fuel, goods vital for the prosperity of the island. The law regulating the trade in charcoal on the island was aimed at guaranteeing the payment of the 2 per cent tax to the authorities and the upkeep of certain conditions in charcoal trading. In particular, it was compulsory to use weights and measures provided by the authorities and not to sell more or less than the declared quantities

Anyone who does not use the weights prescribed for wood is not allowed to sell either charcoal or logs or wood; he is not allowed to sell them on Delos even if he has bought them in there or even if they are cargo board on ship; he may sell only what he has registered on his own name. It is prohibited to sell goods (i.e. wood and charcoal) bought in a public auction, once these have been awarded to the purchaser, or to sell wood or poles or charcoal belonging to another person. Only the importers are permitted to sell their goods and they may not sell more or less than the amount they declared to the *pentekostologoi**. Before any sale the importers shall register with the *agoranomoi** the amount they have registered with the *pentekostologoi*; and whoever contravenes these provisions shall owe fifty drachmas, and any citizen shall have the right to denounce him to the *agoranomoi*; who shall produce the information to the Thirty-One[8] in the same month; and the fee of the court is to be paid by the informer; if the defendant loses his case, he shall pay the court fee and two-thirds of the penalty to the prosecutor and one-third to the treasury, and the *agoranomoi* shall exact the penalty within ten days from the publication of the decision, without bearing any responsibility; if they cannot do this, they shall swear a negative oath, handing over the defendant and his property to the informer, and seeing that it is recorded on the board where other records are written, and will hand it over to the public archive office in the *Boule*.

Those who import, free of duty, wood or logs or charcoal to be sold, according to the weights of the wood, shall register, before the sale, with the *agoranomoi* the amount they are going to sell and they shall not be allowed to sell more or less than the declared quantities; and the *agoranomoi* shall not provide the weights and measures for the charcoal to anyone who is not complying with the law and they shall have to remove their wood or poles or charcoal from where they lie, otherwise they shall owe one drachma per day to the *polis*, and the *agoranomoi* will exact the penalty, without bearing any responsibility.

Relevant texts

Kyzikos (Mysia – Asia Minor): possible mention of charcoal, *AM* 9 (1884) 14–5; for other merchandise, above nos. 36–8; **Sardeis (Lydia – Asia Minor):** use of wood in building, *SEG* xxxvi 1087 (213 BC); **Oropos (Boiotia),** *SEG* xxxvii 100 (*c.* 330 BC); **Athens:** decree on weights and measures, *IG* ii² 1013 (*c.* 100 BC); magistrates responsible for weights and measures (*metronomoi*), *AthPol* 51.2; prototype weights and measures, *SEG* xxxvi 233 (1st century AD).

Further reading

Discussion of sources and trade of timber, R. Meiggs (1982) *Trees and timber in the ancient Mediterranean world*, Oxford; Velissaropoulou (1980: 204); C. Vial (1984) *Delos indépendante*, Paris (*BCH* Supplément 10); brief examination of the purpose of the law, G. Reger (1994) *Regionalism and change in the economy of independent Delos, 314–167 B.C.*, 173–5, Berkeley, Calif.

---

8 The Thirty-One was a court with thirty-one members deciding commercial cases. See as well, *ID* 144 A ii 37 (304 BC) in which the expenses for this court are mentioned.

41 Olbia (S. Russia), Law on trading

IKalchedon 16   *4th century BC*

This law establishes the exclusive use of the coinage, silver and bronze of Olbia for all the transactions concluded in Olbia. It is also enacted that all commercial transactions should take place in a particular location and sets out the exchange rate of the local coinage to the coinage of Kyzikos, which was used widely in the area of the Black Sea from the 6th to the 4th century BC.

These are the conditions for those entering Borysthenes[9] by sea; the Council and the people decided; Kanobos, son of Thrasydamas, proposed; it is permitted to import and export coins with the stamp of authenticity, gold and silver; anyone willing to buy or sell coins, gold or silver, he can do so on the stone in the place where the assembly of the people is convened; whoever sells or buys coins in another place, the seller will be fined to the amount of the sale and the buyer will be required to pay an amount equal to the value of the purchase; all the purchases and sales are to be paid in money issued by the *polis*, bronze and silver coins of Olbia; if anyone sells or buys in another currency the seller will lose the object sold and the buyer the price paid; those who violate the law will have to pay a fine to the magistrates, following the decision of a lawcourt. As far as the buying and selling of gold is concerned, the stater of Kyzikos[10] will be exchanged for no more and no less than ten staters and a half of Olbia; any other recognized gold or silver coins will be exchanged in a commonly agreed price; no tax is to be imposed on anyone buying or selling unacceptable gold or silver coins [. . .]

Relevant texts

Decree prohibiting exports: **Salamis (Cyprus)**, *SEG* xxix 1580 (Imperial); harbour regulations: **Ephesos (Ionia – Asia Minor)**, *SEG* xix 684 (AD 161/2); **Xanthos (Lycia – Asia Minor)**, *FXanthos* vii 86 (mid 2nd century AD); exclusive use of coinage: **Athens**, *SEG* xxvi 72 (below, no. 50); ban on selling anywhere else but in the marketplace (*agora*): **Thourioi (S. Italy)**, Theophrastos frg. 97 iv; **Erythrai (Ionia – Asia Minor)**, *IErythrai* 15 (above, no. 38).

9 Borysthenes was the name of the region where Olbia was founded and after the foundation it was designated the territory of Olbia.

10 *Polis* on the asiatic coast of Propontis founded by the Milesians in the late 7th century BC. Cf. F.W. Hasluck (1910) *Cyzicus*, Cambridge.

Further reading

Trade and the economy of Olbia, J.G. Vinogradov and S.D. Krzyzickij (1995) *Olbia. Eine altgriechische Stadt im nord westlichen Schwarzmeerraum*, 85–97, Leiden (Mnemosyne Suppl 149); trade in ancient Greece and Rome, M.I. Finley (1973) *The ancient economy*, London; P. Garnsey, K. Hopkins and C.R. Whittaker (eds) (1983) *Trade in the ancient economy*, London.

42 Thasos, Harbour regulations

IG xii *Suppl. 348*   *3rd century BC*

Since the Thasians controlled a large portion of the trade of the northern Aegean, regulations for the proper function of their port were necessary. This law reveals that there were, at least, two separate areas designated for ships of a high tonnage. It is also of interest that special officials (*apologoi**), under the supervision of judges, were responsible for upholding the law.

No ship is to be hauled into the delineated areas, in the first one of less than 3,000 talents (= *c.* 78 tons) cargo, and in the second one of less than 5,000 talents (= *c.* 130 tons) cargo; anyone violating this rule shall pay five staters to the *polis*; and the *epistatai** shall exact the fine. And if any dispute arises, the *apologoi* shall decide about it, in the presence of judges; they are to hand their decision to impose a penalty to the *epistatai* who are to exact the penalty. If they do not do so, they themselves shall be liable for the fine. And if the *apologoi* do not reach a decision or do not transmit the decision to the *epistatai*, they shall be accountable to the incoming *apologoi* [. . .] to the *epistatai* who contrary to the decree allow ships to be hauled into the defined areas; anyone wishing to do so can inform [. . .]

Relevant texts

Athens: regulation about ships approaching Sounion, *SEG* x 10 (455/4 BC); regulation on keeping the harbour in good condition, **Ephesos (Ionia – Asia Minor)**: *IEph* 23 (AD 148).

Further reading

Tonnage of ships, Velissaropoulou (1980: 62–4); harbours in Roman Mediterranean, J. Rougé (1966) *Recherches sur l'organisation du commerce maritime en Méditerranée sous l'Empire Romain*, 147–73, Paris.

FINANCES

43 Delphoi (Central Greece), Law regulating the rate of interest

Epigraphica III 41   *early 4th century BC*

The law, also known as the law of Kadys, sets the legal interest rates for public and private loans in Delphoi, together with provisions concerning officials, procedures and women borrowers. There are seven columns surviving; column II is translated from the original publication in *BCH* 50 (1926) 3–106. The remaining columns, except column VII, are so fragmentary that no text can be established. In the first column, the legal interest rate is set together with the penalties for anyone charging more or less. Column II pertains to the procedure used for denouncing any transgressor of the law, while in column III the ability of women to borrow is delimited as well as the amount of produce given as pledge.

Col. I: God. Fortune. This law was passed in a plenary assembly in the archonship of Kadys with four hundred and fifty-four votes in favour. The interest on debts arising from a contract, public and private, shall be paid in the month of Bysion[11] in the archonship of Kadys. From the month of Theoxenios[12] onwards nobody is permitted to charge more than three oboloi per mina[13] for each month by any means, device or pretext, on *patriai*,[14] worshippers of heroes, religious groups (*thiasotai*) or any other group, neither privately nor to a man, a woman, a boy or a girl, man and woman slave, resident or foreigner in Delphoi. And if anyone charges more than the legal rate on public or private debts, he shall be deprived of the owed money and he shall pay fifty drachmas on each mina, as many minas as he lent. And if he charges less minas against the law, he shall be deprived of the money owed and he shall pay twenty drachmas; however, it is permitted to lend without fine six staters for a quarter of an Aiginetan obol per month.

11 Bysion was the eighth month in the calendar, corresponding to our February.
12 Theoxenios was the ninth month in the Delphian calendar. It corresponds to modern March.
13 In Athenian standards one mna was equal to 600 obols. Assuming that in Delphoi the Athenian standards were used, the interest rate was approximately 6 per cent.
14 *Patriai* were a subdivision of the *phratry* in Delphoi. They are also attested in Tenos and Miletos. Cf. D. Roussel (1976) *Tribu et cité. Études sur les groupes sociaux dans les cités grecques aux époques archaiques et classique*, Paris (Centre de Recherches d'Histoire Ancienne 23).

Col. II: Anyone wishing can denounce the transgressor and keep half of the loan. The denouncer shall exact the amount of the loan within thirty days from the denouncement and pay half of it to the public treasury. If the denounced creditor objects, each shall choose ten men who are going to be presented to the Council; from them the Council shall allot eleven trustworthy men, who shall swear that they are going to decide the case with fairness. Any of the councillors who does not keep the promise shall pay fifty drachmas. Anyone who wishes can collect the amount of money and the injured party can charge him with lack of patron? The Council should initiate the procedure within ten days from the denouncement; if not, the denouncer shall force the Council to start the procedure, to allot the judges and summon the witnesses to swear the oath. The Council should have arranged everything according to the law within a month, otherwise each councillor shall owe fifty drachmas.

Col. III: [. . .] by the prosecutor and having exacted the money he will be entitled to keep it. And if anyone [. . .] or prosecutes for anti-patriotism, the action and the trial will be brought before the then current magistrates. A woman is not allowed to lend if her husband does not consent, and if she is a widow, without the consent of her adult son or of the closest relative of her husband [. . .] of these, the pledges which the council accepted and he shall be deprived of the owed money. Produce is not to be counted in any other way but [. . .] Interest because it is annual [. . .] in thirty days to exact, and if he does not exact, he is not permitted to pledge it for more than a year and if the exactor wants to use it as security for more than a year, he shall be liable to pay double the amount he used as security.

Relevant texts

Megara: interest on interest (*palintokion*), Plu. *Mor.* 295c, d (?6th century BC); **Byzantion (Thrace)**: partial repayment of loans, [Aristot.] *Oec.* 1347b (4th century BC); **Olynthos (Chalkidike)**: loan with surety, *SEG* xxxviii 637 (352/1 BC), 639, 640 (4th century BC); **Hyampolis (Phokis – Central Greece)**: record of a loan, *SEG* xxxvii 422 (450–425 BC); loan contracted between individuals and *poleis*: **Thespiai (Boiotia)**, *L'émprunt* 13 (223 BC); **Delphoi (Phokis – Central Greece)**, *SEG* xlii 472 (end 2nd century BC); loan contracted between *poleis*, *L'émprunt* 11 (*c.* 200–190 BC).

Further reading

Athens: interest, Millett (1991: 91–109) and Cohen (1993: 44–6); women and lending, Schaps (1979: 63–7) and E.M. Harris (1992) 'Women and lending in Athenian society', *Phoenix* 46, 309–21;

attempts to resolve problems arising from debts, Asheri (1969); overview of the workings of a bank in the Greek world, R. Bogaert (1968) *Banques et banquiers dans les cités grecques*, Leyden.

44 Athens, Law on loans for cargoes of grain

Demosthenes xxxv (Against Lakritos) 51   *mid 4th century BC*

The law appears in a lawsuit of commercial character; the plaintiff lent money for carrying wine to the Black Sea and on the return journey bringing wheat to Athens. According to the law it was illegal to contract a loan on a ship which would not bring wheat on the return journey to Athens. The law is cited as a proof of the severity of the consequences the plaintiff would have suffered had he violated the law.

Athenians and *metics* living in Athens and any persons over whom they have control are not allowed to lend money on any vessel which is not going to bring to Athens grain and other articles specifically mentioned. And whoever contracts a loan contrary to this law, information and an account[15] of the money shall be provided to the *epimeletai** in the same way as it is provided for the ship and the grain. And the transgressor shall not have any legal redress for recovery of the loan made for a voyage to anywhere other than Athens, and no magistrate shall introduce any such suit to the lawcourts.

Relevant texts

Athens: violation of the law, Dem. xxxiv 37; agreement for a maritime loan, Dem. lvi 6; law on loans for cargo of wheat, Lyc. *Leocr.* 27; unpublished law imposing tax on grain trade mentioned in *SEG* xxxvi 146 (374/3 BC); dispute about grain sellers (*sitopolai*), Lys. xxii; guardians of the grain (*sitophylakes*), *AthPol* 51.3; *sitophylakes* registering imports of grain, Dem. xx 32; interstate agreements for provision of grain from abroad, Dem. xx 31 and Tod ii 167 (346 BC); **Samos**: grain law, *Syll*[3] 976 (below, no. 45); **Teos (Ionia – Asia Minor)**: prohibition of obstructing provision of grain, *Nomima* I, 104 (below, no. 70); receipts of maritime loans in **Kerkyra**, *SEG* xxx 519–26 (6th/5th century BC).

15 For the term *phasis*, D.M. MacDowell (1990) 'The Athenian procedure of phasis', *Symposion 1990*, 187–98; for the term *apographe*, MacDowell (1978: 58) and Todd (1993: 118–19).

Further reading

Athens: maritime loans as professional lending, P. Millett (1983) 'Maritime loans and the structure of credit in fourth-century Athens' in P. Garnsey *et al.* (eds) *Trade in the ancient economy*, 36–52, London, and Millett (1991: 188–96); Cohen (1973: 100–14) and (1993: 42–4); comparative account, R. Bogaert (1965) 'Banquiers, courtiers et prêts maritimes à Athènes et à Alexandrie', *CE* 40, 140–65; food supply and crisis management, P. Garnsey (1988) *Famine and food supply in the graeco-roman world. Responses to risk and crisis*, 89–164 and especially 139–42, Cambridge; role of *sitophylakes* in Athens, Ph. Gauthier (1981) 'De Lysias à Aristote (*AthPol* 51.4): le commerce du grain à Athènes et les fonctions de sitophylaques', *RHD* 59, 5–28.

45 Samos, Grain law

*Syll*³ 976 (= *Choix 34*)   *c. 260 BC*

Most of the Greek cities were ridden by chronic dependence on import of grain. This law from Samos provides for the election of, often wealthy, individuals to administer the fund created by the contributions and the distribution of grain bought with that money; in case of surplus, it can be lent out. The grain law was regarded till recently as an example of the efforts of the *polis* to guarantee grain for its citizens and the procedure to control effectively the distribution of wheat. However, it is now claimed that the importance of the law lies in the administration of the stocked grain collected as tax in the temple of Hera.

Col. A: [. . .] of the most rich. And the nomination of the archons will take place in the second assembly of the month Kronion;[16] the *prytaneis** are to convene this assembly in the theatre and they are to order the participants to sit according to *chiliastys**, having marked the place where each *chiliastys* will sit; whoever does not obey and does not sit with his own *chiliastys*, he shall pay a *polis*-stater; and if he claims that he was unjustly punished, he can bring a special plea and the judgement will be given by a civic court within twenty days; the nomination and the election shall be done by the members of the *chiliastys* themselves; the members of *chiliastys* themselves shall present and select the mortgaged property and the guarantors; the *prytaneis* are to write down in the public archives the scrutinized property and

16 Kronion corresponds to our May/June.

guarantors, which were approved; similarly they are to record the selected *meledonoi**; when the moment of selection comes, the herald of the *polis* will pray for the selectors to choose those who think they are going to administer the fund in the most beneficial way; and the selected persons will take the interest from the borrowers and they shall give it to the men selected for the grain supply; and these men shall buy grain, from the one-twentieth tax levied from the district of Anaia,[17] giving to the goddess a price not lower than the one that the *polis* fixed beforehand, five drachmas and two obols; the remaining amount of money is to be kept until their successors are appointed, unless the *polis* decides to buy grain; and then they are to give it to them; if the *polis* decides to buy grain, they are to give the remaining amount to the selected *sitones**; and the *sitones* shall buy grain from the land of Anaiis, under whatever conditions seem to him the most advantageous for the *polis*, unless the *polis* decides to buy grain from another region; otherwise, let it happen in the way the *polis* decides; and the *prytaneis* of the month Artemision[18] shall put these questions in the assembly having given public notice; and the assembly of the citizens, every year in the first assembly, after electing magistrates, is to select two men responsible for the supply of grain, one from each phyle, whose property will not be less than three talents; these two persons, having received the interest from the *meledonoi*, they will pay the price of the grain and any other expense and they will distribute the wheat; in the same assembly the citizens are to select a person with property no less than two talents as *sitones*; if it seems good, the produce of the interest can be lent out, if there are citizens who, having provided sufficient mortgages and guarantors, wish to buy earlier and offer grain at a more advantageous price to the people; and the men selected for the grain will scrutinize the guarantors at their own risk; all the produce bought shall be distributed to the residing citizens by *chiliastys*, two measures of grain for each month as a gift; the distribution will start in the month of Pelousion[19] and every month until the stocks of grain are consumed; nobody shall take a share on behalf of another citizen, unless someone is sick; the distribution will take place from the first of the month to the tenth, and for those returning to the thirtieth of the month; they are going to account for those who received grain every month submitting a list with their names in a *chiliastys* order; and the magistrates of a *chiliastys* will be able to select the same *meledonos* for five years in succession; and if anyone from the borrowers does not pay back the money, all or part of it, the *chiliastys* will sell the guarantees, and if there is a surplus it will be given to

---

17 Anaia was a fertile area in the mainland opposite Samos. See Shipley (1987: 34–7).

18 Artemision was the ninth month of the Samians and corresponds to our April/May.

19 Pelousion was the first month in the Samian calendar, corresponding to our June/July.

the guarantor; and if there is a deficit the *chiliastys* shall exact it from the guarantor; the *chiliastys* shall pay the accrued interest to the commissioners of the grain; and if they do not pay, the magistrates of the *chiliastys* will not receive the grain until they pay their fair share; and if any one of the selected *meledonoi*, having the money he is supposed to lend, does not lend the money, but keeps it for himself, he shall pay ten thousand drachmas to the *polis*; and similarly if he does not give the interest to the persons selected as grain commissioners, he shall pay an equal fine and the auditors of his *chiliastys* will have his property auctioned up to the amount of his debt; and besides the penalty he will be deprived of his civic rights until he pays the fine; and the magistrates of the *chiliastys*, whose *meledonos* has not paid the money, will not receive the grain distribution; and if the magistrates of a *chiliastys*, all or some of them, pay the debt of the *meledonos* or of any borrower, they shall be able to receive the grain distribution from the moment they paid the debt; nobody is allowed to use this fund or the interest from it but for the free distribution of grain; and if any *prytanis* or orator suggests or the *epistates** puts in vote a proposal to use the fund or to transfer it for another purpose, he shall pay ten thousand drachmas; any treasurer or *meledonos* or grain commissioner or *sitones* shall have to pay the same fine if he gives this money or lends it for any other purpose apart from the free distribution of wheat.

Col. B and C: A list of names and amounts, partly damaged, follows.

Relevant texts

Similar funds set up in different cities: **Athens**, Dem. xviii 248; **Tauromenion (Sicily)**, *IG* xiv 427–30 (2nd–1st century BC); **Iasos (Caria – Asia Minor)**, *IIasos* 244 (mid 2nd century BC); **Erythrai (Ionia – Asia Minor)**, *IErythrai* 28 (*c.* 275–270 BC); **Prousa (Bithynia – Asia Minor)**, Dio Chrys. xlvi 8; **Paros (Cyclades)**, *IG* xii (5) 135 (early 1st century BC); **Thespiai (Boiotia)**, *IG* vii 1719–44 (191–172 BC); **Samothrake**, *ISamothrace* 5 (3rd/2nd century BC).

Further reading

Date: S.V. Tracy (1990) 'The date of the grain decree from Samos. The prosopographical indicators', *Chiron* 20, 97–100; process described in the law, G. Thür and Ch. Koch (1981) 'Prozessrechtlicher Kommentar zum "Getreidegesetz" aus Samos', *AAWW* 118, 61–88; L. Migeotte (1992) *Les souscriptions publiques dans les cités grecques*, 185–91, Genève (Hautes Études du monde grèco-romaine 17); *poleis* did not establish monopolies in grain trade but intervened only in emergencies, L. Migeotte (1991) 'Le pain quotidien dans les cités hellénistiques. À propos des fonds permanent pour l'approvisionnement en grain', *Cahiers Glotz* 2, 19–41; law aiming at simplifying the financial administration of the temple of Hera and not at improving living standards or providing subsistence, D.J. Gargola (1992) 'Grain distributions and the revenue of the temple of Hera on Samos', *Phoenix* 66, 12–28; Shipley (1987: 218–21); collection of evidence on provision of grain in Asia Minor during Principate, J.H.M. Strubbe (1987) 'The sitonia in the cities of Asia Minor under the Principate (I)', *EA* 10, 45–82, and (1989) 'The sitonia in the cities of Asia Minor under the Principate (II)', *EA* 13, 99–122; on *chiliastys*, P. Debord (1984) 'Chiliastys', *REA* 86, 201–11, and N.F. Jones (1987) *Public organization in ancient Greece. A documentary study*, 198–9 (Memoirs of the American Philosophical Society 176).

LEASES

46 Samos, Law on leasing the shopkeepers' stalls (*kapeleia*) in Heraion

SEG xxvii *545*   *c. 246–221 BC*

With this law the Samians endorse the proposals of the administrators of the temple of Hera about the renting out of four stalls for retailers in the temple. These stalls shall be used exclusively by the lessor, who is not allowed to sublease them, to provide work or shelter to certain categories of people such as slaves, mercenaries, the unemployed or suppliants. If a dispute arises between a lessor and a citizen, the administrators of the temple will refer the dispute to the courts of the *polis*.

[In the year of . . .] on the eleventh day of the month Kronion,[20] in the customary assembly and the elections having taken place in the theatre, when [. . .] was *epistates**. The *neopoioi**, having corrected the delineation of the retailers' stalls in the sanctuary in line with the decree, proposed as follows and the assembly has approved: four stalls for retailers shall be leased into the sanctuary of Hera; on each of them the lessor will settle throughout the year and not more than one person will have right to the tenancy; no more than one person is to trade next to these posts [. . .] nor soldier nor

20 See above, fn. 16.

unemployed person nor suppliant nor [. . .] in any way or means except the lessors. Anyone who trades next to these posts will pay a fine of [. . .] drachmas; and the lessors are not allowed to transfer [. . .] to an unemployed person nor to a suppliant in any way or by any method [. . .] to any of these people, he shall pay to the goddess sacred drachmas [. . .], and the fine will be exacted by the *neopoioi* and the treasurer of the sacred funds; and the lessors shall not accept anything from a slave, a suppliant, a soldier or an unemployed person and they shall not buy [. . .] produced in the countryside? nor anything else by any other means or method, some of the landowners or [. . .] sell some of the fruits; the lessors are not permitted to provide shelter to the slaves sitting in the temple, to provide them with work or food or accept from them anything on whatever pretence; and if any of those responsible for the stalls? shall sell any of the prohibited items he shall be liable to pay to the goddess drachmas [. . .] and if a citizen accuses a lessor or a lessor accuses a citizen, suits are to be submitted to the *neopoioi* till [. . .] and the *neopoioi* are to bring the suits submitted [. . .] before the court, subsequently to the day on which they were legally authenticated [. . .] concerning the submission they are to act according to the [. . .] the legal fee will be paid according to the law [. . .] the suit and the penalty will be paid by the defeated party; and if the *neopoioi* fine someone unjustly about something prohibited within the sanctuary and the persons fined object, the submitted objections are to be brought before the citizens' civil court by the *exetastai** in the same way; and the legal fee will be paid by the lessors to the treasurer of the sacred funds [. . .] not to do any wrongdoing nor to be liable?; the lessors [. . .] to the treasurer of the sacred funds will be free of tax [. . .] in the sanctuary; the servants (*hieroi paides*) are not allowed to trade.

Relevant texts

Arkesine (Amorgos – Cyclades): lease of temple land, *IG* xii (7) 62 (4th century BC).

Further reading

Various comments and readings: L. Koenen (1977) 'The Samian statute on kapeloi in the precinct of Hera', *ZPE* 27, 211–18; F. Sokolowski (1978) 'The kapeloi in the Heraion of Samos', *ZPE* 29, 143–7; detailed commentary, L. Soverini (1990–91) 'Il "commercio nel tempio": osservazioni sul regolamento dei kapeloi a Samo (SEG xxvii 545)', *Opus* 9–10, 59–121.

47 Keos (Cyclades), Leasing regulation of Poiassioi

IG xii (5) 568   *5th or 4th century BC*

Poiassa was one of the small *poleis* on the island of Keos. The inscription preserves the terms on which the inhabitants of Poiassa rent their common land; the lessor is obliged to pay the rent regularly, to provide a building and to preserve the existing fruit trees.

Gods. The land of Poiassioi. The lessee shall give on the tenth of the month Bakchion[21] thirty drachmas; if not, he shall evacuate the land; taxes will be paid in Poiassa; the lessee shall provide a straight and roofed building; he is not allowed to cut down cultivated trees.

Relevant texts

Athens: demes, *IG* ii² 2497 (Prasiai, 4th century BC); lease of theatre, *IG* ii² 1176, *SEG* xix 117 and *SEG* xxxiii 143 (324/3 BC); *phratry*, *IG* ii² 1241 (300/299 BC); *orgeones*, *IG* ii² 2499 (306/5 BC), 2501 (end 4th century BC), *SEG* xxiv 203 (333/2 BC); mine leases, *The Athenian Agora* xix P5–16, 18–30, 32–41, 43–4, 50–1 (mid 4th century BC); **Thespiai (Boiotia)**: *IG* vii 1739–41 etc.; **Delos (Cyclades)**: *IG* xi (2) 287 A, 143–74 etc. (Hellenistic era); **Chios**: *phratry* of Klytidai, *SEG* xxii 508 (early 4th century BC); leasing contract: **Klazomenai (Ionia – Asia Minor)**, *IErythrai* 510 (3rd century BC); lease of land: **Mylasa (Caria – Asia Minor)**, *IMyl* 810 and 818 (end 2nd century BC).

Further reading

Leases from Athens, D. Behrend (1970) *Attische Pachturkunden. Ein Beitrag zur Beschreibung der Misthosis nach der griechischen Inschriften*, Munchen (Vestigia 12); leases of Athenian demes, Whitehead (1986: 152–8); leases of mines, M.K. Langdon (1991) 'Poletai records', *The Athenian Agora* xix, 57–143; comparative approach to leases from Athens, Thespiai and Delos, R. Osborne (1988) 'Social and economic implications of the leasing of land and property in classical and Hellenistic Greece', *Chiron* 18, 279–323; discussion of leases between

---

21 Bakchion corresponds to modern February/March.

individuals, G. Casanova (1981) 'I contratti d'affito fra privati nelle epigrafi greche' in E. Bresciani *et al.* (eds) *Scritti in onore di O. Montevecchi*, 89–97, Rome; lease of Klytidai in Chios, D. Behrend (1988) 'Die Pachturkunden der Klytiden', *Symposion 1988*, 231–50.

48 Thasos, Law on leasing public property

IG xii (8) 265   *end 4th century BC*

This text regulates the terms for renting one of the gardens of Herakles. It was public property and the *polis* decided the terms of the lease. There is a preoccupation with cleanliness, as one would expect in a sacred garden.

When Lysistratos, son of Aischron, was archon; Good fortune; The garden of Herakles, the one next to the gate shall be leased on the following terms: The lessee of the garden is to maintain in a clean state the plot around the gates where the manure has hitherto been thrown out. If any of the slaves throws dung into the plot, the lessee shall be obliged to clean it and the slave, after being whipped, shall go without further punishment. The *agoranomos** and the priest of Asklepios shall take care, so that the lessees will provide the plot clean; if they do not, they shall owe a twelfth of a stater for each day, sacred to Asklepios; the *apologoi** are to put them in trial or they shall be liable; the lessee will owe a sixth of a stater for each day to the priest and to the *agoranomos*.

Relevant texts

Athens: procedure of leasing, *AthPol* 47; failure to pay rent, [Dem.] xliii 48; lease of the temple of Neleus, Kodros and Basile, *IG* i^3 84 (418/17 BC); **Thasos**: obligation to keep the leased property clean, *IG* xii Suppl. 353 (early 3rd century BC); law on cleanliness, *SEG* xlii 785 (below, no. 85).

Further reading

Athens: M.B. Walbank (1991) 'Leases of public lands' in *The Athenian Agora* xix, 149–207; keeping public property clean, Vatin (1976).

55

49 Gazoros (Makedonia), Decree about the lease of public land

SEG xxiv 614 (= *Epigraphica I 49*)   *AD 158/9*

This decree is an example of an otherwise unknown community granting rights of *emphyteusis* on fertile land for cultivation to individuals. It lays down that in return the holders of these rights shall keep a percentage of the produce for themselves, according to the type of trees cultivated. This arrangement is known under Roman law (Byzantine law included) as *emphyteusis* – that is, the right of the person who planted them to the fruits of trees and the trees.

Good fortune. From Syros, son of Eualkes, Kozeimazos, son of Polucharmos, Doules, son of Beithys the elected presidents, on the 10th of the month Artemeisios[22] of the 190th Augustan year which is the 306th (provincial) year,[23] to Dioulas, son of Heron, was *mnemon** in Gazoros.[24] We send to you the decision approved by the people and the council according to the law. Alkimos, son of Taralas, proposed that since the public lands need to be planted with vines and fruit-trees, those wishing to do so may undertake the cultivation and retain part of the fruits; the councillors after consideration found his proposal suitable and proceeded with the scrutiny of the cultivators and those who will enjoy the usufruct on the following conditions: those planting vines will keep half of their produce and the other half will remain with the public treasury; people who have planted olive trees will keep two portions, those who have planted fig trees and other fruit trees and grapes will keep all their produce and the public treasury will receive nothing. And in the ensuing vote all voted in favour. The assembly has ratified this decision.

22 Artemeisios was the tenth month in the Makedonian calendar. It corresponds to our April.
23 The Augustan (Sebastos) years mean that years following are counted from the victory of Octavius at Aktion in 31 BC, while the following date indicates the provincial era, the chronology starting off with the annexation of Makedonia into the Roman state in 148 BC. For the problem of dates in Makedonia, see F. Papazoglou (1963) 'Notes d'épigraphie et de topographie macédoniennes', *BCH* 87, 517–26.
24 For Gazoros see F. Papazoglou (1988) *Les villes de Macédoine à l'époque romaine*, 382–5, Paris (*BCH* Suppl 16).

Relevant texts

Athens: ban on uprooting olive trees, Dem. xliii 71 (above, no. 33); **Thasos**: ban on selling the fruits of the vine, *IG* xii Suppl. 347 (above, no. 36); **Thisbe (Boiotia)**: letter of a Roman official allowing and regulating the planting of trees, *Syll³* 884 (3rd century AD); **Lokris (Central Greece)**: guarantee of rights to whatever was planted, *Nomima* I, 44 (below, no. 94).

Further reading

Summary account of *emphyteusis*, H.F. Jolowicz (1952) *Historical introduction to the study of Roman Law*, 2nd edn, 283, Cambridge, and Biscardi (1982: 216); for the development of *emphyteusis* in late Roman law, D. Simon (1977) 'Das frühbyzantinische Emphyteusrecht', *Symposion 1977*, 365–422.

COINAGE

50 Athens, Law on silver coinage

SEG xxvi 72   *375/4 BC*

The law on the silver coinage was introduced during the second Delian League (founded in 378 BC), an alliance of Greek cities under the leadership of the Athenians. The purpose of this law was to strengthen the Athenian currency from the fear of counterfeits or foreign imitations. The law lays down the procedure for testing in the markets of Athens and Peiraieus, threatening corporal punishment for the testers and fines for magistrates who are charged with the supervision of the testers.

The *nomothetai** have decided in the year of the archon Hippodamas; Nikophon proposed: Attic silver coins are to be accepted [. . .] silver and has the impress of the *polis*. And the public tester, sitting between the tables, will test according to these provisions everyday except the day of cash payment, in the *Bouleuterion*.[25] If anyone brings [. . .] having the same

25 *Bouleuterion* was the headquarters of the Council. The old *Bouleuterion* was situated in the west side of the *Agora*; after the building of a new *Bouleuterion* at the turn of the 5th century BC the old one was used as an archive. See Rhodes (1981: 522) and Travlos (1970: 191).

impress with the Attic [. . .] it will be given back to the person who brought it. If it contains less copper or lead or it is counterfeit, it shall be cut [. . .] and it will be sacred to the Mother of the Gods and it shall be deposited in the Boule. If the tester does not sit or he does not test according to the law, the public *syllogeis** are to give him fifty lashes with the whip. If anyone does not accept the silver coin that a tester has tested, he will be deprived of everything he has for sale at that day. Denouncements about events occurring in the grain market shall be brought before the *sitophylakes**, and for events in the market and in the rest of the *polis* to the public *syllogeis*, and for events occurring in the *emporion** and in Peiraieus to the superintendents of the *emporion*, except for offences in the grain market; denouncement for these shall be brought before the *sitophylakes*. And about the denouncement, if the value of the denounced action does not exceed ten drachmas, the magistrates will decide the case; if it is worth more than ten drachmas the case shall be introduced to a lawcourt. The *thesmothetai** shall assist them by allotting the lawcourt whenever it is requested; if they do not, they will be liable to a fine [. . .] drachmas [. . .] and the denouncer will get half, if he succeeds [. . .] and if the seller was a slave, man or woman, he shall suffer fifty lashes with the whip from the magistrate to whom the case has been assigned. And if any of the magistrates does not act according to the law, any Athenian wishing to do so can indict him to the Council, and if he is succesful in the prosecution, the magistrate will be dismissed and the boule can impose a fine of up to five hundred drachmas. In order that there may be a tester in the Peiraieus for the captains of ships, traders and all the others, the Council shall appoint from among the public slaves [. . .] or to buy one, and the price will be paid by the receivers. And the super-intendents of the market will have to take care that the tester will be sitting next to the stele of Poseidon and apply the law pertaining to the tester in Athens in the same way. And this law is to be inscribed on a stone stele and be placed in Athens between the tables and in Peiraieus in front of the stele of Poseidon. And the secretary of the Council will report the price to the *poletai** and the *poletai* are to introduce it in the Council. And the salary of the tester in the *emporion* for the year of the archon Hippodamas (375/4 BC) will be paid from the moment he is appointed, and the *apodektai** will give him an amount of money equal to that given to the tester in the *polis* and in the future his salary will be drawn from the same fund as for the mint workers. And if any decree is written on a stele contrary to this law, the secretary of the Council will bring it down.

Relevant texts

Dyme (Achaia – Peloponnese): judgement on counterfeiters, *SEG* xiii 274 (*c*.190 BC); **Athens**: laws about counterfeiting, Dem. xx 167 and xxiv 212; imposing the use of Athenian coins, weights and measures on the members of the first Delian League (478–404 BC),

IG i³ 1453 (*c.* 425–415 BC); treaty between **Mytilene and Phokaia** on the coinage of *elektron*, *IG* xii (2) 1 and *SEG* xxx 1040 (early 4th century BC); Amphictyonic law on Athenian tetradrachms, *FD* III (2) 139 (below, no. 52).

Further reading

Edition and commentary of the law, R. Stroud (1974) 'An Athenian law on silver coinage', *Hesperia* 43, 157–88, and G. Stumpf (1986) 'Ein athenisches Münzgesetz des 4. Jh. v. Chr.', *Jahrbuch für Numismatik und Geldgeschichte* 36, 23–40; historical significance of the law, S. Alessandri (1984) 'Il significato storico della legge di Nicofonte sul dokimastes monetario', *ASNP* 14, 369–93; collection of evidence on counterfeiting, G. Thür and G. Stumpf (1989) 'Sechs Todesurteile und zwei plattierte Hemidrachmen aus Dyme', *Tyche* 4, 171–83; terminology, M. Caccamo-Caltabiano and P. Radici-Colace (1983) 'Argyrion dokimon (Pollux, 3, 87)', *ASNP* 13, 421–47.

51 Gortyn (Crete), Law on bronze coins

IC iv 62   *end 3rd century BC*

This law sanctions the use of bronze coins instead of silver ones. Any dispute shall be submitted to a special magistrature called *neotai**; a board of seven of them will decide the case.

Gods. This is the decision of the assembly of the *polis*, three hundred citizens being present. It was decided that bronze coins issued by the *polis* are to be used and not the silver coins. Whoever uses silver coins or refuses to accept bronze coins or sells in natura, he shall pay five staters of silver. The indictment should be submitted to the *neotas*. The seven *neotai* allotted to supervise the marketplace will reach a decision after swearing an oath. The litigant who gets the majority of their votes, after they take an oath, will be the winner. The judges will exact the fine; they shall give half to the winner and half to the *polis*.

Relevant texts

Athens: testing of coins, *SEG* xxvi 72 (above, no. 50); penalties for illicit exchange: **Mylasa (Caria – Asia Minor)**, *IMyl* 605 (AD 209/10).

Further reading

Neotai as an institution similar to associations of *neoi*, R.F. Willetts (1954) 'The neotas of Gortyn', *Hermes* 82, 494–8.

52 Delphoi (Central Greece), Decree about the use of the Athenian tetradrachm

FD iii *(2) 139*   *end 2nd century BC*

Amphiktyonies were something like modern confederations of sovereign states. This decree from an era when most Greek *poleis* have been scaled down to autonomous cities imposes the use of the Athenian tetradrachm throughout the *Amphiktyony*.

When the archon in Delphoi was Polyon, on the thirteenth day of the month Daidaphorios;[26] it was resolved by the *Amphiktyones* who have come to Delphoi; all the Greeks shall accept the Attic tetradrachm as equal to four silver drachmas; if any inhabitant of a *polis* or foreigner or citizen or slave, man or woman, does not accept or does not give as it is written, the slave shall be whipped by the archons while the free man shall pay two hundred silver drachmas; and the archons in the *poleis* and the *agoranomoi** will help, so that the fine imposed on those not conforming with the decision will be collected; and of the collected fine half shall belong to the person who prosecuted the transgressor and the other half to the *polis*; and if the archons in charge in the *poleis* or the festivals do not support the persons who prosecute the non-obedient to the resolution, the *Amphiktyones* will judge them, the decision for each of them being reached according to the laws of the *Amphiktyony*; likewise if the bankers working in the *poleis* and in the festivals do not conform with the resolution, anyone wishing can prosecute them to the archons; and the judgement against the archons who do not support the prosecutors shall be as it is written against others. A sealed copy of the resolution shall be carried by each *hieromnemon*[27] to his home country; and the secretary shall send this resolution to all the Greeks and it shall be written in Delphoi on the Athenian treasury [. . .]

26 The fifth month in the Delphian calendar.
27 *Hieromnemon* (lit. 'sacred recorder') was an individual sent by the *polis*-member of the *Amphiktyony* to Delphoi, to participate in the deliberations of the *Amphiktyony*. Lists of *hieromnemones*, *BCH* 45 (1921) pp. 1–70.

Relevant texts

Law of Amphiktyony, *Syll*³ 145 (380/79 BC); law of the Achaian confederacy, *IG* iv² (1) 73 (end 3rd century BC); decree of the Aitolian league for the cult of Artemis Leukophryene, *SEG* xxxviii 412 (208/7 BC).

Further reading

Analysis of the structure of *Amphiktyonies* in the archaic era, K. Tausend (1992) *Amphiktyonie und Symmachie. Formen zwischenstaatlicher Beziehungen im archaischen Griechenland*, Stuttgart (Historia Einzelschriften 73); brief historical account, F. Lefevre (1995) 'L'Amphiktyonie de Delphes: mythe et réalité', *Cahiers du centre G. Glotz* 6, 19–31.

SALE

53 Gortyn (Crete), Responsibility for the actions of slaves after sale

IC iv 72 *col. VII 10–15*   *c. 480–460 BC*

This brief provision regulates the responsibility for damages caused by slaves; even if the sale was not concluded, the buyer of a slave remains responsible for the damages caused by the slave. The aim of the provision is to resolve differences about damages caused by a slave when one claims that he sold the slave responsible for it and the purchaser claims that the purchase was never completed. At the same time, the right of the purchaser to ask for the restitution of the sale is restricted.

If anyone having bought a slave from the marketplace does not conclude the purchase within sixty days, any damage the slave has caused before or after the purchase, the person who bought him shall be liable.

Relevant texts

Gortyn: liability in sale, *IC* vi 41 VII; prohibition on buying a slave who was already pledged, *IC* iv 72 col. X 25–32; **Abdera (Thrace)**: fragmentary regulation on restitution of sale, *BCH* 66–7 (1942–3) p. 180 no. 2 (mid 4th century BC); **Athens**: Hyp. iii 15, 22; Pl. *Laws* 916a; **Gortyn**: *IC* iv 41 VII (above, no. 30); sale of landed property:

Stolos-Kellion (Chalkidike – Makedonia), *SEG* xxxviii 670–3 (357–349 BC); Amphipolis (Makedonia), *SEG* xli 555–66 (mid and late 4th century BC); registration of sale agreements: Tenos (Cyclades), *IG* xii (5) 872 (4th–3rd century BC); Erythrai (Ionia – Asia Minor), *SEG* xxxvii 917–19 (5th–4th century BC); Kimmerian Chersonesos (S. Russia): sale of plots of land, *SEG* xl 615 (*c*. 270–250 BC) and *SEG* xlii 694; sale of a house with a shop: Kamarina (Sicily), *SEG* xxxiv 940 (350–250 BC); purchase of land: Morgantina (Sicily), *SEG* xxxix 1008–13 (4th–3rd century BC); sale of property after confiscation: Athens, *IG* i³ 421–30 (end 5th century BC); Kyzikos (Mysia – Asia Minor), *SEG* xxxvi 1115–16 (4th century BC).

Further reading

IC iv 41 vii and *IC* iv 72 vii 10–15 contain rules for responsibility for actions of the slave and not restitution of the sale, E. Jakab (1989) 'Zwei Kaufvorschriften im Recht von Gortyn', *ZSS.RA* 106, 535–44; H. Meyer-Laurin (1974) 'Die Haftung für den noxa non solutus beim Sklavenkauf nach griechischen Recht', *Symposion 1974*, 263–82; F. Pringsheim (1950) *The Greek law of sale*, Weimar, and M.I. Finley (1951) 'Some problems of Greek law. A consideration of Pringsheim on sale', *Seminar* 9, 72–91; H.J. Wolff (1966) 'La structure de l'obligation contractuelle en droit grec', *RHD* 44, 569–83; sales of land in Makedonia, M. Hatzopoulos (1988) *Actes de vente de la Chalcidique centrale*, Athens (Meletemata 6), and (1991) *Actes de vente d'Amphipolis*, Athens (Meletemata 14); undisclosed defects of merchandise, J. Triantaphyllopoulos (1971) 'Les vices cachés de la chose vendue d'après les droits grecs à l'exception des papyrus', *Studi in onore di E. Volterra* V, 697–719, Milano.

54 Gortyn (Crete), Law of a plantation

IC iv 43   *early 6th century BC*

Although called law of a plantation, this provision contains four different kinds of rules pertaining to pledges and the treatment of slaves, leasing of land and water management. These brief rules provide that the person accepting land as pledge has to care for it, that a slave given as pledge has to be treated properly, that land given for planting shall not be mortgaged and, finally, that the water in the river used for irrigation shall remain at the same level.

Aa: If anyone unfairly accepts threshing-floor as pledge and he does not collect the harvest from it, he shall pay the value of the securities taken, as it is written for each case.

Ab: If anyone takes unjustly a slave, man or woman, as a pledge or strips off his/her clothes or ornaments, he shall pay half the prescribed fine for a free man and one-third of the value of clothes and ornaments, as it is written for a free person.

Ba: Gods. The *polis* gave the lands for planting in Keskoria and Palai[28] to be planted. If anyone has bought or received as mortgage any of them, the transaction shall not be valid. It shall be impossible to take it in pledge before the usufruct is measured.

Bb: Gods. If anyone puts anything to divert partially the flow of the river to his property, he shall not be punished. The flow of the river shall remain as wide as in the level of the bridge in the agora or more but not less.

Relevant texts

Gazoros (Makedonia): grant to plant trees in public lands, *SEG* xxiv 614 (above, no. 49); **Athens**: building a bridge, *IG* I³ 79 (below, no. 100); **Eleutherna (Crete)**: *Nomima* I, 46 (end 6th century BC); **Gortyn**: law on liability of a slave given as pledge, *IC* iv 47 (above, no. 27).

Further reading

Metzger (1973: 37–41); *epikarpia* as establishing an emphyteutic relation, M.R. Cataudella (1976) 'Aspetti del diritto agrario greco: l'affrancazione', *IURA* 27, 88–101 and especially 96–100; R. Koerner (1987) 'Zur Landaufteilung in griechischen Poleis in älterer Zeit', *Klio* 69, 443–9.

28 Localities at the outskirts of Gortyn.

ANIMALS

55 Gortyn (Crete), Regulations about liability
for animals?

IC iv 41 I   *5th century BC*

The following regulations come from what is called the 'small code' of Gortyn and they concern different aspects of liability for animals. In particular in the first fragment, exchange of animals is prescribed possibly in cases in which there is contention about the liability for the injury. In the second fragment (no. 56), matters concerning horses, mules and donkeys are regulated; the owner of the injured animal has to produce it in court.

[. . .] the owner of the injured animal has the right, if he wishes, to exchange his animal with the animal of his adversary. If the adversary does not agree to the exchange, he shall pay the simple value. If the owner does not bring the injured animal or does not bring it dead or does not prove the injury, he shall not have any legal remedy. If a pig injures or kills cattle, the pig shall belong to the owner of the cattle [. . .]

56 Gortyn (Crete), Regulation about animals

IC iv 41 II   *5th century BC*

Disputed ownership of animals was probably regulated in this fragmentary provision. What survives is the right of the owner to demand to see the stolen? animal in the presence of two witnesses.

[. . .] he shall pay an equal amount. And if it is a horse or a mule or a donkey, the injured owner shall take them, if possible, as it is written; if the animal is dead or it is not possible to take it, within five days and in the presence of two witnesses, he shall summon his adversary to show where the animal is; and they shall testify under oath himself and the witnesses that he took the animal or brought the animal or he is summoned. Dogs which were beaten [. . .]

57 Gortyn (Crete), Regulation about animals

IC iv 41 III   *5th century BC*

This fragment regulates the responsibility and the fines to be paid in case someone has received animals as security. He shall have to pay double the value of the animal if he denies that he cannot return it, and single once he cannot return it or returns it intact.

[. . .] if anyone has received a four-legged animal or a bird as a pledge or in usucaption or for any other purpose and he is not in a position to return it, he shall pay the simple value; and if he goes to the court and denies that fact, he shall pay double the value and a fine to the *polis*. [. . .] he shall pay four times the amount. And if anyone restitutes the thing intact, he shall pay the simple value.

58   Knossos (Crete), Regulations about animals

IC i p. 59, no. 5   *3rd century BC*

Although the first column of this inscription is fragmentary, there is no doubt that the second concerns payments to be made for damaging an animal and restitution of the sale of an animal.

Col. B: [. . .] he shall pay the fine?. And if a man breaks the horns of an ox, he shall pay five *lebetes** to the owner of the ox. And if anyone buying wild cattle, wants to reverse the purchase, according to the law, he shall not be liable to pay more than three obols per day, as compensation. And if anyone wants to return the animal he bought, he must do so within five days since the purchase and pay three obols for each day per animal? [. . .] and if he does not want the animal [. . .] in the presence of witnesses shall give it back.

Relevant texts

Abdera (Thrace): defects of an animal sold, *BCH* 66–7 (1942–3) p. 180 no. 2; **Athens**: damages to animals (*blabe tetrapodon*), Plu. *Sol.* 24.1.

Further reading

Gortyn: injuring animals, Metzger (1973: 42–5); pledging animals, Metzger (1973: 97–101).

3

POLIS

PENAL REGULATIONS

59 Athens, Law on male prostitution

Aischines i (Against Timarkhos) 21   *?5th century BC*

In the feud between Demosthenes and Aischines, Timarkhos, a close
ally of Demosthenes, had prosecuted Aischines for his role in the
conclusion of the peace of Philokrates in 346 BC, between Philip
II and the Athenians. Aischines retorted by prosecuting Timarkhos
for prostitution, a charge which, if proven, would debar him from
speaking in the assembly and participating in any other public
activity. The law sanctioned a comprehensive ban on the citizen who
prostituted himself; if he disobeyed the imposed ban the penalty was
death.

If any Athenian prostitutes himself, he shall not be allowed to become one
of the nine archons, to exercise any priesthood, to serve as an advocate for the
people or hold any office, in Athens or abroad, by lot or by vote; he shall not
be permitted to be sent as herald, to make any proposal in the assembly
of the citizens and in public sacrifices, to wear a garland when everybody
else wears one, to enter the purified meeting place for the assembly. Anyone who, having been convicted of prostitution, disobeys any of these
prohibitions shall be put to death.

Relevant texts

Athens: reference to a law of prostitution, Dem. xxii 21; And. i 100;
Isoc. xii 140; prohibition to procure children, Aisch. i 13 and 18;
prohibition from speaking in the assembly, Aisch. i 29; ban on male

prostitutes from participating in a *gymnasion*: **Beroia (Makedonia)**, *La loi gymnasiarchique* (below, no. 98).

Further reading

Summary account, Dover (1974: 213–16); law and homosexuality, Cohen (1991: 171–203); male prostitution, K.J. Dover (1978) *Greek homosexuality*, 19–39, London; homosexuality in Athenian law, E. Cantarella (1985) 'L'omosessualita nel diritto ateniese', *Symposion 1985*, 153–75; purification, Parker (1983: 94); loss of civic rights for male prostitutes, J.M. Rainer (1986) 'Zum Problem der Atimie als Verlust der bürgerlichen Rechte insbesondere bei mannlinchen homosexuellen Prostituierten', *RIDA* 33, 106–14; interrelation of gender and politics in the example of prostitution, D.M. Halperin (1990) 'The democratic body: prostitution and citizenship in classical Athens' in *One hundred years of homosexuality and other essays on Greek love*, 88–112, New York; J.J. Winkler (1990) *The constraints of desire. The anthropology of sex and gender in ancient Greece*, 45–70, New York; female prostitution, V. Vanoyeke (1990) *La prostitution en Grèce et à Rome*, Paris (Collection Realia).

60 Athens, Law on *hybris*

Demosthenes xxi (Against Meidias) 47   *?6th century BC*

Demosthenes in his speech 'Against Meidias' tried to convince the jury that Meidias' behaviour during the festival of Dionysia of the year 348 BC was insolent, although the prosecution he brought forward was not a *graphe hybreos*. Demosthenes wanted to make his point more forceful by invoking the severity of the law on *hybris*. This law is a classical example of Athenian legislating. There is no definition of what constitutes a hybristic act but anyone committing such an act could have been denounced and tried by the popular court (*Heliaia*). Although modern scholars disagree about the exact meaning of the term, any action inflicting dishonour and shame could have been considered hybristic. However, conscious of the possible pitfalls and in order to control malicious prosecution, the legislator sanctioned that the denouncer had to obtain one-fifth of the votes or he had to pay a fine (as happened in other cases of public prosecution).

If anyone commits *hybris* against any person, either a child or a woman or a man, free or slave, or commits any unlawful act against any of these, any eligible Athenian wishing to do so may indict him to the *thesmothetai**; and the *thesmothetai* are to introduce the case within thirty days from the submission of the indictment to the lawcourt (*Heliaia*), if no public affair prevents it, but if there is any other public business, as soon as possible. Whoever is found guilty, the lawcourt (*Heliaia*) shall immediately decide the penalty which he deserves to suffer or to pay. If those submitting an indictment, according to the law, do not proceed or fail to obtain one-fifth of the votes, they shall pay a thousand drachmas to the public treasury. If anyone, who has committed *hybris* against a free person is fined, he shall be imprisoned until the fine is paid.

Relevant texts

Athens: law on *hybris*, Aisch. i 16 (spurious); prosecutions for *hybris*, Is. viii 40–6; Aristot. *Rhet.* 1374b 35–1375a 2; [Dem.] liii 16; Dein. i 23; hybristic behaviour, Dem. xxi 36–40, 71–6 and 175–81; mention of *hybris*: **Nesos (Aiolis – Asia Minor)**, *IAdramyt* 36.24 (4th century BC); *hybris* in **Alexandreia (Egypt)**, *PHal I*, 115–20 (3rd century BC); *hybris* against a manumitted person in Roman times: **Beroia (Makedonia)**, *SEG* xlii 609 (AD 171).

Further reading

Summary account, MacDowell (1990: 263–8); exhaustive examination of literature, Fisher (1992); *hybris* in archaic Athens, O. Murray (1990) 'The Solonian law of hybris' in *Nomos*, 139–46; an explanation of the discrepancy between sparing use and frequent reference to the law, N.R.F. Fisher (1990) 'The law of hybris in Athens' in *Nomos*, 123–38; *hybris* and sexual offences, Cohen (1991: 176–80) and (1995: 143–62); *hybris* as a state of mind and intention together with violent action, D.M. MacDowell (1976) 'Hybris in Athens', *G & R* 23, 14–31; *hybris* as another means of prosecution for other offences, E. Ruschenbusch (1965) 'Hybreos graphe. Ein Fremdkorper im athenischen Recht des 4. Jahrhunderts v. Chr.', *ZSS.RA* 82, 302–9; law of *hybris* as a law not attached to any particular behaviour but covering potentially many offences, providing different and stricter ground for prosecution, M. Gagarin (1979) 'The Athenian law against hybris' in *Arktouros*, 229–36; re-assessment of Fisher's theory, D. Cairns (1996) 'Hybris, dishonour, and thinking big', *JHS* 116, 1–32.

61 Athens, Law on bribery

Demosthenes xxi (Against Meidias) 113   *?6th century BC*

The law quoted is generally agreed to be genuine and it is to be dated possibly in the 6th century BC. The citation of the law introduces another attack of Demosthenes against Meidias, in his homonymous speech; the implication is that while Demosthenes was in trouble convincing witnesses to come forward, Meidias did not have any qualms in convincing witnesses to testify in his favour, using intimidation and possibly bribery as Demosthenes implies. The law is more general than other laws banning special forms of bribery; the penalty is disenfranchisement.

If any Athenian accepts a bribe, or himself offers one to another (Athenian), or corrupts anyone with promises to the detriment of the people or of any of the citizens individually, by any means or device, he shall be deprived of his rights, himself and his children and his property will be confiscated.

Relevant texts

Athens: bribing magistrates, *AthPol* 54.2; Dein. i 60; Hyp. v 24, Isoc. viii 50; speakers in the assembly, Dein. ii 17; jurors, speakers, advocates, Dem. xlvi 26, Hyp. iv 7–8 and 29; ambassadors, Dem. xix 273–7; foreigners using bribes to acquit themselves from the charge of usurping citizenship (*doroxenia*), *AthPol* 59.3; accusation for bribery, Lys. xxi, Dem. xviii 114 and xix 343, Dein. i 42, Aisch. iii 259; clause against bribery in the heliastic oath, Dem. xxiv 150; mention of bribery and punishment, *IG* ii² 110.39–47 (410/9 BC); **Sparta**: *ephors* susceptible to bribing, Aristot. *Pol.* 1270b; **Klazomenai (Ionia – Asia Minor)**: clause on bribery, *SEG* xxix 1130bis (early 2nd century BC).

Further reading

Comprehensive discussion of the evidence, D.M. MacDowell (1983) 'Athenian laws about bribery', *RIDA* 30, 57–78; F.D. Harvey (1985) 'Dona ferentes. Some aspects of bribery in Greek politics' in P. Cartledge and F.D. Harvey (eds) *Crux. Essays in Greek History presented to G.E.M. de Sainte Croix*, 76–117, Exeter and London; corruption in the orators, a topos in attacking the opponent, H. Wankel (1982) 'Die Korruption in der rednerischen Topik und in der Realitat des klassischen Athen' in W. Schuller (ed.) *Korruption im Altertum*, 29–47,

Wien (Konstanzer Symposium Oktober 1979); uses of bribery, J. Ober (1989) *Mass and elite in democratic Athens. Rhetoric, ideology, and the power of the people*, 236–8, Princeton; bribing of ambassadors was not as widespread as sources suggest, S. Perlman (1976) 'On bribing Athenian ambassadors', *GRBS* 17, 223–33.

62 Athens, Law on theft

Demosthenes xxiv (Against Timokrates) 105   *?6th century BC*

In 353 BC Timokrates proposed a law with the provision that state debtors who give guarantees shall remain free till the ninth prytany of the year (see below, no. 91). Demosthenes' strategy is to show, through a comparison of Timokrates with Solon, who was considered as the lawgiver *par excellence* in fourth-century Athens, that the proposed law was designed to serve the interests of a few individuals. According to the Solonian law, thieves were punished with a hefty fine and sometimes with the additional, humiliating penalty of being kept in the stocks.

If stolen property is recovered, the penalty shall be double the value of the property, if it is not, ten times the value of it in addition to the lawful punishment.[1] The thief shall be kept in the stocks for five days and nights, if the lawcourt decides to impose an additional penalty. Whoever wishes may propose the additional penalty, when the matter is raised.

Relevant texts

Athens: reference to law, Lys. x 16; [Aristot.] *Problemata* 952a; public prosecution for theft (*graphe klopes*): Dem. xxiv 113; Pl. *Laws* 854, 855, 857, 914, 933–4, 941–2 and 946; procedures available for prosecution in case of theft, Dem. xxii 26–7; thieves treated as criminals (*kakourgoi*), *AthPol* 52.1; punishment for accomplices in

---

1 Some scholars have emended the phrase 'ten times the value . . . ' to 'twice the value . . . ' on the ground that the former was not supported by other pieces of evidence. However, in the most recent discussion on theft, Cohen (1983: 62–8) argued that the original reading should not be dismissed. The expression 'penalties' (in Greek, *epaiteiois*) is not very clear; does it suggest that in case the property is not recovered the person responsible shall pay ten times its value on top of twice the value of the property or that the tenfold repayment would have been accompanied by any additional penalty such as keeping the thief in stocks?

theft, Lys. xxix 11; conditions for searching one's house for stolen goods, Is. vi 42; stealing water, *LSCG* 178 (*c.* 400 BC); Pl. *Laws* 845 d4–e9; stealing sacred property, Dem. xix 293 and xxiv 111–12; sacrilege (*hierosylia*), Dem. xxiii 26, X. *Hell.* i 7.22 and Cohen (1983: 105–7) with a list of instances of *hierosylia* from other regions; theft by public officials, *AthPol* 48.4–5, 54.2 and 59.2; Dem. xxiv 114; **Beroia (Makedonia)**: theft in the *gymnasion*, *La loi gymnasiarchique*, 99–101 (below, no. 98); clauses for punishment of thieves in the judicial agreement (*symbolon*) between **Stymphalos and Sikyon-Demetrias (Peloponnese)**, *IPArk* 17.111–29 (below, no. 106); **Delphoi and Pellana**, *Staatsvertrage* 1558 (early 3rd century BC); **Korope (Thessaly)**: theft of harvest, *IG* ix (2) 1202 (mid 6th century BC); **Arkades (Crete)**: imprecation against thieves, *Nomima* II 83 (5th century BC); **Phalanna (Thessaly)**: law on embezzlement, *IG* ix (2) 1226 (*c.* 450 BC).

Further reading

Private prosecution for theft (*dike klopes*) and exhaustive discussion, Cohen (1983) and D.M. MacDowell in *CR* n. s. 34 (1984) 229–31; brief discussion of the law, Todd (1993: 283–4); thorough discussion of the Platonic regulation, T.J. Saunders (1990) 'Plato and the Athenian law of theft' in *Nomos*, 63–82.

63 Athens, Law on unintentional homicide

Nomima I, 02 (= *IG* i³ 104)   *409/8 BC*

Although we cannot be sure that this law was really part of the early Draconian legislation, Athenians in the late fifth century BC clearly believed so. What is preserved is the reinscription of the law during the revision of the laws initiated in the aftermath of the first oligarchic coup in 410 BC. The law starts by awkwardly sanctioning the punishment for unintentional killing. There are also provisions about the grant of pardon, the prosecution of the killer and the killing of a fugitive convicted for murder.

Diognetos from the deme of Phreattys was secretary, Diokles was archon. The council and the assembly decided, the tribe Akamantis was presiding, Diognetos was secretary, Euthydikos was *epimeletes**, [. . .] said: The inscribers are to take the law of Drakon on homicide from the *basileus** and

71

inscribe it on a stone stele and deposit it in front of the *Basileios Stoa;*[2] the *poletai*[3] have to agree, according to the law and the *Hellenotamiai*[4] have to provide the money.

First column: Even if anyone kills without intention, he shall be exiled; the *basileis* are to judge the culprit [. . .] or conspired; the *ephetai** will issue the decision. For granting pardon, the consent of all, father or brother or sons (of the victim), is needed, but the refusal of one of them is enough for not granting it. If there are not any of the above-mentioned relatives, the consent of relatives to the degree of cousins and sons of cousins will be sufficient for granting pardon, but the refusal of one of them is enough for withholding it. If there is no relative and the homicide is unintentional and the Fifty-One *ephetai* have acknowledged it, ten members of the deceased's *phratry* will be selected on the basis of merit by the Fifty-One *ephetai* to grant pardon. This law applies to homicides committed before the introduction of the law. The relatives to the degree of cousin and sons of cousins will proclaim the accusation in the marketplace, helped by cousins, children of cousins, son-in-law, father-in-law and members of *phratry* [. . .] responsible for homicide [. . .] the Fifty-One [. . . .] If anyone conspires to kill or kills the culprit, while the culprit abstains from the marketplace, games, panhellenic sanctuaries (*hiera*), let him be punished with the same penalty as that for the homicide of an Athenian citizen; and the *ephetai* shall decide the case [. . .] and the *ephetai* shall decide the case [. . .] be free. And if anyone whose property is seized by force and unlawfully, kills in defence, he will not have to pay any compensation [. . .]

Relevant texts

Adjudication in case of a dispute over a homicide, Homer, *Il.* 18.497–508; **Athens**: speeches for different cases of homicide, Antiphon i–vi; jurisdiction of Areiopagos on homicide cases, Dem. xxiii 22; hostage taking (*androlepsiai*), Dem. xxiii 28, 44 and 82; killing the killer who abstains from the prohibited areas, Dem. xxiii 37; justifiable homicide, Dem. xxiii 53; homicide courts, Dem xxiii 65–80, Aristot. *Pol.* 1300b 27–30 and *AthPol* 57.3; private prosecution for homicide (*dike phonou*), Dem. xlvii 68–73 and Pl.

---

2 The place (lit. 'the portico of the Basileus') where the results of the codification of 410 BC would have been inscribed. It lies in the Agora; see Travlos (1970: 580).

3 Public officials responsible for the selling of confiscated property at auction, leasing out public lands, mines and taxes. Cf. *AthPol*. 47.2–5.

4 *Hellenotamiai* were Athenian officials responsible for keeping fiscal account of the tribute of the allied *poleis* during the first Delian League (478–404 BC).

Euthyphro 4a–e; Aristot. *Pol.* ii 1269a 1–3; **Sicily**: fragmentary regulations about killers, *Nomima* I, 01 (525–500 BC); **Lokris (Central Greece)**: mention of a law on homicide, *Nomima* I, 44 (below, no. 94); **Mantineia (Arkadia – Peloponnese)**: decision of a court imposing the death penalty, *IPArk* 7 (*c.* 460 BC); **Miletos (Ionia – Asia Minor)**: prescription of death penalty, *Nomima* I, 103 (5th century BC); fragmentary rules touching upon aspects of homicide: Gortyn **(Crete)**, *IC* iv 89 (5th century BC); **Mantineia (Arkadia – Peloponnese)**, *IPArk* 6 (460–450 BC); **Kyrene (N. Africa)**: purification of killers, *SEG* xi 72 (end 4th century BC).

Further reading

Comprehensive overview of punishment in classical Athens, E. Karabelias (1991) 'La peine dans Athènes classique', *Recueils de la société Jean Bodin pour l'histoire comparative des institutions* 55.1, 77–132; intentional homicide covered by the law for unintentional homicide, M. Gagarin (1981) *Drakon and early Athenian homicide law*, New Haven; conspiracy to kill (*bouleusis*): M. Gagarin (1988) 'Bouleusis in Athenian homicide law' in *Symposion 1988*, 81–99; grant of pardon (*aidesis*): E. Heitsch (1984) *Aidesis im attischen Strafrecht*, Mainz (Akademie der Wissenschaften Mainz 1); enlightening discussion of modern bibliography, A. Maffi in *RHDFE* 66 (1988) 111–15 Chronique; defilement (*miasma*): Parker (1983: 104–43 and Appendices 5–7) and I. Arnaoutoglou (1993) 'Pollution in the Athenian homicide law', *RIDA* 40, 109–37; role of *ephetai*, E.M. Carawan, (1991) 'Ephetai and Athenian courts for homicide in the age of the orators', *CPh* 86, 1–16; role of *basileis* on deciding the intentional (or otherwise) character of homicide, E. Heitsch (1985) 'Der Archon Basileus und die attischen Gerichtshofe für Totungsdelikte', *Symposion 1985*, 71–87; jurisdiction of Areiopagos based not on the intentional character but on killing by one's own hand, G. Thür (1990) 'The jurisdiction of the Areopagos in homicide cases', *Symposion 1990*, 53–72 and the response of R.W. Wallace; original jurisdiction of the court at Phreatto, E.M. Carawan (1990) 'Trial of the exiled homicides and the court at Phreatto', *RIDA* 37, 47–67; meaning of '*dikazein*', G. Thür (1990) 'Die Todesstrafe im Blutprozess Athens (Zum dikazein in IG I³ 104, 11–13; Dem. 23, 22; Aristot. AP 57, 4)', *JJP* 20, 143–56; diachronic study of penalties in homicide cases, J. Méleze-Modrzejewski (1990) 'La sanction de l'homicide en droit grec et hellénistique', *Symposion 1990*, 3–16; S. Humphreys (1990) 'A historical approach to Drakon's law on homicide', *Symposion 1990*, 17–45 and the response by S. Todd; status and treatment of killers, E. Grace (1973) 'Status distinctions in the Drakonian law', *Eirene* 11, 5–30; the Tetralogies of Antiphon as reversal of topics and technics used in lawcourt speeches, E.M. Carawan (1993) 'The Tetralogies and Athenian homicide trials', *AJPh* 114, 235–70; relation of Tetralogies to homicide law, Ch. Eucken (1996) 'Das Totungsgesetz des Antiphon und der Sinn seiner Tetralogien', *MH* 53, 73–82; testimonia and physical remains of lawcourts, A.L. Boegehold (1995) *The lawcourts at Athens. Sites, buildings, equipment, procedure and testimonia*, Princeton (Athenian Agora xxviii); private prosecution for murder could be brought only by relatives or the master of the killed, A. Tulin (1996) *Dike Phonou. The right of prosecution and Attic homicide procedure*, Stuttgart (Beiträge zur Altertumskunde 76).

CONSTITUTION (*POLITEIA*)

64 Athens, Decree of Demophantos against tyranny

Andocides i (On the Mysteries) 96–8   *410 BC*

Andocides was prosecuted in 400/399 BC for attending the Eleusinian Mysteries after being convicted of impiety in 415 BC; in his attack against Epichares, one of his prosecutors, he claims that Epichares was a member of the Council during the oligarchic regime of the Thirty in 404/3 BC and, therefore, anyone could kill him with impunity. The decision of the people allowing such a course of action was a decree passed after the abolition of the regime of the Four Hundred sanctioning the killing of anyone attempting to overthrow the democratic institutions of the *polis* or serving under an oligarchic administration. The decree also provided the text of an oath to be sworn.

The Council and the assembly decided; Aiantis was the presiding tribe; Kleigenes was secretary; Boethos was chairman; Demophantos proposed the following: The date of this decree is the Council of the Five Hundred,[5]

5 The Council established by Kleisthenes in 508/7 BC. As the name implies it comprised five hundred members, fifty from each of the ten Athenian tribes (*phylai*). Their duties included consideration of proposed laws, scrutiny of magistrates, jurisdiction over cases of wounding with intent to kill. Cf. *AthPol* 43–4ff.

chosen by lot, for whom Kleigenes was the first secretary. Whoever abolishes the democracy in Athens, or serves in any public office, while democracy is abolished, he shall be enemy of the Athenians and he shall be slain with impunity and his property shall be confiscated and one-tenth shall be given to the goddess; the person who has killed him, or conspired to, shall be free of defilement; all the Athenians are to swear over unblemished sacrifices by tribes (*phylai*) and demes that they will kill him. And this shall be the oath: 'I will kill by word and deed and vote and my own hand, if it is in my power, anyone who overthrows the democracy in Athens, who holds any public office while democracy is abolished, who attempts to become a tyrant or helps to establish one. And if someone else kills such a person, I will consider him to be pure in the eyes of gods and deities, because he has killed an enemy of the Athenians, and I will sell all the property of the killed and give half of it to his killer, without depriving him of anything; and if anyone dies when killing or attempting to kill such a person, I will treat him and his children in the same way as Harmodios and Aristogeiton[6] and their descendants. And I declare null and void all the oaths against the Athenian democracy sworn in Athens or in a camp or anywhere else.' All the Athenians shall swear this oath over unblemished sacrifices before the festival of Dionysia.[7] And they shall pray that those observing the oath may be blessed, while those breaking it may perish, themselves and their descendants.

65 Athens, Law against tyranny

SEG xii 87   *336 BC*

Almost seventy-five years after the decree of Demophantos (above, no. 64), the Athenians thought it necessary to pass another resolution which was designed to protect the constitution of the *polis*. The reason this time was the advance of the Makedonians after the defeat of the Athenians in the battle of Chaironeia in 338 BC. Members of the *Areiopagos* seemed to have had pro-Makedonian leanings and, therefore, clauses appeared punishing those members of the *Areiopagos* collaborating with a tyrannical regime or exercising their duties when such a regime was installed.

---

6 The slayers of the tyrant's brother Hipparchos, son of Peisistratos in 514 BC. This event led to the eventual demise of the tyranny after Spartan intervention in 510 BC. The descendants of the tyrant-slayers were given free meals at the *prytaneion*, administrative centre of the *polis*. Cf. *AthPol* 18.

7 The festival of the Great (or City) Dionysia in honour of Dionysus was celebrated in spring (approximately March). Discussion of its introduction, Parker (1996: 92–5); survey of the evidence, Parke (1977: 125–36).

When Phrynichos was archon, the tribe Leontis held the ninth prytany and Chairestratos, son of Ameinias, from the deme of Acharnai, was secretary; from the chairmen Menestratos from the deme of Aixone has put this decree to the vote; Eukrates, son of Aristotimos, from the deme of Peiraieus proposed; Good Fortune of the Athenian people; the *nomothetai** have decided; if anyone revolts in order to install a tyrannical regime or helps to this aim or abolishes democracy or deprives the Athenian people of their constitution, whoever kills this person shall not need purification; and it is not permitted to the members of the *Areiopagos** while the Athenian democracy is abolished to go to the *Areiopagos*, to sit together in session, to take any decision on any affair; if any member of the *Areiopagos*, while democracy is abolished in Athens, goes to the *Areiopagos* or sits in session or takes any decision, he will be disenfranchised, himself and his descendants and that his property will be confiscated and one-tenth will belong to the goddess; and the secretary of the council shall have this law inscribed on two stone *stelai* to be set up, one in the entrance to the *Areiopagos*, which leads to the assembly hall, and the second in the assembly of the people; the treasurer will pay twenty drachmas for inscribing of the *stelai*, from the funds reserved for decrees.

Relevant texts

Athens: Solonian law against tyranny: *AthPol* 8.4 and 16.10, Plu. *Solon* 19.3 (= Ruschenbusch F70); provision in the law about denunciations, Hyp. iv 7–8; provisions in oaths, Dem. xxiv 144 and 149; provisions against attempts to install a tyranny in the alliance between Athens and Erythrai, *IG* i^2 10.31–7 (*c.* 455 BC); alliance between the Arkadian league and Athens: Tod ii 144.25 (362/1 BC); alliance between Athens and Thessalians, Tod ii 147.28 (361/0 BC); decrees against tyranny: **Ilion (Troas – Asia Minor)**: *Illion* 25 (3rd century BC); **Eretria (Euboia)**: *IG* xii (9) 190 and *BE* 1969, 449 (*c.* 340 BC); reward for informers of a plot to abolish the *polis'* constitution, **Thasos**: *Choix* 31 (below, no. 72); results of tyrannical regime in **Eressos (Lesbos)**: Tod ii 191 (4th century BC); **Kimmerian Chersonesos (S. Russia)**: resistance to a tyrannical regime as a clause in an oath, Schwyzer 173 = *IOSPE* iv 79 (3rd century BC); **Erythrai (Ionia – Asia Minor)**: restoration of the statue of a tyrannicide, *IErythrai* 503 (beginning 3rd century BC).

Further reading

Summary account on Solon's law against tyranny, Rhodes (1981: 220–2); discussion of the earliest tyranny law as reported by *AthPol*, M. Gagarin (1981) 'The thesmothetai and the earliest Athenian tyranny law', *TAPhA* 111, 71–7; M. Ostwald (1955) 'The Athenian legislation against tyranny and subversion', *TAPhA* 86, 103–28; Demophantos' decree as a political event, political tool: J.F. McGlew (1993) *Tyranny and political culture in ancient Greece*, 183–212, London; the function of the image of a tyrant in the ideology of the Athenian *polis*, V.J. Rosivach (1988) 'The tyrant in Athenian democracy', *QUCC* 30, 43–57; J. Engels (1988) 'Das Eukratesgesetz und der Prozess der Kompetenzerweiterung des Areopagos in der Eubullos-und Lykurgära', *ZPE* 74, 181–209; role of the *Areiopagos* in cases of imposing a tyrannical regime, O. de Bruyn (1995) *La compétence de l'Areopage en matière de procès publics. Des origines de la polis athènienne à la conquête romaine de la Grèce (vers 700–146 avant J.-C.)*, Stuttgart (Historia Einzelschriften 90); law of Ilion against tyranny, Chr. Koch (1996) 'Die Wiederherstellung der Demokratie in Ilion. Zum Wandel der Gesetzgebung gegen die Tyrannis in der griechisch-makedonischen Welt', *ZSS.RA* 113, 32–63.

66 Arkesine (Amorgos – Cyclades), Regulation of procedural affairs after internal conflict

IG xii (7) 3   *end 4th century BC*

At the beginning of this text there are twenty-seven severely damaged lines, from which only words on the left-hand side are preserved, not sufficient for a better understanding of the text. It is followed by an even more damaged fragment of a decision of which only four lines survive. The most likely interpretation is that the regulation concerns arrangement of debts after a period of internal strife. Conciliators (*diallaktai*)[8] have been already appointed and they have left written instructions about the resolution of disputes. Any official contravening these arrangements shall pay a hefty fine. Disputes worth less than a hundred drachmas shall be resolved following the normal procedure.

[. . .] the deadline agreed by the *eisagogeis** before [. . .], Sokrates and Timokles; suits registered when *eisagogeis* were those around Eurudikos shall not be tried, neither in this nor in any other special court in another *polis* called to judge nor anywhere else, if the *diallaktai*[8] do not leave any written

---

8 Conciliators or mediators appointed for resolving disputes created by civil strife in a *polis*. They were usually appointed by both parties and their decisions were binding. In Arkesine, it seems that they left instructions how to proceed in actions brought to court and they may have imposed fines.

instructions to the appropriate magistrates about which actions shall be brought into a *polis* court, those who do not pay according to the decision of the *diallaktai* or according to the agreement they have concluded with their adversaries or they do not write a recognition of their debt to the *chreophylakes*,[9] they shall be liable to prosecution similar to defaulters or to those who do not recognize their debts. No *prytanis** is to propose or to vote for, no *eisagogeus* is to bring such a proposal for discussion; if he does bring it or does anything despite the law, he shall owe three thousand drachmas to Hera and he will be disenfranchised; and each *eisagogeus* shall owe three thousand drachmas and he will be disenfranchised and be liable to prosecution as introducing court proceedings against this decree and the appointed time.

Teisomenos proposed: The remaining affairs shall be arranged according to the proposals of the Council; but it is permitted to decide the suits written on the whitened boards in a *polis* court, if the dispute does not exceed a hundred drachmas [. . .]

Relevant texts

Regulation of debts: **Ephesos (Ionia – Asia Minor)**, *IEph* 4 (early 3rd century BC); **Tegea (Arkadia – Peloponnese)**, *IPArk* 5 (324 BC); **Phlyous (Korinthia – Peloponnese)**, X. *Hell.* v 2, 10.

Further reading

Interpretation of this decree, Gauthier (1972: 333–7); collection of literary and epigraphical testimonia about indebtedness, Asheri (1969).

67 Athens, Amnesty decree of Patrokleides

Andocides i (On the Mysteries) 77–9   *405 BC*

The decree is mentioned in the context of Andocides' effort to defend himself against an accusation of impiety. The thrust of that accusation pertains to the events of 415 BC when groups of prominent individuals were involved in the profanation of the Eleusinian

---

9 *Chreophylakes* (lit. 'guardians of debts') were officials appointed to, among other things, register debts. In other *poleis* they may have played the role of maintaining the archives.

mysteries and in the mutilation of the *stelai* of Hermes. Andocides claims that his case is included in the amnesty provided by the decree of Patrokleides in 405 BC. The decree provided amnesty for all disenfranchised persons; individuals convicted in the homicide courts and those involved in overthrowing democracy were exempted from the amnesty.

Patrokleides proposed: Since the Athenians have decreed to allow the disenfranchised and the public debtors to speak and put proposals to the vote in the assembly, the Athenians shall pass the same decrees as the ones during the Persian wars (i.e. 490–480 BC) which benefited the city. Concerning those listed by the revenue collectors or the treasurers of the Goddess and of the other Gods or the *basileus** or anyone whose name had not been removed till the end of the term of the Council for the year of the archon Kallias (i.e. 406/5 BC): all those who were disenfranchised or were public debtors or were condemned for maladministration during their term in office by the auditors and the assessors at the auditors' office or those about whom prosecution for maladministration is pending or restrictions have been imposed on those who have been condemned as guarantors of persons who failed to appear in court up to this same date; and all inscribed as members of the Four Hundred[10] or for whom anything else is somewhere inscribed about any act committed during the oligarchy, except the names of fugitives recorded in *stelai*; or those tried by *Areiopagos* or *ephetai* or *prytaneion* or *Delphinion*,[11] presided over by the *basileis*, or who are in exile for homicide or sentenced to death; or those guilty of massacre or of being a tyrant. The revenue collectors and the Council shall remove all the other names from every public document according to the above mentioned, and if there is any copy anywhere, it shall be produced by the *thesmothetai** and by other officials. This shall be done within three days following the

10 The regime of the Four Hundred was the outcome of a short-lived oligarchical coup in 411 BC. The leaders of the coup abolished jury pay, replaced the Council of Five Hundred with a new one of four hundred members and set property criteria for those who would retain their full citizenship. The regime collapsed in early 410 BC after defeat of the fleet and revolt of the Athenian fleet stationed in Samos. Cf. *AthPol* 29–33.

11 These were the most important homicide courts in Athens. In *Areiopagos* cases of intentional homicide, poisoning and arson were tried. In *Delphinion*, cases of homicide were tried, for which the culprit was already in exile. *Ephetai* were judges involved in many different homicide courts; the *prytaneion* was a court which dealt with cases in which the killer was unknown or death had been caused by an inanimate object. The court of Palladion, where cases of justifiable homicide were heard, is missing from the list. For an overview, D. M. MacDowell (1963) *Athenian homicide law in the age of the orators*, Manchester, and references in no. 63 above.

decision of the assembly. Nobody is allowed to keep privately any copy of the documents to be destroyed or to recall grievances. Anyone doing this shall be liable to the same penalty as the fugitives from the *Areiopagos*,[12] so that the Athenians may live in trust with each other, now and in the future.

Relevant texts

Amnesties reported in literary sources: **Athens**, *AthPol* 22.8 (481/0 BC), 39.1–6 (403/2 BC), And. i (On the Mysteries) 87–91, [Dem.] xxvi 11 (338 BC); **Corinth (Peloponnese)**, X. *Hell.* v 1.2–8 (392 BC); **Erythrai (Ionia – Asia Minor)**: decree banning the prosecution of exiles, *IErythrai* 10 (second half 4th century BC); **Olympia (Elis – Peloponnese)**, Schwyzer 424 (4th century BC); **Tegea (Arkadia – Peloponnese)**: restoration of exiles, *IPArk* 5 (324 BC), **Chios: Tod ii 192 (332 BC), Mytilene (Lesbos)**: *IG* xii (2) 6 (below, no. 68); **Alipheira (Arkadia – Peloponnese)**: amnesty, *IPArk* 24 (273 BC); **Cyprus**, *SEG* xxxvii 1372 (145/4 BC); **Klazomenai (Ionia – Asia Minor)**, *SEG* xxix 1130bis (early 2nd century BC); **Iasos (Caria – Asia Minor)**: confiscation of property of those who participated in an abortive attempt to overthrow the regime, *IIasos* 1 (mid 4th century BC).

Further reading

T.C. Loening (1987) *The reconciliation agreement of 403/402 BC in Athens: Its content and application*, Stuttgart (Hermes Einzelschriften 53); on the accountability of magistrates (*euthyna*), M. Pierart (1971) 'Les euthunoi athéniens', *AC* 40, 526–73 and especially 531–41, and J.T. Roberts (1982) *Accountability in Athenian government*, Madison, Wisconsin; relation of accounts to procedures of accountability, J. Davies (1994) 'Accounts and accountability in classical Athens' in R. Osborne and S. Hornblower (eds) *Ritual, finance, politics. Athenian democratic accounts presented to D. Lewis*, 201–12, Oxford; discussion of disenfranchisement, Hansen (1976: 54–98), MacDowell (1978: 73–5).

---

12 Fugitives from the *Areiopagos* were people prosecuted for major offences such as intentional homicide, attempts to overthrow democracy, etc. and condemned to death. The penalty envisaged here is presumably death. Cf. R. W. Wallace (1989) *The Areopagos council to 307 B.C.*, Baltimore.

68 Mytilene (Lesbos), Regulation about the return of exiles

SEG xxxvi 752 (= *IG* xii (2) 6)   ?c. 332 BC

Civil strife was a well-known characteristic of the individualistic, competitive Greek *poleis*. The domination of one or the other party led to expulsions and the need to restore the exiles. This fragmentary decree addresses some of these questions, but more significantly it makes clear the commitment for equality between the exiles and those who remained, the establishing of a reconciliation committee and a ritual re-unification. Its date provides significant evidence about the relationship of the Makedonian kings with the Greek *poleis*. It is dated in the turbulent 330s BC when the island of Lesbos was 'captured' by the Persians and 'liberated' by the Makedonians twice in three years.

[. . .] and the *basileis** will help the exiles as being contrived by those who remained in the *polis*. And if any of the exiles does not conform with these decisions, he shall neither have any land granted by the *polis*, nor wait to be granted any transferred land from those who remained in the *polis*; but these people, from those who remained in the *polis* and who had property transferred, will be waiting for this land and the *strategoi** immediately will give back the land to those remaining in the *polis* as if they had never transacted with the exiles and the *basileis* will help those who remained in the *polis* as being contrived by the exiles. And if any suit is brought about these affairs, no *peridromos*[13] and *dikaskopos** and no other authority is permitted to introduce it. If something is not done as it is written in the decree, the *strategoi* and the *peridromoi* and the *dikaskopoi* and the other authorities shall punish the transgressor of the stipulations of the decree, with no regard of him being either one of the exiles or one of those who remained in the *polis*; but the parties in the agreement shall behave to each other without suspicion and conspiracy and they shall obey the inscribed decision of the king *(diagramma)*[14] and the agreement included in this decree. The assembly of the citizens shall elect twenty men, ten from the exiles and ten from those who remained in the *polis*; these men shall earnestly guard and take care so that the exiles will not be treated differently

---

13 Officials with authority to introduce suits to courts.
14 *Diagramma* was a decision of the king, of an impersonal character. It took precedence over customary law and the laws of the *polis*. It did not necessarily regulate only one affair. It was used in the Makedonian kingdom to differentiate legislation for the kingdom from either customs or laws of the *polis*. See Hatzopoulos (1996, vol. 1: 405). For a *diagramma*, see no. 111 below.

from those who remained in the *polis* evermore. And as for the disputed property, the twenty men shall take care to reconcile the exiles with those who remained in the *polis* and with each other, and if not, they will be as fair as possible and everybody shall comply with the reconciliation which the king decided and they will live in harmony with one another, in the *polis* and in the countryside; and about money, the reconciliation will be carried out as much as possible; and about the oaths that the citizenry will swear, about all these the elected men will bring to the assembly their recommendation, and the assembly having heard the case will decide, if it is beneficial, it will consider ratifying whatever was recommended as being advantageous, as similarly it was decreed by the assembly for those exiles who returned in the year of the *prytanis** Sminthinas. And if something is omitted in this decree, the council will decide about it. The decree having been ratified by the assembly, in the twentieth of the month, after the sacrifice, the whole citizenry shall pray to the gods, so that the agreement will bring safety and prosperity to the citizens, the exiles and those who remained in the *polis*; and all the public priests and priestesses shall open the temples and the people will assemble to pray. The *basileis* shall offer every year to the gods the promised sacrifices by the assembly when messengers were sent to the king; and the people and the messengers sent to the king, those from the exiles and from those who remained in the *polis*, shall be present in the sacrifice. And the treasurers shall have this decree inscribed on a stone *stele* and erected in the temple of Athena.

Relevant texts

Mytilene (Lesbos): decree on concord, *SEG* xxxvi 750 (*c.* 340–330 BC); exiles, Isoc. *Letters* vii 3; return of exiles: **Chios:** Tod ii 192 (332 BC); **Tegea (Arkadia – Peloponnese),** *IPArk* 5 (324 BC); **Selinous (Sicily),** *Nomima* I, 17 (*c.* 500 BC); **Hierapytna (Crete):** agreement between two groups of Hierapytnians, *SEG* xxxvi 811 (2nd century BC); **Amphipolis (Makedonia):** individuals condemned to exile, Tod ii 150 (357 BC); **Athens:** restitution of property, Lys. *Hippoth.* frg. 2 37–44.

Further reading

Historical account and date, A.J. Heisserer (1980) *Alexander the Great and the Greeks. The epigraphic evidence*, 118–41, Norman, Oklahoma; judicial comments on property disputes and the role of the commission, A. Wittenburg (1988) 'Il ritorno degli esuli a Mitilene', *Symposion 1988*, 267–76; strategies of dealing with the problem of restoring property to exiles, Lonis (1991); civil strife (*stasis*), Gehrke (1985); exiles in literature and history, J. Seibert (1979) *Die*

politischen Fluchtlinge und Verbannten in der griechischen Geschichte,
Darmstadt (Impulse der Forschung 30); P. McKechnie (1989)
Outsiders in the Greek cities in the fourth century BC, 16–34, London.

69 Erythrai (Asia Minor), Law protecting democracy

Nomima I, 106 (= *IErythrai* 2)   *465–452 BC*

It is assumed that this law aimed at protecting the new democratic
regime. However, what we have in column A is the end of a paragraph concerning prosecution of officials; it is not clear whether it
concerns officials of an abolished regime or new rules to be enforced.
In the second column, people usually excluded from *polis* affairs are
allowed to prosecute; unfortunately the next line is broken. In the
third column, there is a passing reference to scrutinies of citizenship;
an illegitimate son shall be enslaved.

Col. A: [. . .] not [. . .] selected by lot [. . .] not magistratures. If he violates
any law, he shall owe ten staters; anyone wishing can prosecute him and the
successful prosecutor will have half of the fine and the other half will belong
to the *polis*. If the prosecutor withdraws the charges, he shall owe whatever
he would have received had he won the case and he could be prosecuted in
the same manner. Nine members from each tribe (*phyle*), from those whose
property is worth more than thirty staters, will be selected to judge after
having sworn the same oath as the councillors (*bouleutai*), according to the
laws and the decrees. The full composition of the court will include at least
sixty-one judges; they will judge according to the law which lies near.[15] The
*prytaneis** will introduce the case and direct the hearing, writing down the
name of the debtor; if they do not, they will owe [. . .]

Col. B: [. . .] inscribe this decree on a stone *stele* and set it up in the circle of
Zeus Agoraios in the second *prytaneia*. The right to prosecute will belong to
any person who was not brought up according to the tradition, to son of
freedman or foreigner; for the one whose father has exercised a magistrature
or was selected by lot [. . .]

Col. C: [. . .] if he is a son of an illegitimate his case will be examined and he
will be put in yoke (i.e. he shall be enslaved). And if any of the true citizens

15 This information is a good piece of evidence of where laws were set up. The law
   in discussion was inscribed and erected close to the lawcourt, in the same way
   the law on homicide in Athens was to be set up in the portico of Basileus (above,
   no. 63).

does not appear, although called by the *prytaneis*, he shall owe half a stater, which will belong to the *prytaneis*, unless he is impeded by necessity.

Relevant texts

Thasos: reward for slave informers, M–L² 83 (below, no. 72); **Miletos (Ionia – Asia Minor)**: political expulsions, M–L² 43 (*c.* 470–440 BC).

Further reading

Summary account of internal strife in Erythrai, Gehrke (1985: 66–9).

70 Teos (Ionia – Asia Minor), Public imprecations

Nomima I, 104 (= M–L² 30)   *c. 475 BC*

The invocation of divine powers for the enforcement of an oath or a law was an alternative strategy and not necessarily an indication of primitiveness. In legislative texts of the late 5th and 4th centuries BC the imprecation follows the civic penalty. Invocation of divine powers continued to be used, especially where oaths were involved. The text from Teos demonstrates that sometimes imprecations may have been considered as an exclusive strategy. These imprecations cover a wide range of actions such as poisoning citizens of Teos, obstructing the import of grain (i.e. effectively starving the population), disobedience and betrayal. Van Effenterre and Ruze (1994) think that the issue of these imprecations was dictated by the fear of imminent trouble.

A. Anyone who prepares and administers poisonous potions to Teians or to a single Teian, let him perish, himself and his descendants. Whoever obstructs the import of wheat to Teos with any means or method, at sea or on the land, or refuses grain when it is imported, let him perish, himself and his descendants.

B. [. . .] any of the Teians revolts to *aisymnetes** [. . .], let him perish, himself and his descendants. Anyone who henceforth will be an *aisymnetes* in Teos or in lands belonging to Teos [. . .] or betrays the *polis* and its countryside or the men on the island or in the sea, or the guard in Aroe[16] or

16 Locality in the countryside of Teos.

henceforth betrays or steals or gives refuge to thieves or plunders or plays host to brigands knowing that they come from the land or the sea of the Teians, or does something harmful to the community of Teians or to Hellenes or to barbarians, let him perish, himself and his descendants. Those magistrates, who have not pronounced this curse during the festivals of Anthesteria, Herakleia and Dieia,[17] shall be liable to this curse. Whoever writes on, breaks, defaces the *stele* on which the curse is inscribed, let him perish, himself and his descendants.

71 Teos (Ionia – Asia Minor), Measures against public enemies

Nomima I, 105   *c. 470 BC*

In the same vein as the previous text but a few years later, these imprecations provide useful information about the relations between Teos and Abdera, a Teian foundation in Thrace, the text of the civic oath and different offices in Teos.

A. [. . .] does this, let him perish, himself and his descendants. Anyone who in the exercise of an office wrongs a neighbour, let him perish, himself and his descendants. [What follows is the text of a civic oath.] I am not going to conspire or revolt or instigate strife and division. I am not going to persecute anyone or to confiscate property or arrest or kill, unless he is condemned by at least two hundred citizens in Teos, according to the laws or at least five hundred citizens in Abdera. I am not going to appoint any *aisymnetes** not with many [. . .]

B. [. . .] let him perish, himself and his descendants from Teos and the territory of Teos and from Abdera. [. . .]

C. [. . .] if the community of the Abderitans demand it back, should he not return it, let him perish, himself and his descendants.

D. [. . .] at the festival of Anthesteria, Herakleia and Dieia; in Abdera Anthesteria, Herakleia and at the festival of Zeus.[18] Anyone who, elected as *timouchos*[19] or treasurer, does not pronounce what is inscribed on the *stele*, for

---

17 The festival of Herakleia was celebrated in honour of Herakles, and Dieia in honour of Zeus. The festival of Anthesteria was celebrated in spring and was common to all Ionians. For the celebration in Athens see Burkert (1978: 237–42).

18 See above fn. 17.

19 The title of the major magistrate in Teos.

the purpose of reminding and applying it, or anyone elected as secretary (*phoinikographos*),[20] in the order of *timouchos* [. . .]

Relevant texts

Athens: judicial cursing tablet, *SEG* xxxvii 214 (early 4th century BC); **Selinous (Sicily)**: private legal imprecations in *defixiones*, *Nomima* I, 5 (500–475 BC); mention of imprecations: **Argos (Argolid – Peloponnese)**, *Nomima* I, 100 (575–550 BC); **Atrax (Thessaly)**, *Nomima* I, 102 (*c.* 475 BC); **Athens**: imprecations to be pronounced against anyone exporting grain illegally, Plu. *Solon* 24.

Further reading

Distinction between supplication (requests to the god(s) for vengeance and/or justice) and the *defixio* (request to the god(s) to inflict pain on the cursed), H.S. Versnel (1987) 'Les imprecations et le droit', *RHD* 65, 5–22; collection of recently published tablets, D.R. Jordan (1985) 'A survey of Greek defixiones not included in the special corpora', *GRBS* 26, 151–97; in the political sphere, Gehrke (1985: 209 and 248); collection of judicial curse tablets in translation, J.G. Gager (ed.) (1992) *Curse tablets and binding spells from the ancient world*, 116–50 and 175–99, Oxford; relationship between Teos and Abdera, A.J. Graham (1992) 'Abdera and Teos', *JHS* 112, 44–73.

72 Thasos, Law rewarding informers

M–L² 83 (= Choix 31) ?411–409 BC

The island of Thasos was a member of the first Athenian League (478–404 BC) but revolted in 411 BC. The new regime was anti-Athenian and oligarchic (for the restoration of democracy in Thasos in 407 BC see *SEG* xxxviii 851). The law provided generous rewards as incentives to anyone, except the initiator of the plot, for providing information on a plot to revolt in Thasos or in its colony Neapolis (modern Kavala). There are particular provisions when more than one person from the plotters denounces such a plot; a special court of 300

---

20 A magistrate subordinate to *timouchos* and whose duties were akin to that of a secretary.

men will decide about it. The denouncer is guaranteed judicial and religious immunity. This law reveals uneasiness on behalf of the oligarchic regime in Thasos.

I. Whoever denounces a conspiracy to revolt in Thasos and proves it to be true, he shall have a thousand staters from the *polis*; and if the denouncer is a slave, he will be freed; if more than one person denounce, three hundred men will hear the case and will decide; if any one of the plotters reveals the plot, he shall have the money and no charge, based on a religious or secular oath, will be brought against him, no public imprecation is to be pronounced against him, unless he is the initiator of the plot. The law will come into force from the twenty-ninth of the month Apatourion,[21] in the year of the archons Akryptos, Aleximachos and Dexiades.

II. Whoever denounces a conspiracy to revolt in the colonies or to betray the *polis*, by a Thasian or a colonist, and it was proved to be true, he shall have two hundred staters from the *polis*; and if the property of the plotter exceeds the amount of two hundred staters, the denouncer shall have four hundred staters from the *polis*; and if the denouncer is a slave he will be freed; if more than one denounce, three hundred men will hear the case and will decide; if any one of the plotters reveals the plot, he shall have the money and no charge, based on a religious or secular oath, will be brought against him, no public imprecation is to be pronounced against him, unless he is the initiator of the plot. The law will come into force on the third of the month Galaxion,[22] in the year of the archons Phanodikos, Antiphanes, Ktesillos.

Relevant texts

Abdera (Thrace): fragmentary regulation for denunciation, *BCH* 66–7 (1942–3) p. 189 no. 3 (3rd century BC); **Athens**: informers in the case of profaning the Eleusinian mysteries and the mutilation of *Hermai*, And. i 11–18 and 20, Th. vi 60.2–4; reward for informers, Antiphon v 34; freeing slaves who denounce a plot against democracy: **Ilion (Troas – Asia Minor)**, *Illion* 25 (3rd century BC); public imprecations: **Teos (Ionia – Asia Minor)**, *Nomima* I, 104–5 (above, nos. 70, 71).

---

21 Probably the first month in the Thasian calendar. For the Thasian calendar see F. Salviat (1992) 'Calendrier de Paros et calendrier de Thasos: Boedromia, Bodromia et la solidarité des armes', *Mélanges P. Levêque 6. Religion*, 261–7, Paris.
22 Probably the third month in the Thasian calendar.

Further reading

Commentary and historical interpretation, Pouilloux (1954: 139–49).

73 Athens, Ratification of laws

Demosthenes xxiv (Against Timokrates) 20–3
early 4th century BC

The speech was written for the prosecution of Timokrates on proposing an unconstitutional law. The procedure of legislating in fourth-century Athens was partly regulated by the law quoted in this passage. The existing laws were to be examined and ratified, first those concerning the workings of the Council, then the general ones and finally those concerning magistracies. If any law was not ratified, any Athenian could propose a new law; he should have it written on a whitened board and displayed in the *agora*, where statues of the eponymous heroes stood. A committee of five Athenians was to be elected to defend the laws under repeal.

On the eleventh day of the first presiding tribe (*phyle*) in the assembly; the herald having prayed, the ratification of laws will proceed as follows: first those laws concerning the Council, second the general ones, then those concerning the nine archons and then those affecting the remaining authorities. First, those content with the laws about the Council will raise their hands and then those who are not content, and later in the same way they will vote about the general statutes. The ratification of the laws shall be conducted according to the existing laws. If some existing laws are rejected, the *prytaneis**, in whose term the voting takes place, shall devote the last of the three assemblies to discuss the rejected laws; the chairmen of this assembly shall, immediately after the religious observances, put the question about the sessions of *nomothetai** and the fund from which their payment is to be drawn. Only persons who have sworn the judicial oath can be appointed as *nomothetai*. If the *prytaneis* do not convene the assembly as above or the chairmen do not put the question in discussion, each *prytanis* shall owe a thousand drachmas sacred to Athena and each chairman forty drachmas sacred to Athena. And an indictment (*endeixis*)[23] shall be lodged with the *thesmothetai** as in the case of anyone who holds an office while in debt to the public treasury; and the *thesmothetai* are to introduce the cases of those against whom information was given to the court according to the

---

23 For the procedure of *endeixis* see MacDowell (1978: 58) and Todd (1993: 117).

law, otherwise they are not going to become members of the *Areiopagos** on the ground of obstructing the rectification of the laws. Before the day of the assembly any Athenian who wishes may display, in front of the monument of the eponymous heroes,[24] the laws he proposes, in order that the assembly may vote about the time allowed to the *nomothetai* with due regard to the number of the proposed laws. Anyone proposing a new law, shall write it on a white board, and display it in front of the eponymous heroes as many days as remain until the meeting of the assembly. The assembly, on the eleventh of the month Hekatombaion,[25] shall elect five persons from all the Athenians who will defend the laws under repeal in front of the *nomothetai*.

74 Athens, Law prohibiting the passing of conflicting laws

Demosthenes xxiv (Against Timokrates) 33

early 4th century BC

At this point of his speech, Demosthenes claims that Timokrates not only violated procedural provisos (see below, no. 91) but more significantly that he proposed an unconstitutional law. The penalty in this case was the same as in the case of proposing an unsuitable law. What this law regulates is not the submission of an indictment for proposing a decree contravening a law (*graphe paranomon*) but the indictment for proposing a law in conflict with existing laws (*graphe nomon me epitedeion theinai*).

It is prohibited to repeal any existing law except at a session of *nomothetai**. And then, any Athenian who wishes to repeal a law, shall propose a new law to replace the one repealed. And the chairmen (*proedroi*) shall take a vote by showing of hands about those laws, first about the existing one, if it seems that the law is advantageous to the Athenian people or not, and then about the proposed one. The law which the *nomothetai* vote for shall be the valid one. It is not allowed to introduce a law in conflict with existing laws, and if anyone, having repealed an existing law, proposes a new law not advantageous to the Athenian people or in conflict with any of the existing laws, indictments may be lodged against him according to the existing law regarding the proposer of an unsuitable law.

24 The ten eponymous heroes have given their names to the *phylai* of Athens, after the reforms of Kleisthenes in 508/7 BC. Their statues stood in the Athenian Agora.

25 Hekatombaion was the first month in the Athenian calendar and corresponds to our July/August.

Relevant texts

Athens: Ratification of the appointment of officials, *AthPol* 43.4, 55.6 and 61.2; alleged law of Zaleukos: Dem. xxiv 139; **Olympia (Elis – Peloponnese)**: precautions against changing laws, *Nomima* I, 108 (end 6th century BC); prohibition on amending laws: **Megalopolis (Arkadia – Peloponnese)**, *IPArk* 30 (end 2nd century BC); **Demetrias (Thessaly)**, *SEG* xxiii 405, 12 (1st–2nd century AD); **Alexandreia Troas (Mysia – Asia Minor)**, *IPriene* 44, 18 (2nd century BC); **Labraunda (Lydia – Asia Minor)**, *ILabraunda* 56, 2 (?1st century AD).

Further reading

Athens: legislative procedures, M.H. Hansen (1980) 'Athenian nomothesia in the fourth century BC and Demosthenes' speech "Against Leptines"', *ClMed* 32, 87–104; different procedures of legislating used at different times, D.M. MacDowell (1975) 'Law-making at Athens in the 4th century B.C.', *JHS* 95, 62–74, and the criticism and objections by P.J. Rhodes (1985) 'Nomothesia in fourth-century Athens', *CQ* 35, 55–60 and M.H. Hansen (1985) 'Athenian nomothesia', *GRBS* 26, 345–71; detailed discussion of suit for proposing an illegal decree (*graphe paranomon*), J. Triantaphyllopoulos (1960) 'Graphe paranomon', *Neon Dikaion* 16, 229–33 and H.J. Wolff (1970) *Normenkontrolle und Gesetzbegriff in der attischen Demokratie. Untersuchungen zur graphe paranomon*, Heidelberg (Sitzungsberichte der Heidelberger Akademie der Wissenschaften, Philosophisch-historische Klasse); discussion and collection of cases of *graphe paranomon*, M.H. Hansen (1974) *The sovereignty of the people's court in Athens in the fourth century BC and the public action against unconstitutional proposals*, Copenhagen (Odense University Classical Studies 4); political arguments and legal pleas in judging cases of *graphe paranomon*, H. Yunis (1988) 'Law, politics, and the graphe paranomon in fourth-century Athens', *GRBS* 29, 361–82; *graphe paranomon* outside Athens, J. Triantaphyllopoulos (1985) 'Graphe paranomon fuori di Atene' in F. Broilo (ed.) *Xenia. Scritti in onore di P. Treves*, 219–21.

75 Athens, Law on the validity of laws and decrees

Andocides i (On the Mysteries) 87   *?403 BC*

This law provides the cornerstone of the Athenian legislative process in the aftermath of the restoration of democracy (404/3 BC). In particular, no decree of the assembly of the citizens shall supersede any law; moreover, an implicit criterion of distinction between decree and law is established – laws concern all the citizens of the *polis*. Any law concerning an individual should be approved, in a secret vote, unanimously in the assembly.

The authorities are not allowed to use an unwritten law in any case. No decree of either the council or the assembly is to prevail over a law. It is not permitted to make a law for an individual if it does not extend to all Athenian citizens and if it is not voted by six thousand people, in a secret vote.

Relevant texts

Athens: law quoted, Dem. xxiii 87, xxiv 30 and xlvi 12; reference to the law, Dem. xxiv 59; distinction between law (*nomos*) and decree (*psephisma*), Aristot. *Pol.* 1292a; **Olympia (Elis – Peloponnese)**: no violation of written law, *Nomima* I, 109 (end 6th century BC).

Further reading

Hierarchical relation between law and decree, F. Quass (1971) *Nomos und Psephisma. Untersuchung zum griechischen Staatsrecht*, 23–44, München (Zetemata. Monographien zur klassischen Altertumswissenschaft 55); summary account, MacDowell (1978: 43–6); J. Triantaphyllopoulos (1985) *Das Rechtsdenken der Griechen*, 5–7, München (Münchener Beiträge zur Papyrusforschung und antiken Rechtsgeschichte 78).

76 Erythrai (Ionia – Asia Minor), Regulation against re-election in secretaryship

IErythrai 1   *5th–4th century BC*

One of the major principles in the constitutions of several ancient Greek cities was the rotation on an annual basis of almost every public office. In most of the cases, the discharge of an official was preceded by an account of his activity while in office. The inscription from Erythrai provides a good example of the rotation principle. According to this regulation, secretaries are to be appointed for only one term in office. It seems that the regulation marks a break with what was happening earlier in Erythrai.

Apellias has proposed: People who were secretaries from the year when Chalkides was archon and onwards, no one of them is allowed to be secretary or to hold any other office. No one is allowed in the future to become a secretary more than once for the same office or treasurer more than once or to be elected in two offices simultaneously. Anyone who becomes a secretary or is elected or proposes or votes for such a proposal, he shall be damned and disenfranchised (*atimos*) and he shall owe a hundred staters. The *exetastai** shall exact the money, otherwise they will owe the same amount of money themselves. This law shall take effect from the month of Artemision[26] when Posis was *hieropoios**. The council has decided: anyone who selects a secretary in conflict to the provisions on the stele shall owe [. . .] staters.

Relevant texts

Ban on re-election of magistrates: **Gortyn (Crete)**, *IC* iv 14 (6th century BC); of *kosmoi**: **Dreros (Crete)**, M–L² 2 (end 7th century BC); in a *polis'* subdivision, **Erythrai (Ionia – Asia Minor)**, *IErythrai* 17 (5th/4th century BC); annual offices in **Athens**: *AthPol* 4.4, 62.3; annual tenure a feature of democratic regimes: Aristot. *Pol.* 1317b 20–5; exemptions from the rule of rotation: *AthPol* 43.1, 61.

Further reading

For a discussion of the rule and its exceptions in Athens, see Rhodes (1981: 116 and 696) and Todd (1993: 292).

77   Thasos, Law granting citizenship

IG xii *Suppl. 264: 7–16*   *5th or 4th century BC*

In ancient Greek *poleis* the assembly of the citizens could grant citizenship to an individual or to citizens of other *poleis* in exceptional circumstances. With this law the Thasians extend the right to

---

26 See Text no. 45.

Thasian citizenship to all those, men and women, born by Thasian women living in Neapolis[27], one of their colonies in the mainland, as part of the reorganization following the political upheavals of the late 5th century BC.

The assembly of citizens has decided; decision identical for the remaining (affairs) with the decision of the Council; pray to Herakles and to all the other gods; Good fortune, the inhabitants of Neapolis, who descend from Thasian women, will be considered Thasians and they can participate, themselves and their children, in everything that Thasians take part in; and when they reach the same age as the other Thasians, they shall swear an oath (of allegiance) according to the law; this decree shall be inscribed next to the law about disenfranchisement in the market and in the port and the *prostatai***** with the secretary will bring down the decree about Apemantos[28] and the *hieropoioi***** will have this decree inscribed in the sanctuary of Herakles;[29] the same regulation applies to women, too; if any magistrate or citizen violates this provision, he shall be disenfranchised and his property will be consecrated to Herakles.

Relevant texts

Athens: Perikles' citizenship law, *AthPol* 26.4; citizenship for Plataians, [Dem.] lix 94–106; for Samians, *IG* i^3 127 (405/4 BC); for metics who helped to restore democracy in Athens, *IG* ii^2 10 (401/400 BC); grant of citizenship: **Athens**, *IG* ii^2 226 (342 BC); **Larisa (Thessaly)**, *IG* ix (1) 516 (*c.* 210 BC) and 517 (214 BC); **Phalanna (Thessaly)**, *IG* ix (2) 1228 (3rd century BC); **Pharsalos (Thessaly)**, *SEG* xl 486 (*c.* 230–200 BC); **Triphyllia (Messenia – Peloponnese)**, *SEG* xl 392 (400–369 BC); union (*synoikismos*) between **Orkhomenos and Euaimon (Arkadia – Peloponnese)**, *IPArk* 15.40–3 (*c.* 360–350 BC); conditions of granting citizenship:

27 Neapolis lies under the modern Kavala, opposite the island of Thasos. It was founded by the Thasians as a trading station, providing access to the inland. For a summary account see Isaac (1986: 66–9).

28 Apemantos was a pro-Athenian Thasian accused of being a staunch supporter of Athenian policy. His property was confiscated and he was exiled by the Thasian oligarchic regime in 411 BC. He went to Athens where his children had tax-free status (*ateleia*) and *proxenia*. See Tod ii 98 (*c.* 403 BC) and Dem. xx 59. For a recent, fragmentary, testimony of Thasian exiles in Athens see M. B. Walbank (1995) 'An inscription from the Athenian agora: Thasian exiles at Athens', *Hesperia* 64, 61–5.

29 For the sanctuary of Herakles see M. Launey (1944) *Le sanctuaire et le culte d'Herakles à Thasos*, Paris (Études Thasiennes 1).

Dyme (Achaia – Peloponnese), *SEG* xl 394 (3rd century BC); citizenship awarded to an individual whose mother was a citizen: **Aigiale (Amorgos – Cyclades)**, *IG* xii (7) 392 (1st century BC); **Ephesos (Ionia – Asia Minor)**: award of citizenship for those fighting with the Ephesians against Mithridates, *IEph* 8 (below, no. 90).

Further reading

Athens: collection and discussion of cases of naturalization, M. Osborne (1981–3) *Naturalization in Athens*, 4 vols, Brussels; citizenship law of Perikles, C. Patterson (1981) *Pericles' citizenship law of 451/0 B.C.*, New York; origins of citizenship in Solon's era, P.B. Manville (1990) *The origins of citizenship in ancient Athens*, Princeton; motives and modes of replenishing (*anaplerosis*) the civic body, R. Lonis (1991) 'L'anaplerosis ou la reconstitution du corps civique avec des étrangers à l'époque hellénistique' in R. Lonis (ed.) *L'étranger dans le monde grec* II, 245–70, Nancy; questions on citizenship arising from the summary of a play, D. Gofas (1988) '"Troizenian koren poloumenen erastheis epriato". Amour et citoyenneté à Trézène', *Eros et Droit en Grèce classique*, 55–66, now in *Meletes*, 103–10; exceptional character of the grant of citizenship to Samians, Chr. Koch (1993) 'Integration unter Vorbehalt-der athenische Volksbeschluss über die Samier von 405/4 v. Chr.', *Tyche* 8, 63–75; reliability of the evidence on the naturalization of the Plataians, K. Kapparis (1995) 'The Athenian decree for the naturalization of the Plataeans', *GRBS* 36, 359–78.

78 Thasos, Law on the honours awarded to dead soldiers

LSCG Suppl. 64 (= Nouveau Choix 19)   *c. 350 BC*

This fragmentary law sets out the honours awarded to the war dead. It resembles, in a way, modern provisions for public funerals. It is interesting to note the differentiation of these honours from the normal format of a funeral; public officials are charged with certain duties, the duration of the mourning is restricted, and, more significantly, at a symbolical level the *polis* is to provide armour to the sons of the dead and dowry to their daughters, thus playing the role of their dead fathers.

[. . .] the *agoranomos** shall not neglect anything on the day of the funeral, before the funeral; nobody is allowed to mourn the Brave men (*Agathoi*) for more than five days; it is not allowed to carry the customary rites; those who do will be considered impure; and the *gynaikonomoi** and the magistrates and the *polemarchoi** shall not neglect and they shall impose the penalties provided by the laws; the *polemarchoi* and the secretary of the council are to have the names of the dead followed by their fathers' names inscribed in the list of the Brave (*Agathoi*) and they are to call their fathers and their children when the *polis* sacrifices to the war dead. The *apodektes** is going to give to each one what is given to a dignitary. Their fathers and children are to be invited to the games and occupy an honorary place; the organizer of the games will reserve a place and will provide them with a seat; when the children, whom the dead left behind, reach the majority age, the *polemarchoi* will give them each, if they are boys, a pair of greaves, a breastplate, a dagger, a helmet, a shield, and a spear valued at no less than three minas, on the occasion of the festival in honour of Herakles in the contest and they will proclaim the names; and if they are daughters, a dowry [. . .] when they reach the fourteenth year [. . .]

Relevant texts

Athens: taking care of children, Th. ii 46; public funeral, Th. ii 34.1–8; duties of *polemarchos* for the war-dead, *AthPol* 58.1; speech made in a public funeral, Lys. ii; decree of Theozotides about orphans of war, *SEG* xxviii 46 (403/2 BC); casualty lists, *IG* i² 929 (460/59 BC); **Rhodes**: public funerals, D. S. xx 84; **Sparta**: writing the name of the dead on the tombstone, if he fell in battle, Plu. *Lyc.* 27.3; **Makedonia**: honours and immunities to relatives of the dead in Alexander's campaign, Arr. *Anab.* i 16.5 and vii 10.4.

Further reading

Public burial of the war-dead contributes to the attenuation of inequalities, N. Loraux (1986) *The invention of Athens: The funeral oration in the classical city*, 17–42, English translation, Cambridge, Mass.; discussion of epigraphical and archaeological evidence in Athens, C. Clairmont (1983) *Patrios nomos. Public burial in Athens during the fifth and fourth centuries B.C.*, Oxford (BAR 161); useful recapitulation of evidence on war-dead in ancient Greece, W.K. Pritchett (1985) *The Greek state at war*, vol. 4, 94–259; iconography of state burials, R. Stupperich (1994) 'The iconography of Athenian state burial in the classical period' in W.D.E. Coulson *et al.* (eds) *The archaeology of Athens and Attica under the democracy*,

93–103, Oxford (Oxbow Monograph 37); summary account, Parker (1996: 131–40).

PROCEDURE

79 Athens, Law on *probolai*

Demosthenes xxi (Against Meidias) 10   *?c. 350 BC*

Demosthenes, having been punched in public during the festival of Dionysia, complained in the assembly; the procedure whereby anyone could lodge a complaint about misdemeanours during a festival was called *probole* (lit. 'putting forward'). The decision of the assembly was only pre-judicial and had no binding force. If the complainant so wished, he could pursue the affair further and go to court. Demosthenes reminds the jury of one of the provisions of the law on *probolai*, which prohibits any seizures, either of property or of persons, during the festivals.

Euegoros proposed: When the procession takes place in honour of Dionysus in Peiraieus and the comedies and the tragedies, and the procession at the Lenaion[30] with the tragedies and the comedies, and the procession at the City Dionysia[31] and the boys and the *komos*[32] and the comedies and the tragedies and the procession and the contest of Thargelia,[33] nobody is allowed during these days to distrain or to seize anything from another person, not even for debts overdue. Whoever violates any of the above shall be liable to prosecution by the aggrieved, and a complaint (*probolai*) against the offender may be introduced in the assembly in the precinct (i.e. theatre) of Dionysus, as it is provided in the case of other offenders.

30 The whole phrase is considered fossilized by MacDowell (1990: 232–3), reflecting the older state of affairs when plays were performed in a makeshift theatre. The festival of Lenaia was held approximately in January.
31 The most important festival in honour of Dionysus; it was held approximately in March.
32 MacDowell (1990: 232–3) considers that it may refer to the men's choruses, or it may denote some other part of the festival.
33 Festival in honour of Apollo held approximately in May. The contest did not include plays but only singing (dithyrambic) competition.

80 Thasos, Law on the adjournment of legal procedures

SEG xix *415*   *end 4th century BC*

The festival days were regarded as sacred days and no legal business was conducted. This law from Thasos corroborates evidence from Athens. It provides that on certain listed festivals no legal action is to be taken or procedures to be continued. Another interesting aspect of this law is the existence of a special procedure for cases tried within the space of a month (*emmenoi*), parallel to the Athenian evidence.

[. . .] in these days it is not permitted to denounce or to capture anyone and hand him to magistrates; in the festival of Apatouria[34] [. . .] all gods, Maimakteria, Posideia, when [. . .] Anthesteria, Soteria, Dionysia, Diasia, Great Herakleia, Choreia, Duodekatheia, Alexandreia [. . .] supplication day in Thesmophoria, Great Asklepieia, Demetria, Heroxeineia, Dioskouria, Great Komaia [. . .] neither on the days when public arbitrators register the preliminary declaratory oaths of the litigants and when they receive testimonies and pieces of evidence and have a preliminary hearing, nor when the lawcourts are hearing 'monthly cases', nor when they register the oaths of the litigants in a 'monthly case', nor in inquests, nor in help, nor in protection, neither to denounce nor to capture nor the *epistates** to accept.

Relevant texts

Athens: monthly cases, *AthPol* 52.3 and 59.5; **Arkesine (Amorgos – Cyclades)**: mention of *probolai*, *IG* xii (7) 3 (above, no. 66); regulation about complaints for offences committed during the festival of City Dionysia (*probolai*), Dem. xxi 8; cases of *probolai* brought against foreigners and citizens, Dem. xxi 175–81 and 218; no judicial action to be taken during the festival of Asklepieia, **Lampsakos (Mysia – Asia Minor)**, *ILamps* 9.24–8 (2nd century BC); selection and training of choruses, Antiphon vi 11–13, Dem. xxi; period during which legal business is adjourned (*ekecheiria*): **Ilion (Troas – Asia Minor)**: *OGIS* 212, 15 (*c.* 281 BC); **Magnesia on Meander (Ionia – Asia Minor)**, *IMM* 100 (end 2nd century BC);

34 The inscription refers to a series of festivals held in Thasos at different dates throughout the year. For a discussion, F. Salviat (1958) 'Une nouvelle loi thasienne: institutions judiciaires et fêtes religieuses à la fin du IVe siècle av. J.-C.', *BCH* 82, 193–267 and especially 212–63. For *Thesmophoria* see Burkert (1978: 242–6).

Sparta: *IG* v (1) 18 B, 8 (Imperial); **Ephesos (Ionia – Asia Minor)**: *IEph* 24 (AD 162–4).

Further reading

Athens: meaning of monthly cases as those which can be submitted every month, Cohen (1973) and the objections of M.H. Hansen (1979) 'Two notes on the Athenian dikai emporikai', *Symposion 1979*, 165–75; relation of the Thasian inscription to the Athenian regulation, D. Gofas (1974) '"Emmenoi dikai" à Thasos', *Symposion 1974*, 175–86 now in *Meletes*, 71–7; legal nature of the accusation against Meidias, G.O. Rowe (1994) 'The charge against Meidias', *Hermes* 122, 55–63; *probolai*, MacDowell (1990: 13–16 and 230–5); laws about choruses in the festivals, D.M. MacDowell (1982) 'Athenian laws about choruses', *Symposion 1982*, 65–77; *ekecheiria* as adjourning all legal business, L. Robert (1937) *Études Anatoliennes. Recherches sur les inscriptions grecques de l'Asie Mineure*, 177–9, Paris; H. van Effenterre (1993) 'Modernité du droit grec: un patrimoine', *Cahier G. Glotz* 4, 1–12.

81   Gortyn (Crete), Regulation about pledged property

IC iv 81   *5th century BC*

The fragment preserves part of a regulation regarding procedures in case of dispute over pledged property. The plaintiff is to summon his adversaries for the measurement and if they do not appear he is entitled to proceed and announce the result in the agora. He shall also have to swear that the property belongs to his adversary. Witnesses are the decisive factor, for resolving disputes both of identity and ownership.

[. . .[of trees and houses [. . .] the nine closest of the neighbours [. . .] summon in the presence of witnesses three days before the [. . .] to mark off; and if people summoned according to the law do not appear, he shall himself mark off and shall declare four days before, in the presence of two witnesses, in the agora. In order to avoid litigation the person who accepted the pledge shall swear an oath that the property belonged to the person who gave it as a pledge. The person who gave a pledge shall swear that he is not the owner. The litigant for whom most people shall testify under oath shall be the winner. And if a house is pledged and the person who provided the pledge claims that the house does not belong to him, three from his nine neighbours shall confirm the pledger's claim; and if any of the neighbours [. . .]

82 Gortyn (Crete), Regulation about pledged property

IC iv 75   *5th century BC*

The inscription survives in four portions of which only two provide reasonably restored texts. The first fragment concerns the procedure of measuring and declaring the result in public when property was pledged and most probably repeats, in part, the previous regulation. The second fragment includes a list of objects excluded, most probably, from sequestration.

Frg. A: [. . .] summon in the presence of two witnesses three days before the one who pledged, to mark off; and if the individual does not come while he has been [. . .]

Frg. B: [. . .] weapons of a free man, which he carries at war, except animals, produce, iron tools, plough, two oxen, container, millstone, donkey for ploughing, from the *andreion** whatever is provided to members, the bed of a man and a woman, free [. . .]

Relevant texts

Land surveyors (*geodotai*): **Lykia (Asia Minor)**, *SEG* xl 1062 (early 2nd century BC); **Athens**: land dividers (*geonomoi*), *IG* i^3 46 (below, no. 96).

Further reading

Athens: pledging property, Harrison (1968: 253–304); discussion of overlap of regulations in the Gortynian legislation, J.K. Davies (1996) 'Deconstructing Gortyn: When is a code a code?' in L. Foxhall and A.D.E. Lewis (eds) *Greek law in its political setting. Justifications not justice*, 33–56, Oxford.

83 Kyme (Aiolis – Asia Minor), Law of *dikaskopoi*

IKyme 11   *3rd century BC*

This fragmentary law describes the duties of *dikaskopoi**, major officials at Kyme. The officials were involved in prosecutions for serious offences, from which, in case they succeeded, they could retain half of the imposed fine. They were obliged to inscribe this law on three *stelai* and set it up in three different places, the political and religious centres of the community.

[. . .] of interests [. . .] and if the prosecutor is defeated, he shall pay [. . .] of which penalty half shall belong to the *polis* and half to the *dikaskopos* [. . .] and if the *dikaskopos* is defeated [. . .] of the trial, the *dikaskopos* [. . .] since the judge? will pronounce [. . .] in thirty days the fine [. . .] and shall exact the money; if not, he shall be killed without punishment; anyone willing is allowed to kill him, and the killer will be considered pure and free of any defilement; and if anywhere else in another law something else is proposed contrary to this law, it will be void; this law is to be inscribed by the future *dikaskopoi* in three *stelai* in [. . .] days [. . .] from the day the law is ratified by the people and set up one in the *prytaneion*, the other in the altar [. . .] and the other in the temple of Artemis [. . .] when *prytanis** was [. . .]

Relevant texts

Mytilene (Lesbos): mention of *dikaskopoi*, *IG* xii (2) 6 (*c.* 332 BC).

84 Athens, Law on prosecution of draft-dodgers and those who harm their parents

Demosthenes xxiv (Against Timokrates) 105   *?6th century BC*

This law does not regulate in a modern sense any offence but rather sets out a procedure to be followed once someone is arrested for the ill-treatment of his parents or for draft-dodging or for violating the ban on entering particular sacred places. The process involves imprisonment before trial.

And if anyone is put under arrest as ill-treating his parents or draft-dodging or entering places from where he is banned according to the law, the *Eleven** are to put him in jail and bring him before the lawcourt. Any eligible person may prosecute him. If he is found guilty, the lawcourt shall assess what penalty he is to suffer or to pay. If he is to pay a fine, he shall be kept in prison until he pays.

Relevant texts

Athens: providing for parents, Lys. xiii 91, Aesch. i 28; imprisonment for those who maltreat parents, Dem. xxiv 60 and 102; suits for maltreating parents: *AthPol.* 56.6; **Delphoi (Phokis – Central Greece)**: law on maltreatment of parents, *RPh* (1943) p. 62 (above, no. 22); draft-dodging, Lys. xv; alleged legislation of Charondas: D. S. xii 16; desertion, Lys. xiv; **Nesos (Aiolis – Asia Minor)**: mention of *liponautai, IAdramyt* 36 (late 4th century BC).

Further reading

Attitudes towards parents, Dover (1974: 273–8); father–son relationship and a general discussion, B.S. Strauss (1993) *Fathers and sons in Athens. Ideology and society in the era of the Peloponnesian war*, London; failure to perform military service, MacDowell (1978: 159–61) and D.M. MacDowell (1993) 'The case of the Rude Soldier (Lysias 9)', *Symposion 1993*, 155–60; procedure of private arrest and indictment against criminals (*apagoge*), Hansen (1976) and E.M. Harris (1993) '"In the Act" or "Red Handed"? Apagoge to the Eleven and Furtum Manifestum', *Symposion 1993*, 169–84.

CLEANLINESS

85 Thasos, Regulation concerning public cleanliness

SEG xlii 785   *early 5th century BC*

This is one of the earliest regulations concerning cleanliness and its maintenance in a *polis*. It was found in the port of Thasos and it contains provisions about building restrictions, responsibilities for street cleaning and the penalties for non-compliance.

From the street on the bank [. . .] the sanctuary of Herakles; from the road of the sanctuary of Graces; it is not permitted to build a threshold on this street or to take water to [. . .] or to dig a cistern or [. . .] put or [. . .] does; anyone acting against this law shall owe a hundred staters to the Pythian Apollo and a hundred to the *polis*; the magistrates, in whose term the violation occurred, shall exact the penalty; if they do not, they shall owe double the amount of the penalty to the god and to the *polis*; and if the penalty is not written, the wrongdoer may not pay it; anyone who has not done any wrong [. . .] prove [. . .]; when he shall be reinstated, let him use the building. Every inhabitant shall keep the street in front of his house clean; if nobody lives in, the person to whom the building belongs shall; and the *epistatai** shall keep clean every month; and if something falls, they will make [. . .]; the street stretching from the sanctuary of Herakles to the sea will be kept clean by the *epistatai*; litter from the houses and from the streets is to be removed when the magistrates order so; if anyone does not comply with the law, he shall owe one-twelfth of a stater for each day to the *polis*; the *epistatai* shall exact the penalty and they shall keep half of it; nobody is allowed to climb up on the roofs of public buildings on this street to watch (a procession?) and no woman is permitted to watch from the windows; the inhabitant of the property where such illegal acts were committed shall pay a stater for each (act) to the *polis*; the *epistatai* shall keep half of it; nobody is allowed to put a pipe for running water to the relief which comes up in this street; if he does, he shall owe half one-twelfth of a stater for each day, of which half shall belong to the *polis* and the other half to the *epistatai*, who shall exact the penalty; from the temple of Graces to the area of money-changers and the *symposion** and the street beside the *prytaneion*; in the middle of these streets it is not permitted to pile up or to throw dung; if anyone does, he shall owe one-twelfth of a stater for each time to the *polis*, the *epistatai* are to exact the penalty retaining half of it; if not, they shall owe double the amount to Artemis–Hekate.

86 Paros (Cyclades), Regulation concerning cleanliness

IG xii (5) 107   *early 5th century BC*

The regulation might have been part of a lengthier regulation on cleanliness, similar to those surviving in Thasos or in Keos. It probably concerns the disposing of the waters after a blood sacrifice. Interestingly, the whole of the fine is paid to the prosecutor and not to the *polis* or the god.

Anyone who throws the dirty waters after the sacrifice from the top of the street shall owe fifty-one drachmas to the person who will prosecute him.

87 Athens, Regulation concerning cleanliness

IG i³ 257   *c. 440–430 BC*

This fragmentary inscription may have been part of a larger regulation concerning sacral places. What is interesting is the attested activity of tanners near the river Ilissos and the prohibition of disposing of hides and other litter in the river.

[. . .] drachmas. And the *basileus** shall take care of it. It shall be written on a stone *stele* and shall be put up in both sides; it is not permitted to allow hides to rot in the Ilissos above the temple of Herakles; nobody is permitted to tan hides or to throw litter into the river [. . .]

88 Keos (Cyclades), Regulation on cleanliness

IG xii *(5) 569*   *early 3rd century BC*

With this joint decision of the *Boule* and the people, the local magistrate is charged with the duty of keeping the water in the fountain clean, so that it can be used for cultic purposes in the sanctuary of Demeter. The imposed penalties reflect distinction according to status.

Hegistos said: the council and the assembly decided; when the *epimeletes** is in charge of the fountain in the upper part in order that the covered pipe will work, he shall take care of the fountain at the lower end, so that nobody will clean himself or wash in the fountain but the water will run clean to the sanctuary of Demeter; if anyone cleans himself or washes anything in the fountain, the *epimeletes* shall have the authority to impose a penalty of ten drachmas to a free man and to the children of free men and to whip the slaves; this *stele* shall be erected next to the fountains where the council thinks appropriate; the treasurer shall pay the expenses.

Relevant texts

Fountains: **Pergamos (Aiolis – Asia Minor)**, *SEG* xiii 521.159–89 (below, no. 99); **Athens**, Pl. *Laws* 764 b1–c2, Plu. *Themistokles* 31, *AthPol* 50.1, Pl. *Laws* vi 779c; **Andania (Arkadia – Peloponnese)**: *LSCG* 65.103–6 (92 BC); **Delos (Cyclades)**: *LSCG* Suppl. 50 (end 5th or early 4th century BC); **Kos**: *LSCG* 152.4–9 (4th century BC); **Athens**: obligation to keep a sanctuary of a cult group clean, *SEG* xxi 530 (333/2 BC); *IG* ii² 380 (end 4th century BC), Aristot. *Pol.* 1321 b4–5, *AthPol* 50.2; **Thasos**: *kopros, -onai*, *IG* xii (8) 265 (above, no. 48) and *SEG* xxvi 1029 (4th/3rd century BC).

Further reading

Edition and full commentary of the law from Thasos, H. Duchene (1992) *La stéle du port. Fouilles du port 1: Recherches sur une nouvelle inscription thasienne*, Paris (Études thasiennes 14); relation between the Platonic regulation on fountains and actual laws, Klingenberg

(1974); duties of property owners in regard to street cleaning and hygiene, D. Hennig (1995) 'Staatliche Anspruche an privaten Immobilienbesitz in der klassischen und hellenistischen Polis', *Chiron* 25, 235–82; difference in the solutions adopted in Thasos, in regard to responsibility for cleaning, Vatin (1976); discussions of different urbanistic regulations, Martin (1974: 57–72); locating the sanctuary of Herakles near Ilissos, in Athens, H. Lind (1990) *Der Gerber Kleon in den 'Rittern' des Aristophanes. Studien zur Demagogenkomödie*, 155–60, Frankfurt (Studien zur klassischen Philologie).

PROPERTY AND DEBTS

89   Gortyn (Crete), Procedure resolving land border disputes

IC iv 42B   *5th century BC*

Delineation of property, individual or public, boundaries was a source of disputes. Boundary disputes were common among Greek *poleis*, usually resolved by arbitrators, called upon by both *poleis* and later by the Romans. The fragmentary provision from Gortyn gives little information about the procedure but it centres upon the responsibility of the magistrates to adjudicate.

[. . .] within fifteen days, which are the borders of the two lands according to the claims. If the plaintiff claims that the fifteen days have passed, the judge and the *mnemon** will decide after having sworn an oath. And if, although summoned, they do not swear the oath, their property shall be disposed of as in the case of someone refusing to judge. And if public office or death prevents them, none of them shall suffer any penalty. The judges of *etaireia** and the judge about pledges, if they judge on the same day or the next, they shall not be punished.

Relevant texts

Boundary disputes between *poleis*: **Athens–Megara**, *IG* ii² 204 (352/1 BC); **Epidauros–Hermione (Argolis – Peloponnese)**, *SEG* xxxi 328 (3rd/2nd century BC); **Alipheira (Arkadia – Peloponnese)**, *SEG* xxv 449 (3rd–2nd century BC); **Klazomenai –unknown** *polis* **(Ionia – Asia Minor)**, *SEG* xxviii 697 (end 4th century BC); **Priene–Samos**, *IPriene* 37 (2nd century BC); **Ambrakia–Charadros (Epiros)**, *SEG* xxxv 665 (*c.* 160 BC) and *BE*

1988, no. 265; **Metropolis–Oiniadai (Aitolia)**, *IG* ix² (1) 3B (*c.* 250 BC); **Kondaia**–unknown *polis* **(Thessaly)**: *IG* ix (2) 521 (3rd/2nd century BC); demarcation of boundaries: **Mygdonia (Makedonia)**, *SEG* xl 542 (mid 4th century BC); **Mylasa (Caria – Asia Minor)**, *SEG* xxxix 1123 (2nd century BC); boundaries settlement: **Stiris–Phanotheus (Thessaly)**, *SEG* xlii 479 (3rd century BC); **Phrygia (Asia Minor)**, *SEG* xxxii 1287 (AD 253–60); **Numidia**, *SEG* xxx 1781 (AD 111); boundary stones: temples, **Athens**, *SEG* xli 123 (2nd century BC), **Sparta**, *SEG* xli 318 (1st century AD), **Kommagene (Asia Minor)**, *SEG* xli 1500 (Imperial), private property: **Dystos (Euboia)**, *SEG* xli 723 (5th–4th century BC).

Further reading

Romans deciding boundary disputes between Greek *poleis*, M. Corsaro (1988) 'Qualche osservazione sulle procedure di recupero delle terre pubbliche nelle citta greche', *Symposion 1988*, 213–29; G. Daverio Rocchi (1988) *Frontiera e confini nella Grecia antica*, Rome; officials involved in resolving boundary disputes, R. Scuderi (1991) 'Decreti del Senato per controversie di confine in eta repubblicana', *Athenaeum* 79, 371–415; D. Rousset (1994) 'Les frontières des cités grecques. Premières reflexions à partir du recueil des documents épigraphiques', *Cahiers Glotz* 5, 97–126; boundary stones in Athens, G.V. Lalonde (1991) 'Horoi', *The Athenian Agora* xix, 5–37.

90 Ephesos (Ionia – Asia Minor), Law regulating debts

IEph 8   86/5 BC

In the early 1st century BC the *poleis* in Asia Minor suffered from the protracted wars of Mithridates, king of Kappadokia, against the Romans (89–85 and 74–63 BC). In the beginning, most of the Greek *poleis* of Asia Minor sided with Mithridates. But a year later, having experienced further upheavals due to the reforms imposed by the king, *poleis* like Ephesos started defecting to the Romans. The Ephesians facing the threat of invasion by Mithridates decided to cancel any debts to the public or sacred treasury, to readmit those excluded from the civic body, and to give the right to citizenship to any foreigner, resident or slave who would fight for the salvation of the *polis*. It is interesting to note the concealment of the initially favourable attitude of the Ephesians towards Mithridates in the preamble of this decision.

[. . .] and the people keeping the old favour towards the Romans, the common deliverers, and promptly obeying whatever was ordered; Mithridates, king of Kappadokia, violating the treaty with the Romans and gathering troops, attempted to dominate over lands not belonging to him and conquered our neighbouring *poleis* by deceit and due to the size of its troops and the suddenness of his attack, conquered our city. Our people, guarding from the very beginning the favour to the Romans, awaiting but the occasion to take up arms for the common salvation, decided to declare war against Mithridates for the hegemony of Rome and for the common freedom. All the citizens have unanimously contributed to this struggle. Therefore, it was decided by the people that, since the whole affair is about war, protection, security and salvation of the temple of Artemis, of the *polis* and its territory, the generals and the secretary of the Council and the presidents shall bring forward immediately a decree and any other action to be taken in these circumstances and the people shall consider them.

The people have decided, following a proposal of the presidents and the secretary of the Council, Asklepiades, son of Asklepiades, who was son of Euboulides, and information provided by the generals. Since the biggest danger is pending over the temple of Artemis and over all the citizens and everyone living in the *polis* and on its territory, it is necessary to be united and face the danger; the people have decided that, because the whole affair is about war, protection, security and salvation of the temple of Artemis, of the *polis* and its territory, those people who were deprived of their citizenship or their names were put forward for expulsion from the citizens' register by the sacred or public treasurers in whatever way, they shall again be citizens and the inscription of their name and their debts shall be cancelled; those who are registered as accused for a religious or public offence or (are threatened by) religious or civil penalties or debts imposed in whatever way, the accusations and penalties shall be waived and any execution against them shall be void. And if anyone leased a sacred place or public property, the exaction will proceed according to the laws and the procedure. Anyone who has borrowed from a temple, he shall be released from the obligation to repay the loan, apart from those who borrowed on mortgage from associations or their representatives; in this case the interest will be charged from the following year till the situation of the people improves. And if anyone was naturalized so far, he will be a citizen and have a share in the benefits. And the religious and public prosecutions are cancelled and are void unless they concern boundary and inheritance disputes. And the resident-foreigners exempted from tax (*isoteleis*) and the resident-foreigners (*metoikoi*) and the sacred slaves and the freedmen and the foreigners and those who shall take up arms and register with the leader (*hegemon*), all of them shall be citizens on an equal footing (as the other citizens) and the leaders (*hegemones*) shall pass their names to the presidents and to the secretary of the Council, who shall allot them into tribes and *chilyastai**; and the public slaves who shall take up arms shall be freed and have the status of a resident-foreigner. And the creditors who have

106

lent money for maritime loans, loan agreements, deposits, mortgages, remortgages, sales, agreements, contracts and instalments came to the assembly of the people and happily and deliberately and in agreement with the people absolved the debtors from all the debts, and possession shall remain with the people who possess now unless anyone, in Ephesos or abroad [. . .] has contracted a loan or concluded an agreement. And regarding bank affairs, those who have deposited money or given or received pledges during the current year, the exaction of the debts shall follow the law. As for deposits or pledges of earlier years, the bankers and the depositors shall arrange the payment from the following year and for the following ten years and the interest shall be in proportion [. . .]

Relevant texts

Ephesos: law on abolition of debts, *IEph* 4 (297/6 BC); **Alipheira (Arkadia – Peloponnese)**: provisions on cancelling debts, *IPArk* 24 (273 BC).

Further reading

Asheri (1969).

91 Athens, Law about public debtors

Demosthenes xxiv (Against Timokrates) 39   353 BC

This law was proposed by Timokrates aiming at releasing his friends from jail, according to Demosthenes. The proposed law provided that state debtors could remain at liberty till the ninth prytany of the year (April–May) if they provided guarantees. If not, they should be jailed and their guarantees should be confiscated.

On the twelfth day of the first presidency (*prytaneia*), that is of Pandionis, Timokrates has proposed: and if any of the public debtors is put in jail in addition to a fine, according to a law or a decree, he shall be allowed to appoint, himself or others on his behalf, as guarantors for the debt, persons approved by the assembly who will pay off the debt in full. And the chairmen are required to put the request to the assembly, whenever a debtor wishes to nominate guarantors. And the debtor who appointed guarantors shall be released from jail once he has paid off the debt for which he appointed guarantors. But if the debtor does not pay off the debt either himself or his guarantors till the ninth presidency (*prytaneia*), the debtor shall be jailed and the guarantors shall have their property confiscated. With the exception of tax-farmers and their guarantors and their collectors and the lessees of leased property and their guarantors, the *polis* may exact the payments according to the laws in force. If anyone incurs a debt on the ninth presidency (*prytaneia*), he shall pay it off in full in the ninth or tenth presidency of the following year.

Relevant texts

Procedure of exacting public debts, *AthPol* 47.3–48.1.

Further reading

Summary account, MacDowell (1978: 164–7); Rhodes (1981: 555–9).

92 Zelea (Phrygia – Asia Minor), Decree on delimiting and registering public land

Syll³ 279 (= Schwyzer 733)   *334/3 BC*

The decree, probably issued soon after the passage of Alexander the Great, provides for the setting up of a committee to find public land occupied illegally and to impose fines. In case of objections being raised there will be a panel of judges to decide each case. It resembles more an administrative ordinance than a law in a modern sense.

Resolution of the people. Kleon to be *epistates** Timokles proposed. Nine men from among the citizens shall be elected, as inspectors on behalf of the people, to find out if any individual has occupied the part of the public land which the Phrygians were occupying without paying tax, since the acropolis was captured by the citizens; the inspectors should be elected among those who do not possess any public land. The elected shall swear to Artemis that they shall find anyone occupying public land according to the decree and they shall impose a fine according to the value, rightly and justly, according to their opinion. And when those elected by the people impose a fine, the individuals should pay it to the *polis*, otherwise they shall be ejected from the land. The search and the imposition of fines should end on the month Heraion and the payment of the fines on the month Kekyposios. If anyone objects, claiming that he bought (the land) or took it as an owner (?) from the *polis*, there should be a trial (*diadikasia*) and if it is proven that he does not possess it legally, he shall pay the fine increased by fifty per cent. And the magistrates shall give the plots of land (to the *polis*?) from where individuals were ejected by the month Akatallos. And the people who are away, when they return to the *polis*, they shall pay the fine in a month's time, otherwise they shall be liable, according to this decree. Eleven of the citizens shall be judges, elected by the people from among those who do not possess any public land. Three persons out of the eleven shall be allotted to act as advocates. And the judges and the advocates shall swear by Artemis according to the law. And the magistrates shall have the decree and the fines to be paid about the plots of land inscribed on a *stele* and erected in the sanctuary of the Pythian Apollo. The magistrates shall spend the money on the public temples and whatever the *polis* needs.

Further reading

Commentary, M. Corsaro (1984) 'Un decreto di Zelea (Mysie) sul recupero dei terreni pubblici (Syll³ 279)', *ASNP* 14, 441–93; judicial aspect of land disputes, G. Thür (1977) 'Kannte das altgriechische Recht die Eigentumdiadikasie?', *Symposion 1977*, 55–69.

93 Halikarnassos (Caria – Asia Minor), Law on resolving property disputes

Nomima I, 19   *475–450 BC*

The inscription preserves a common decision, on the one hand, of the inhabitants of Halikarnassos and Salmakis in Caria and on the other hand of Lygdamis, a local dynast, about land disputes. The identity of this Lygdamis is still debated. The most likely explanation for the issue of this law is the return of exiles. It provides that there shall be an initial period of freezing of claims on land and only then will disputes about land be discussed, according to rules laid out in the inscription. The role of the *mnemones** was decisive in this process.

These were decided at the meeting of the Halikarnassians and Salmakiteans and Lygdamis in the sacred assembly the fifth day of the month Hermaion, when Leon, son of Oatatios, was *prytanis** and Sarytollos, son of Thekuileos, was *naopoios**. For the *mnemones*. No land or building shall be handed over to the (incoming) *mnemones* when Apollonides, son of Lygdamis, is *mnemon* and Panamyes, son of Kasbollis, and in Salmake when Megabates, son of Aphyasis, and Phormion, son of Panyassis, are *mnemones*. Whoever wants to start court proceedings about land or buildings, he has to introduce his demand within eighteen months since this law was passed. A legal oath shall be sworn, as presently, in front of the judges. Anything the *mnemones* know will prevail. If anyone wants to start court proceedings, after the passing of the deadline, the possessor of the land or of the buildings will have to swear an oath; the judges will receive one-twelfth of a stater; the possessor will swear the oath in front of the plaintiff. Owners of the land and of the buildings will be the people who had them when Apollonides and Panamyes were *mnemones*, unless they lost ownership after a suit. Anyone who wants to abolish this law or puts forward a proposal for its abolition, his property will be sold, the money will be consecrated to Apollo and he shall be exiled for ever. And if his property is not worth ten staters, he shall be sold as a slave abroad, without any possibility of returning to Halikarnassos. And the Halikarnassians who respect this decision, as it was sworn on the sacrificial victims and written in the temple of Apollo, are free to initiate legal proceedings.

Further reading

Overview of previous theories and a fresh examination of the legal questions, A. Maffi (1988) *L'iscrizione di Ligdamis*, Trieste; role of *mnemones*, W. Lambrinoudakis and M. Worle (1983) 'Ein hellenistische Reformgesetz über das offentliche Urkundenwesen von Paros', *Chiron* 13, 333–41; discussion of modes of returning property to exiles, Lonis (1991).

94 Lokris (Central Greece), Property law

Nomima I, 44 (= IG *ix.1² 609*)   *?525–500 BC*

The law extends provisions of property law to the distribution of new lands. In particular, it concerns the question of inheritance of the land; the lot will pass from father to son, and if there is no son it will pass to the daughter, and if no daughter survives to the brother of the deceased, and in case there is no brother to the nearest relative. Any motion for redistribution of the lands will incur the curse of the *polis*, unless the *polis* brings in 200 men as colonists to defend the *polis*. The right on planted trees is guaranteed.

This law about landed property will be valid for the division of the land of Hylia and Liskaria,[35] for the reserved as well as for the public lands. The right to the land will belong to the parents and to the son; if there is no son, it will belong to the daughter; and if there is no daughter to the brother; and if no brother exists, the nearest relative will be the owner according to the law; and if there are no relatives [. . .] Whatever will be planted, shall be protected. Anyone introducing a motion for division of land or votes for such a motion in the council of Elders, in the *polis*, or in the elected council or incites civil strife for division of land, he shall be cursed, his property shall be confiscated and his house will be demolished, according to the law on homicide, unless in case of war, a hundred and one citizens from the

---

35 Unknown localities in Lokris.

aristocracy, or the majority decide to bring as new colonists two hundred men of military age and ability. This law is consecrated to the Pythian Apollo and to the other gods worshipped in the same sanctuary. Anyone who transgresses these provisions shall be cursed, himself and his descendants, and anyone respecting them shall be blessed by the gods. Half of the land will belong to the previous occupiers and the other half to the colonists. The valley lots are to be divided. Exchanges will be valid provided that they have taken place in front of a magistrate. If the *demiourgoi** make more profit than is allowed, it will be consecrated to Apollo for nine years as an offering and it will not be inscribed as profit.

Relevant texts

Laws on intestate succession: **Athens**, Dem. xliii 51 (above, no. 2); **Gortyn (Crete)**, *IC* iv 72 col. IV 23–col. VI 46 (above, no. 3); easements, *IC* iv 46b (beginning 5th century BC); easements on water, *IC* iv 52 (beginning 5th century BC).

Further reading

Summary in van Effenterre and Ruze (1994: 188–92) and Graham (1983); S. Audring (1989) *Zur Struktur des Territoriums griechischer Poleis in archaischer Zeit*, Berlin (Schriften zur Geschichte und Kultur der Antike 29); S. Link (1991) 'Das Siedlungsgesetz aus Westlokris (Bronze Papadakis; *IG* ix (i) 3 nr. 609 = Meiggs–Lewis 13)', *ZPE* 87, 65–77; Fr. Gscehnitzer (1991) 'Zum Vorstoß von Acker-und Gartenbaum in die Wildnis: Das "Westlokrische Siedlungsgesetz" (IG, IX, I² 609) in seinem agrargeschichtlichen Zusammenhang', *Ktema* 16, 81–91.

ESTABLISHING COLONIES

95 Chaleion (Lokris – Central Greece), Law about the colony in Naupaktos

Nomima I, 43 (= *IG* ix.1² 718)   *460–450 BC*

This law regulates the setting up of a colony of Hypoknamidian Lokrians in the area of modern Naupaktos and the relation of the colony with its mother-*polis*. The citizens of the colony lose some of their rights as citizens of Lokris but could participate in the sacrifices and other ceremonies of the mother-*polis*, as foreigners. In particular, arrangements were made for the property left behind and *ateleia* was granted, oath of allegiance and alliance was to be sworn, and the citizens of both mother-*polis* and colony would have judicial preference in courts.

Side A: These are the terms for the colony in Naupaktos; if a Hypoknamidian Lokrian[36] becomes Naupaktian, he will be able, while Naupaktian, to participate in the ceremonies and sacrifices as foreigner (in his country of origin) if he wishes so; if he wishes, he can participate in sacrifices and ceremonies in a community, he and his descendants in perpetuity. The colonists from Hypoknamidia Lokris shall not pay taxes in Lokris before they become again citizens of Hypoknamidia Lokris. If anyone wants to return and has left a son who is in the majority age or brother, they are allowed to do so without right of entry (to property?). And if the Hypoknamidian Lokrians are expelled from Naupaktos, they can return to their place without the right of entry. In this case they are not going to pay any taxes apart from those imposed in West Lokris.

A: The colonists in Naupaktos will swear an oath that they will not deliberately distance themselves from the Opountians with any pretence, excuse or trick. The swearing of the oath can be repeated, if they wish so, thirty years later by a hundred citizens of Naupaktos in Opous and a hundred Opountians in Naupaktos.

B: If any colonist leaves Naupaktos without paying any taxes, he is to be excluded from Lokris, unless he is acquitted by the Naupaktians.

C: If there are no descendants or heirs of a Hypoknamidian Lokrian colonist in Naupaktos, the nearest relative from the Lokrians will take possession of the inheritance, whether he is a man or a child, provided that he shall go to Naupaktos within three months; if he does not, the laws of Naupaktos will apply.

D: Anyone returning from Naupaktos to Hypoknamidia Lokris has to proclaim it in Naupaktos in the agora and in Hypoknamidia Lokris in the agora.

E: When Perkatharians and Mysachenoi[37] become citizens of Naupaktos, their property in Naupaktos will be governed by the laws of Naupaktos

---

36 The Hypoknamidian or Opountian Lokrians were living to the north of Boiotia opposite the island of Euboia, in the south of the modern district of Phthiotis.

37 There are no details about the nature, the size and the origin of these groups. Scholars have suggested that they were families of purifiers, a noble clan, or groups of exiles who have returned.

while their property in Hypoknamidia Lokris shall be regulated by the laws of Hypoknamidians, according to the practice of each *polis*. If any of the Perkatharians and Mysachenoi return to their *polis*, they will have to conform with the laws of each *polis*.

Side B. F: If a colonist in Naupaktos dies and has a brother, he (the brother) shall inherit and he shall take anything that he is entitled to, according to the laws in Hypoknamidia Lokris.

G: The colonists in Naupaktos will have priority before the judges; justice is dispensed, against or in favour of them in Opous on the same day. In Hypoknamidia Lokris there will be a guarantor for the colonists and in Naupaktos for the Lokrians, so that they will enjoy their rights.

H: Anyone who leaves his father, leaves to him part of his property; in case of the father's death, the colonist in Naupaktos will recover that part.

I: Anyone who attempts, by any means or method, to abolish these resolutions will be deprived of his civic rights and his property will be confiscated, unless it was agreed between the two parties, the assembly of a Thousand in Opous and the assembly of the colonists in Naupaktos. The magistrate will have thirty days to dispense justice to the plaintiff, provided that he has at least thirty days more in office. If he does not do so, he will be deprived of his civic rights and his property, the land and the slaves will be confiscated,. The legal oath shall be sworn. The votes will be collected into a box. The law instituted for the Hypoknamidian Lokrians will be equally valid for the Chaleians,[38] those together with Antiphatas.

96 Athens, Law on establishing a colony in Brea[39]

IG i³ 46   *c. 445 BC*

Colonization was already a widely used solution to problems of over-population, scarcity of resources or civil strife in the archaic era. The

---

38 Chaleion was a *polis* in the vicinity of modern Galaxidi, in the district of Phokis.
39 Although we have the decree regulating the dispatch of colonists, we cannot locate the site of Brea. It was somewhere in Thrace; but the Athenians of the 5th century BC gave the name Thrace to the whole of the coastline between Thessalonike and Byzantion. It might have been on the valley of lower Strymon, near Amphipolis or on the west coast of mainland Chalkidike, as has been recently suggested in *To Archaiologiko Ergo sten Makedonia kai Thrake* 7 (1994). See Isaac (1986: 51–2).

law about the colony in Brea contains provisions for distribution of land by a commission of ten officials, sacred land and extent of public land, duties of the colony as an ally of Athens and obligation for other neighbouring allies to defend the newly established colony, eligibility of citizens to join the expedition, symbolic connection with the motherland.

Face A: [. . .] the colonists will provide for the colony as much as they wish. They shall elect ten *geonomoi*,[40] one from each tribe (*phyle*), who shall distribute the land. Damokleides shall be governor of the colony and he shall do his best. The land consecrated to the gods will continue to be sacred but no additional land shall be consecrated. The colony will send an ox for the festival of Panathenaia[41] and a *phallos* for the festival of Dionysia.[42] If the colony is attacked, the *poleis* in Thrace shall help with the utmost strength according to the treaties [. . .] when secretary was [. . .] . These shall be inscribed on a *stele* and be deposited on the Acropolis; the colonists shall pay for the cost of the *stele*. And if anyone votes against the provisions on the *stele* or a speaker speaks in public or attempts to modify or to abolish the decree, he shall be disenfranchised, himself and his children and his property shall be confiscated and one-tenth will belong to the Goddess, if the colonists themselves [. . .] need. Soldiers who are enlisted as colonists, when they return to Athens, they should arrive within thirty days in Brea. The colonists should leave in thirty days. Aischines shall go with them carrying the money.

Face B: Phantokles said: Concerning the colony at Brea, let it be done according to what Demokleides said; the *prytaneis** of the tribe Erechtheis shall introduce Phantokles to the council in its first sitting; *thetes** and *zeugitai** are allowed to go as colonists in Brea.

Relevant texts

Agreement of founders of **Kyrene (N. Africa)**, *Nomima* I, 41 (*c.* 630 BC); **Kerkyra**: sending colonists to Issos (Dalmatia), Schwyzer 147 (4th century BC); fragmentary document of a colony of Aitolians in **Same (Kephallenia)**, *IG* ix 1^2 2 (end of 3rd century BC); access to

40 Individuals responsible for the apportioning of land.
41 Festival in honour of Athena, taking place every four years, in July. There was a procession from the Acropolis to Eleusis. For a summary account see Parke (1977: 33–50) and Burkert (1978: 232–3); Parker (1996: 89–92) discusses the reform of the festival in the 6th century BC.
42 See this chapter, fn. 7.

courts: **Chaleion (Lokris – Central Greece),** *Nomima* I, 43 (above, no. 95); **Athens:** fragment of a foundation of a colony, *IG* i^2 46 (*c.* 440 BC) and list of things taken for the setting up of a colony, Tod ii 200 (325/4 BC).

Further reading

Relationship between colony and mother-city as a link between independent *poleis*, Graham (1983); inheritance provisions in the law about Naupaktos, A. Maffi (1986) 'Sulla legge coloniaria per Naupatto (ML 20)', *Festschrift für A. Kränzlein. Beiträge zur antiken Rechtsgeschichte,* 69–82, Graz; religious aspects of colonization, I. Malkin (1987) *Religion and colonisation in ancient Greece,* Leiden; Roman practices, D.J. Gargola (1995) *Lands, laws & Gods. Magistrates and ceremony in the regulation of public lands in republican Rome,* London (Studies in the history of Greece and Rome).

POLIS INSTITUTIONS

97 Paros (Cyclades), Law reforming the archives

SEG xxxiii 679   *late 3rd or early 2nd century BC*

The law concerns the reform of an archive. A committee was appointed and proposed the reforms endorsed by the people. The reforms imposed tighter procedures to eliminate tampering with the material deposited in the archives. No penalty is provided either for offenders or officials; only curses are pronounced and every citizen retains the right to prosecute any offender. Furthermore, procedures for the scrutiny and cross-examination of the contents of the archive are put forward, as well as elaborate procedures of checks and balances.

These were written and proposed by Kleotharses, son of Silenos, Chares, son of Kratistoleos, Eukrates, son of Kriton, elected by the assembly of the citizens, with regard to the archives, the existing ones in the temples of Apollon, Artemis and Leto and the ones to be opened in the future. The archons around Nikesiphon and the *polis*-priests will have to curse anyone abusing, erasing or tampering with entries in the existing archives; if anyone has abused or erased or tampered with any of the entries in the existing archive, since it has been opened in the sanctuary, let him perish. And if anyone knows about it and does not denounce it to the archons and to the *apodektes** taking care of the sanctuary, and likewise if anyone in the future abuses or erases or tampers with the archives referring to sacred matters, let him perish, even when someone knows and does not denounce it. If anyone abuses the archive in the sanctuary, any willing citizen of Paros can prosecute those responsible, without any time limit or the possibility of raising objections; the prosecutor will submit, according to the law, a public suit to the *basileus**, including all the allegations, suggesting what penalty the defendant should suffer or pay; and the prosecution will likewise proceed in case of a later occurred abuse in the archive. In order to avoid as much as possible the repetition of any offence in the future and if this is not possible, cross-examination will be conducted through the summaries; the *mnemones** of the year when Nikesiphon was archon, are to write down on paper summaries of all the archival material that they have brought into the temples of Apollon, Artemis and Leto, and they (the *mnemones*) are to hand down the summaries to the archons when they hand the other archival material to the *apodektes* and to the *mnemon*; and the archon is to put down that the material handed on was identical to the original, and the archons are to hand it down to the *apodektes* who is taking care of the archive in the *polis*, after having received the material from the *mnemones*; and the *apodektes* is to put the archival material immediately, in the presence of the archons, in the box which is in the temple of Hestia. For the cost of these the archons around Nikesiphon are to give to the *mnemones* from the fund of *prytaneia*[43] to each *mnemon* thirty drachmas, half of it in the month of Thargelion and the other half in the month of Apatourion. In the future, after the year of the archon Nikesiphon, the selected *mnemones* shall hand the other archives they received from previous *mnemones*, having written them down, to the *apodektes* in the Pythion, according to the law. As for the documents the *mnemones* manage and those for which summaries were given to them, they have to copy them exactly in a monthly order and give them to the *apodektes* who is taking care of the Pythion, just as the other documents and the archons, as it is written, and these affairs are to be administered as it is written above. For the cost of this, give to the *mnemones* whatever is written in the budget. In order that it will be possible for anyone wanting to check the documents in the temple of Hestia, if anyone claims that documents in the temple of Hestia are not also written in the temple of Pythion, the claimants have to inform the archons in the main assembly where citizens will hear the claim that documents are not also written in the archives kept in the temple of Pythion, and on the fifth of the month the *apodektes* will open the sanctuary and display, in the presence of the archons, and nobody is allowed to bring out any document without the permission of the *apodektes* and of the archons, but the scrutiny will take place while they are there; the archons and the *apodektes* will be liable for committing any offence concerning the documents or the scrutiny of archives according to the rules; and the

---

43 *Prytaneia* was the fund collected by the dues for cases introduced in lawcourts.

apodektes will be liable for any offence committed about the archives in the sanctuary of Hestia in the same manner as if anyone has committed an offence about the archives in the sanctuary of Python. When the assembly of the citizens decides to use a document, in order to be evident to all, the *apodektes* taking care of the archives in the *polis*, Sokleides, is to have this document written on a *stele* and put next to the sanctuary of Hestia; and the cost of the inscription and of the *stele* will be paid to him from the income he has.

Relevant texts

Mykonos (Cyclades): registration of contracts, *Syll³* 1215 (4th century BC); **Tenos (Cyclades)**: *IG* xii (5) 872–3 (4th/3rd century BC); **Thasos**: officials to provide access to archives, *BCH* 50 (1926) p. 226 no. 3 (2nd century AD); **Ephesos (Ionia – Asia Minor)**: charges for the *polis* bureau, *IEph* 14 (1st century BC); **Dyme (Achaia – Peloponnese)**: burning of archives during disturbances, *Syll³* 684 (*c.* 140 BC).

Further reading

Edition and commentary of the law, W. Lambrinoudakis and M. Worle (1983) 'Ein hellenistische Reformsgesetz über das offentliche Urkundenwesen von Paros', *Chiron* 13, 283–368; registration of contracts in archives, A. Christophilopoulos (1979) *Nomika Epigraphika*, 9–69, Athens: orality and archives, R. Thomas (1989) *Oral tradition and written record in classical Athens*, 34–83, Cambridge; R. Thomas (1992) *Literacy and orality in ancient Greece*, Cambridge; temple archive in Epizephyrioi Lokroi (S. Italy), A. De Franciscis (1972) *Stato e societa in Locri Epizefiri (L'archivio dell'Olympieion Locrese)*, Napoli.

98 Beroia (Makedonia), Gymnasiarchical law

La loi gymnasiarchique   *before 167 BC*

This is the only example of a complete law concerning the duties and rights of a gymnasiarch. It is written on two faces of a *stele*. In the first part it records the passing of the law, while the text of the oath to be sworn by the officials of the *gymnasion* and the actual law occupies the second and longest part of the inscription. That second part is organized in sections concerning the qualifications for the office of gymnasiarch, the officials appointed for the award of prizes, the individuals responsible for the provision of olive oil, the organization of athletic contests during the festival in honour of Hermes, the training of the boys frequenting the *gymnasion* and their separation from youths of an older age, the eligibility of participants in the *gymnasion*, and the punishment for different offences committed either by the participants or the officials.

Face A: When Hippokrates, son of Nikokrates, was *strategos**, on the nineteenth of the month Apellaios,[44] the assembly having been convened, Zopyros, son of Amyntas, the gymnasiarch, Asklepiades, son of Heras, Kallippos, son of Hippostratos, have proposed; since all the other magistracies are exercised according to the law and in those *poleis* in which there are gymnasia and anointing,[45] the laws of gymnasiarchs are deposited in the public archives, it is proper the same to be done in our *polis* and to put what we have given to the *exetastai** in the *gymnasion*, being inscribed on a *stele*, in the same manner another copy is to be deposited in the public archives; for, when this has been done, the younger people will be more restrained and will obey the leader and their revenues will not be wasted, the gymnasiarchs elected each year being, according to the law, the officials and liable. The *polis* has decided that the law of gymnasiarchs put forward by Zopyros, son of Amyntas, the gymnasiarch, Asklepiades, son of Heras, Kallippos, son of Hippostratos, will be valid and will be deposited in the public archives, it will be followed by the gymnasiarchs and it will be put in the *gymnasion* on a *stele*. It was approved on the first of the month Peritios.[46]

Law of the gymnasiarch. The *polis* shall elect a gymnasiarch, not younger than thirty years old not older than sixty years old, at the same time that other magistrates are elected, and the elected gymnasiarch shall exercise his magistracy having sworn the following oath: 'I swear by Zeus, Earth (*Ge*), Sun (*Helios*), Apollon, Herakles, Hermes that I shall exercise the duties of gymnasiarch, according to the law of gymnasiarchs, and when there is no provision in the law according to my judgement of what is just and moral, without favouring friends or harming enemies against the law and I shall not myself appropriate the existing revenues of the young people or deliberately allow anyone else to do so, in any way or under any pretext; if I act according to the oath I shall be blessed with abundance, if not, the opposite.' The elected gymnasiarch, when he is to assume his post, shall convene an assembly in the *gymnasion* on the first day of the month

44 The second month of the Makedonian calendar, approximating to November.
45 Anointing, throughout the law, does not mean only the act of applying olive oil to the body; it denotes, more generally, the participation in the activities of the *gymnasion*.
46 The fourth month of the Makedonian calendar, approximating to January.

Dios,[47] in which he will propose three men to be elected by showing of hands; these three, having sworn the following oath, will, together with the gymnasiarch supervise the youths, according to the instructions they receive, and will follow the gymnasiarch every day to the *gymnasion* [. . .] of the gymnasiarch with what he will need [. . .] and the second day of Dios [. . .] the *politarchai** and the *exetastai* [. . .] the *gymnasion* together with the aforementioned men [. . .] from them [. . .] in the anointing and so [. . .] and if anyone does not do any of the above, he will pay [. . .] and the revenue collector (*praktor*) will exact the penalty, the *exetastai* having signed, and if they do not sign they are to pay a fine equal to the penalty and one-third shall go to the denouncer.

Provision of wood: [. . .] together with the *exetastai* [. . .] the existing property [. . .] deciding a case [. . .] we swear by Zeus, Earth (*Ge*), Sun (*Helios*), Apollon, Herakles, Hermes [. . .] and when there is no provision in the law according to our judgement of what is just and moral, without appropriating the existing revenues of the young people or favouring friends or harming enemies, against the law, in any way or under any pretext, if I act according to the oath I shall be blessed with abundance, if not, the opposite [. . .] of the boys and the elected gymnasiarch . . .

Face B: No one younger than thirty years old is allowed to strip himself after the signal has been lowered,[48] unless the leader (*aphegoumenos*) agrees; when the signal is lifted nobody else is to strip himself, unless the leader agrees, and nobody is to be anointed in another athletic arena (*palaistra*) in the *polis*; if he does, the gymnasiarch will reprimand him and will impose a fine of fifty drachmas; the persons frequenting the *gymnasion* will obey the person appointed by the gymnasiarch as the leader, as they obey the gymnasiarch; the person who does not obey, if he is not a free citizen, the gymnasiarch will whip him, and if he is a free citizen the gymnasiarch shall impose a fine. The ephebes and those less than twenty-two years old will practise every day javelin throwing and archery, when the boys are anointed, and likewise, if there is a need, in other disciplines.

About boys. *Neaniskoi*[49] are not permitted either to enter the area of boys or to speak to them; if they do, the gymnasiarch will reprimand and impose a fine to anyone violating this provision; the *paidotribai*[50] shall come twice a day to the *gymnasion*, at the time the gymnasiarch will fix, unless one of them is ill or has any other immediate occupation; if not, he is to inform the gymnasiarch; if it seems that any of the *paidotribai* is negligent and does not come to the boys at the fixed time, the gymnasiarch shall impose a fine of

47 The first month of the Makedonian calendar, approximating to October.
48 Probably a kind of a flag was raised, perhaps accompanied by a sound.
49 In the law, young men 20–30 years old are designated as *neoi* or *neaniskoi*.
50 *Paidotribai* were teachers of gymnastics.

five drachmas for each day; and the gymnasiarch will be responsible for punishing the undisciplined boys and the *paidagogoi*,[51] if they are not free citizens, with lashes, and if they are free, to impose a fine on them; the *paidotribai* have the duty to examine the boys three times a year every four months and the gymnasiarch shall appoint judges who shall award a crown of olive leaves to the winner.

People not allowed to take part in the *gymnasion*: any slaves, freedmen or their sons, any *apalaistros*,[52] any male prostitute, anyone practising a trade in the agora; neither is any drunkard or mentally ill person permitted to strip himself in the *gymnasion*. If the gymnasiarch allows any of the above mentioned to be anointed, deliberately or after being denounced to him, he shall pay a thousand drachmas; in order that the amount will be exacted, the denouncer is to lodge a complaint with the *exetastai* of the *polis*, and they will notify the revenue collector (*praktor*) and if they do not notify or the revenue collector does not exact, they are to pay an equal fine and to give one-third of it to the denouncer; if the gymnasiarch thinks that the complaint is unjust, he can raise objections in ten days and the case will be decided in the appropriate court; and the future gymnasiarchs shall obstruct the people who want to be anointed despite the laws, if not they will be liable to the same fine. Nobody is allowed to insult the gymnasiarch in the *gymnasion*; if anyone does, he shall pay fifty drachmas; if anyone beats the gymnasiarch in the *gymnasion*, the people present shall stop him and not allow him to continue, and likewise the offender shall pay a hundred drachmas and, moreover, he shall be liable to prosecution according to the existing laws; and if anyone present does not help, although he can, he shall pay fifty drachmas.

About the festival of Hermes. The gymnasiarch shall organize the festival in honour of Hermes in the month of Hyperberetaios[53] and he shall make a sacrifice to Hermes and he shall offer as a prize a weapon and three other (prizes) for vigour and discipline and diligence to those up to thirty years of age and the gymnasiarch shall make a list of seven people from those in the *gymnasion*, to judge on the vigour, and from those seven, three will be allotted to judge after swearing by Hermes that they decide fairly, who has the best shaped body, without any favour or enmity; and if the allotted persons do not judge and do not swear that they are not capable (of judging), the gymnasiarch shall impose a fine of ten drachmas to the person who fails and he shall replace him with someone else chosen by lot; the gymnasiarch will decide about discipline and diligence, having sworn by Hermes, about

51 *Paidagogoi* were persons who were accompanying the young men; they could be either freedmen or slaves.
52 The term *apalaistros* means a person who, although of citizen status, cannot practise in the *gymnasion*, perhaps due to a physical infirmity, and is therefore a person exempted. Cf. the discussion in *La loi gymnasiarchique*, 81–4.
53 The twelfth month of the Makedonian calendar, approximating to September.

discipline who was, in his opinion, the most disciplined among those up to thirty years of age, and about diligence who was, in his opinion, the most diligent in this year among those up to thirty years of age; and the winners that day shall wear the crown and they can be decorated with a ribbon; the gymnasiarch shall organize during the festival of Hermes, a torch-race for boys and those between twenty and thirty years of age; the cost of the weapons will be paid by the existing revenue. For the celebration of the festival of Hermes, the *hieropoioi** will receive from every person frequenting the *gymnasion* up to two drachmas and they will organize the feast in the *gymnasion*; they are to elect their successors who will be *hieropoioi* of Hermes the following year. And the *paidotribai* shall sacrifice to Hermes, at the same time as the *hieropoioi*, receiving not more than one drachma from each boy and they will prepare portions of raw meat from the animal to be sacrificed, and the *hieropoioi* and the gymnasiarch shall not provide any spectacle during drinking. The prizes which the winners receive shall be dedicated, within eight months into the term of the next gymnasiarch; if they do not, the gymnasiarch shall impose a fine of a hundred drachmas and he shall punish with lashes and fines those who cheated and competed unfairly, and similarly if anyone hands down victory to someone else.

Election of *lampadarchs*. The gymnasiarch is going to elect three *lampadarchs* from those in the *gymnasion*, in the month of Gorpiaios,[54] and the elected shall provide olive oil to the *neaniskoi*, each for ten days; and he shall elect three *lampadarchs* among the boys, who shall provide olive oil, each for ten days; and if anyone of the elected or his father or his brothers or the *orphanophylakes*[55] objects on the ground that the individual is unable to be a *lampadarch*, he will be excused having sworn an oath within five days after the election; if he does not perform the duties of a *lampadarch* or does not swear the oath, he shall have to pay fifty drachmas and in addition he shall provide olive oil and perform the duties of a *lampadarch*; and equally if the person who was excused seems to have sworn with no valid motive, after having been found guilty by the gymnasiarch and the young men, he shall pay fifty drachmas and he will provide olive oil and perform the duties of a *lampadarch*; and the gymnasiarch shall elect another *lampadarch* to replace the person who presented a valid excuse, and he shall organize the torch-race for boys, selecting among those who frequent the *gymnasion*, those who seem to him to be qualified, and in the same way the torch-race of the *neaniskoi* will be organized.

About *brabeutai*. The gymnasiarch will appoint as judges of the games persons who seem to him to be qualified, in the torch-race of the festival of Hermes and in the long-distance run and in the other games, and if anyone accuses one of the judges and claims that he was wronged, the judge shall be

---

54 The eleventh month of the Makedonian calendar, approximating to August.
55 Guardians of the orphans. It was their responsibility to protect the property of minors from maladministration.

liable to prosecution according to the laws of the *polis*. The gymnasiarch shall administer the revenues of the *gymnasion* and he shall pay the expenses from these revenues; at the end of his term in office, he is to put down the revenue on a board and anything that was paid in the way of fine or of judicial decision and the expenses, and display this board in the *gymnasion* in the month of Dios[56] in the following year, and he shall give his accounts to the *exetastai* of the *polis* every four months and it shall be allowed, if anyone wants, to take part in the scrutiny of his accounts; he shall give any surplus to his successor within thirty days after the end of his tenure; and if he does not provide the accounts or the surplus as it is prescribed, he shall pay to the *gymnasion* a thousand drachmas, and the revenue collector (*praktor*) shall exact the money after notification by the *exetastai* and the gymnasiarch will equally submit his accounts and the surplus. The person who buys the revenue of *gloios*[57] will assume the function of the guardian of the athletic arena (*palaistra*), obeying the orders of the gymnasiarch, for what is proper in the *gymnasion*, and if he does not obey or he is undisciplined, the gymnasiarch shall whip him. And if anyone steals anything from the *gymnasion*, he shall be liable to the same punishment as in the case of being convicted for sacrilege in the appropriate lawcourt. The gymnasiarch shall write the reason for all the fines he imposes, he shall proclaim them in the *gymnasion*, he shall display the names of the fined on a whitened board and he shall notify the revenue collector; and the revenue collector, having exacted the fine, will give it to the gymnasiarch; and if anyone claims that he was unjustly fined, he shall be allowed to raise his objections and be judged by the appropriate authorities and if the fined person wins, the gymnasiarch shall pay back the fine increased by fifty per cent; and in addition the one-fifth and the one-tenth. Anyone willing can hold the gymnasiarch accountable within twenty-four months following the end of his tenure, and the judgement on these affairs will be issued by the appropriate lawcourts. Handed down by the *politarchai*. There was one vote against this decree.

Relevant texts

Amphipolis (Makedonia): an unpublished ephebarchical law is mentioned in *SEG* xxxiv 602 (22 BC) and a gymnasiarchic law mentioned in Hatzopoulos (1996: II no. 16) (182 BC); **Aigiale (Amorgos – Cyclades)**: mention of a law of *gymnasion*, *IG* xii (7) 515, 81 (2nd century BC); **Sestos (Thrace)**: honouring a gymnasiarch, *ISestos* 1 (133–120 BC); **Eressos (Lesbos)**: *IG* xii Suppl.

---

56 The first month of the Makedonian calendar, approximating to October.
57 The mixture of olive oil and sweat was called *gloios*. The right to collect it and dispose of it was sold according to the law.

122, 22–5 (209–204 BC); **Koresia (Keos – Cyclades)**: 30 as the minimum age for a gymnasiarch, *Syll³* 958.21–2 (early 3rd century BC); teaching archery and javelin throwing: **Teos (Ionia – Asia Minor)**, *Syll³* 578 (2nd century BC); **Thespiai (Boiotia)**, *SEG* xxxii 496 (250–240 BC); **Erythrai (Ionia – Asia Minor)**, *IErythrai* 81, 8–12 (1st century BC); **Athens**: opening and closing time of schools and wrestling arenas (*palaistrai*), Aisch. i 10; penalties for abusing magistrates, Lys. ix 6, Dem. xxi 32–3; honouring trainers of ephebes, *IG* ii² 1028 (102 BC); **Kos**: calendar of a *gymnasion*, *LSCG* 165 (2nd century BC).

Further reading

New edition with exhaustive commentary and bibliography, Ph. Gauthier and M.B. Hatzopoulos (1993) *La loi gymnasiarchique de Beroia*, Athens (Meletemata 16); epigraphical testimonia for qualities promoted in the *gymnasion*, N.B. Crowther (1991) 'Euexia, Eutaxia, Philoponia. Three contests of the Greek *gymnasion*', *ZPE* 85, 301–4 ; theft and sacrilege, Cohen (1983: 93–116); Spartan youth education, N.M. Kennel (1995) *The gymnasium of virtue. Education and culture in ancient Sparta*, London (Studies in the history of Greece and Rome).

99 Pergamos (Aiolis – Asia Minor), Law of *astynomoi*

SEG xiii 521 (= *OGIS* 483)   *2nd century AD*

Although the inscription is dated in the 2nd century AD, the law reflects regulations as old as the second century BC. There are detailed regulations on keeping streets, roads and paths clean and in good condition, on the minimum size of streets, on digging up ditches and producing bricks or stones, on repairing common walls and sharing the cost, on keeping clean springs and fountains in the *polis*, on registering and keeping clean all cisterns in town.

Col. A: [. . .] being an *astynomos*** set up the royal law on his own expenses. [. . .] they (i.e. the *astynomoi*) shall inspect and decide as it seems right to them. If, in this manner, the individuals do not observe the decision, the *strategoi*** shall impose the fine prescribed in law and they shall pass the decision for the exaction of the fine to the revenue collector; and the *astynomoi* shall order the restoration of the place in its earlier condition, within ten days and they shall exact the expenses increased by fifty per cent from those who do not comply and they shall give to the contractors (*ergolaboi*) what is due to them and to the treasury the rest. If the *astynomoi* do not act according to the law, the *strategoi* shall issue the order, and the difference of the expenses will be exacted from the *astynomoi*, who shall pay in addition a fine of a hundred drachmas. The *nomophylakes*[58] shall exact the fine immediately. The same procedure is to be followed against other people who do not comply. As for the roads in the countryside, the avenues shall be not less than twenty *pecheis* (*c.* 10 metres) wide and the other roads not less than eight *pecheis* (*c.* 4 metres) wide, apart from the paths used by the neighbours to provide access to each other. The owners of land shall provide the streets next to their houses and in the neighbouring area of up to ten *stadia*[59] in a good and walkable condition, contributing and repairing them with other people. And if they do not comply, the *astynomoi* shall seize them?

Col. B: [. . .] and the persons who throw litter shall be compelled by the *amphodarches** to clear up the place, according to the law; if they do not, they shall be denounced to the *astynomoi*. The *astynomoi* together with the *amphodarches* shall issue an order and the cost increased by fifty per cent shall be exacted from the non-compliant immediately and the *astynomoi* shall fine them ten drachmas. If any *amphodarches* does not act according to the above, the *astynomoi* shall fine him twenty drachmas for each violation. And the fines paid shall be given to the treasurer every month; and the money shall be deposited in a fund for the cleaning of the streets, when need arises; it is prohibited that this amount of money should be transferred to any other account. The *astynomoi* shall be responsible for the exaction and shall take care of everything else. And if they do not act according to the above, the strategoi and the official in the *polis* shall fine them fifty drachmas for each violation. And this fine is to be included in the above-mentioned fund.

About debris: If anyone while flattening digs up a ditch or makes stones or clay or pulls bricks or installs uncovered water pipes in the streets, the *amphodarches* shall prevent him. If he does not comply, the *amphodarches* shall denounce him to the *astynomoi*. The *astynomoi* shall fine the non-compliant five drachmas for each violation and compel him to restore everything to its previous condition and to cover the water pipes. And if the individuals concerned do not comply, the *astynomoi* shall issue a decision within ten days and the non-compliant shall pay the cost increased by fifty per cent. Similarly, the existing water pipes shall be compulsorily covered. If the *astynomoi* do not do any of these, they shall be liable to the same fines.

---

58 *Nomophylakes* (lit. 'guardians of laws') were considered a mainly oligarchic institution (at least in Athens). Their task was to supervise the adherence to the laws. For Athens see Rhodes (1981: 315–17) and G. Cawkwell (1988) 'Nomophylakia and the Areopagus', *JHS* 108, 1–12.

59 A *stadion* was equal to *c.* 190 metres.

About exaction. If anyone does not pay the portion of the cost of the decision providing for the cleaning of the quarters from dung or does not pay the fine, the *amphodarches* shall take pledges and give them to the *astynomoi* the same day or the next. And if nobody reclaims the pledges within five days, these shall be sold either in a *phratry* assembly or in a plenary assembly of the citizens in the presence of *astynomoi*; and the income shall be given to [. . .]

Col. C: [. . .] the *astynomoi* shall inspect and if it seems to them necessary that it be repaired, the owners shall repair it. And if some of them do not want to, the *astynomoi* shall issue a decision together with the help of anyone willing from those affected; and the incurred cost shall be paid immediately, the three-fifths by the non-compliant and two-fifths from the rest and the cost shall be given to the contractor. When the common walls need repair or have fallen, if all the neighbours use them, they shall contribute equally to the construction, and if one possesses buildings adjacent to the wall and the other has a court adjacent, the one who dwells shall pay the two-thirds and the other shall pay one-third; in the same proportion they will pay the person who has a one-floor house and the person who has a ground floor; the person who damages the common walls shall be summoned by the *astynomoi*, and if he is found guilty, after the decision is pronounced, he shall pay damages. It is not allowed to build or to cut through or to cause any other damage to the common walls, without the consent of the owners. And the walls which are a nuisance to the inhabitants of a house, the owners shall dig a trench, without damaging the neighbours. The external sides of the trench should be solid, if there is no stone to support the cover. The cover of the trench should not be higher than the level of the neighbouring court, unless the running of the waters requires. Otherwise the trenches will belong to the individuals who dug them, the place on top of the trenches, if they are covered, shall belong to the neighbours, provided that their use does not damage the walls of anyone else. If it is impossible, after the architect together with the *astynomoi*, has reached a decision, the neighbours shall provide access to those entering to clean and likewise, in case of a fall, when repair is needed. As for those burrowing through the wall, the *astynomoi* shall decide, if they find them guilty, they shall fine them five drachmas. Nobody is allowed to dig a trench, to store wine-jars, to plant or to do anything else, which will damage a common wall or anyone else's wall. If anyone does and the owner prosecutes him, the *astynomoi* shall inspect and decide as it seems right to them. And the walls of other houses about to fall, and the neighbours having warned about the damage [. . .]

Col. D: [. . .] they shall be compelled to clean the sewage.
About springs. The *astynomoi* shall be responsible for taking care of the springs in the *polis* and in the suburbs, so that they shall be clean and the pipes bringing and taking away the water shall have the necessary

width. And if anything needs repair, the *astynomoi* shall inform the *strategoi* and the official in charge of the sacred revenue to arrange the issue of the order. Nobody is allowed to water animals, to wash clothes or utensils or anything else in public springs. And if anyone does any of these, if he is a free man, he shall be deprived of the animals and the clothes and the utensils and he shall be fined fifty drachmas; if he is a slave and has acted under his master's instructions, he shall be deprived of the above and he shall himself be lashed fifty times in the back, and if he has acted without the agreement of his master, he shall be deprived of what he has, and after being lashed a hundred times, he shall be tied in the stocks for ten days and when he is to be released he shall be whipped not less than fifty times. And let anyone willing to seize anyone damaging springs, and the one who shall seize him or report him to the *astynomoi*, shall have half of the imposed penalty and the remaining shall be put aside for the repair of the sanctuary of the Nymphs.

About cisterns. The selected *astynomoi* shall write down the existing cisterns in houses, during the month of Pantheion, and shall give the list to the *strategoi* and shall take care so that their owners shall keep them waterproof and no one shall be filled; if not, the *astynomoi* shall fine anyone who has acted against this order a hundred drachmas and they shall exact the fine and they shall compel them to clear it up. And if some cisterns are already filled, the *astynomoi* shall order their owners to clear them within eight months; and if the owners do not comply, the *astynomoi* shall exact the same fine and they shall force them to clear them. And the amounts of fines shall be given every month to the treasurers and the fines shall be used for the clearing and the construction of cisterns, and they cannot be transferred in any other account. And the *astynomoi* shall impose fines on those who damage their neighbours' property by not keeping their cisterns waterproof. And if some convictions occur for this reason, the *astynomoi* shall exact the fine and give it to the affected and those *astynomoi* who do not file the suit about the cisterns in the archive or do not act according to the law, the *nomophylakes** shall exact a hundred drachmas and shall list the fine into the same category of revenue.

About privies (public toilets)? The *astynomoi* shall be responsible for the public toilets and their sewage and if some of them are not waterproof [. . .]

Relevant texts

For a still unpublished Hellenistic urbanistic law from **Kyrrhos (Makedonia)**, 'Ancient Macedonia' II pp. 7–11; **Skotoussa (Thessaly)**: delimitation and use of public spaces, *SEG* xliii 311 (3rd century BC); designation of streets in **Erythrai**, *IErythrai* 151 (*c.* 340 BC); **Athens**: law on distances, *Digest* x 1.13 (below, no. 101); Plu. *Solon* 33; duties of *astynomoi*, *AthPol* 50.2; judgement for offences connected with building: **Argos (Peloponnese)**: *SEG* xli 308 (*c.* 375

BC); inscriptions about cleanliness: **Thasos**, *SEG* xlii 785, **Athens**, *IG* i³ 257, **Keos (Cyclades)**, *IG* xii (5) 569 (above, nos. 85, 87, 88); digging and preserving ditches, **Alexandreia (Egypt)**: *PHal* 1, 103; prescript concerning protection of an aqueduct: **Nikaia (Mysia – Asia Minor)**, *Ilznik* 1 (early 2nd century AD); restrictions on balconies in **Athens**: Polyaen. *Strat.* iii 9, 30; easements: [Dem.] lv, Pl. *Laws* 844c.

Further reading

Edition and commentary: G. Klaffenbach (1955) *Das Astynomeninschrift von Pergamon*, Berlin (Abh. Deutsch. Akad. Wiss. Berlin. Kl. für Sprachen, Litt. Kunst); the law in its socio-political context, Martin (1974: 48–72); comparison of regulations about fountains in Plato and in Greek cities, Klingenberg (1974); no such thing as Greek water law and relation between water management and cult, R. Koerner (1974) 'Zu Recht und Verwaltung der griechischen Wasserversorgung nach den Inschriften', *AfP* 22/3, 155–202; a synthesis of archaeological evidence with legal regulations on building and water management in the Roman Empire, C. Saliou (1994) *Les lois de bâtiments. Voisinage et habitat urbain dans l'Empire romain. Recherches sur les rapports entre le droit et la construction privée du siècle d'Auguste au siècle de Justinien*, Beyrout (Bibliothèque Archeologique et Historique 116); easements, Harrison (1971: 249–52); A.P. Christophilopoulos (1973) 'Pragmatikai douleiai en attikais epigraphais' in *Dikaion kai Historia*, 55–9, Athens.

BUILDING

100 Athens, Decree authorizing the building of a bridge

IG i³ 79   *422/1 BC*

Ancient Greek *poleis* made decisions on public works projects. The Parthenon at Athens may be the best known example but the Athenians were involved in other building projects, less well known but equally important. This decree authorizes the building of a bridge in order to facilitate the annual procession to Eleusis. The bridge should be wide enough for pedestrians but narrow for carts.

When Prepis, son of Eupheros, was secretary. The Council and the people decided when the tribe Aigeis was presiding, Prepis was secretary and Patrokles was *epistates**; Theaios said: A bridge shall be built on the river Rhetos,[60] next to the town, using stones from Eleusis from the demolished old temple, those left in order to build the wall, so that the priestesses will bring the sacred objects safely. The width should be five feet, so that no cart will go through, but it will be possible for pedestrians to walk to the rituals. And cover the channels of Rhetos with stones according to the plans of Demomeles the architect. And if there are not [. . .]

Relevant texts

Regulating the flow of river: **Gortyn (Crete)**, *IC* iv 43 (above, no. 54); repair of walls: **Athens**, *IG* ii² 244 (337/6 BC) and *IG* ii² 463 (307/6 BC); loan to a *polis* to build walls: *L'emprunt* 9 (*c.* 221 BC); building accounts of the Parthenon and Propylaia, M–L² 59 and 60 (434/3 BC); **Gytheion (Lakonia – Peloponnese)**: protection of a building site, *IG* v (1) 1155 (beginning 5th century BC).

Further reading

Collection of inscriptions referring to building and discussion, F.G. Maier (1959–61) *Griechische Mauerbauinschriften*, 2 vols, Heidelberg.

101 Athens, Law on distances

Digest x 1.13   *?6th century BC*

Gaius, a Roman jurist of the 2nd century AD, in his commentary on the Twelve Tables refers to an allegedly Solonian law on distances. The law provides the minimum distance to be kept in case of building, digging and planting.

If anyone builds a wall or a ridge, he is not allowed to remove the boundary stone; if he builds a small wall, he has to leave space of one foot (*c.* 30 centimetres); if he builds a house, two feet; and if he digs a trench or a pit, he has to leave as much space as the depth of the trench or of the pit; and if he digs a cistern, he has to leave space of an *orgyia* (= *c.* 1.90 metres); olive

---

60 Name of a location on the Sacred way (*Hiera odos*) leading from Athens to Eleusis. The same name is used for the stream. It seems that water flooded from the nearby hills. The Athenians possibly had to channel the water to the sea.

and fig-trees are to be planted at a distance of nine feet from other property and five feet from other trees.

Relevant texts

Athens: collection of references to this law, Ruschenbusch F 60–2; respect of boundaries: Pl. *Laws* 842e 7–9 and 843b 1–6; no violation of borders with neighbours, Pl. *Laws* 843c 6–d 2; distances while planting, Pl. *Laws* 843e 3–844a 1; need for authorities to police building and cleanliness, Aristot. *Pol.* 1321b; **Chios**: *SGDI* 5654.9–15 and 5653a (Hellenistic); regulation on distances: **Alexandreia (Egypt)**, *PHal* 1.79–114 (3rd century BC); **Pergamos (Aiolis – Asia Minor)**, *SEG* xiii 521 (above, no. 99).

Further reading

U. Paoli (1949) 'La loi de Solon sur les distances', *RHD* 27, 503–17; comparisons of the Platonic regulation and the laws in Athens, Klingenberg (1976: 56–61).

NAVAL AFFAIRS

102 Athens, Law about *triereis*

IG i³ *153*   *440–425 BC*

The law defines some of the duties of the trierarch, the Athenian responsible for the upkeep for one year of a *trieres*, a warship with three rows of rowers. This responsibility (called *trierarchia*) was considered as proof *par excellence* of status in classical Athens. This fragmentary law concerns safety as it sets the minimum number of persons required for certain works to be done.

[. . .] of ships [. . .] the *trieropoioi*[61] [. . .] and the *trierarchoi** shall write down the names; it is prohibited to haul up a ship from the sea with less than a hundred and forty men or to launch a ship with less than a hundred and twenty men or to undergird with less [. . .] men or to anchor with less than a hundred men or [. . .] or to [. . .] and the *trierarchos* and the skipper of

---

61 Officials elected among councillors to supervise the building of triremes. Cf. *AthPol* 46.1.

each ship shall take charge of performing these duties; and if any *trierarchos* or skipper or anyone else violates these provisions, he shall owe a thousand drachmas sacred to Athena and the superintendents of the dockyards shall impose the fine. The secretary of the council shall have this decree written on a stone *stele*; and the *kolakretai** shall give the money and the *poletai** shall pay the costs.

103   Athens, Naval law

IG i³ *236*   *410–404 BC*

The law pertains to the duties of the trierach with regard to the equipment of the ship with which he is entrusted. In particular, the trierarch was entitled to use any means to retrieve the equipment of the ship.

[. . .] repair as best as possible and give the ships [. . .] as they received them from the dockyard; and if anyone is elected as an accountable official [. . .] according to the decree proposed by [. . .] if anyone exercises an office while he is still accountable for a previous one. If anyone of the public debtors does not hand to the incoming *trierarchos** money or wooden equipment, the *trierarchos* can summon him within the aforesaid time to the superintendent, with two witnesses for the summoning and write down the name of the witnesses [. . .] and the next day the superintendents shall introduce the case to the lawcourt; and if the defendant does not bring a claim against anyone else, as having the equipment, he shall have to hand it to the wronged; and the execution of the decision shall be as in the case of a private debtor;[62] if the defendant does not pledge anything, despite the request of the *trierarchos*, he shall pay to the treasury whatever the lawcourt fines him. [. . .] and those around the shipbuilder [. . .] of the *trierarchos* eight diobols[63] for each day [. . .] they are to be introduced to the lawcourt within the aforementioned time [. . .] and if anyone obstructs, in the same way; and the *trierarchos* [. . .] so that anyone wishing shall use, and the *trierarchos* shall call [. . .] when it seems proper to the *deme* and the names [. . .]

---

62 Execution of a judgement imposing a fine on a private dispute was the sole responsibility of the winning litigant. If the defeated litigant did not pay, the winner could use a *dike exoules* to confirm his victory at the earlier trial. If the defaulting litigant had lost the second trial, he would have been considered a state debtor. However, the reference to 'private debtor' in this law is to make it clear that a person refusing to hand down naval equipment cannot be considered a state debtor.

63 A diobol was a coin with a value equal to two obols.

Relevant texts

Athens: *trieropoioi*, *AthPol* 46.1; appropriated equipment to be returned, [Dem.] xlvii 20, 44; trierarchs refusing to return equipment, [Dem.] xlvii 25, 28; individual punished for not returning oars, *IG* ii^2 1631 (323/2 BC); naval records (mainly from the period 330–322 BC), *IG* ii^2 1604–32 and recently J.L. Shear (1995) 'Fragments of naval inventories from the Athenian agora', *Hesperia* 64, 179–224; **Thasos:** harbour regulation, *IG* xii Suppl. 348 (above, no. 42).

Further reading

In-depth examination of the origin and the function of trierarchy and the duties of trierarchs (with previous bibliography included), V. Gabrielsen (1994) *Financing the Athenian fleet. Public taxation and social relations*, Baltimore.

INTER-*POLIS* RELATIONS

104 Miletos (Ionia – Asia Minor), *Isopoliteia* agreement with Olbia

Staatsvertrage III 408   *c.* 330 BC

It was not unusual for Greek cities to have bilateral agreements allowing their citizens to enjoy a status higher than that of an ordinary foreigner or resident. These agreements encapsulate the essentials of citizenship as articulated in *polis* discourse. In this agreement there are particular, reciprocal provisions for participating in the religious festivals and celebrations, exemption from taxation for foreigners and election to the offices of the *polis*.

These are the ancestral agreements between the citizens of Olbia and the citizens of Miletos; the Milesian who is in Olbia shall sacrifice as a citizen of Olbia on the same altars and shall frequent the same public sanctuaries as the citizens of Olbia; Milesians are going to be exempted from taxation as they have been; and if he wants to be elected as *timouchos**, he shall appear in front of the council and shall register and be liable to tax as the other citizens; he shall have the privilege to the front seats, to be heralded in the games and to pronounce curses in the festival of *triakas* as they utter in Miletos; and if any Milesian has a contract in Olbia, he shall have recourse to the lawcourts and he shall appear in the public court (*demotikon* *dikasterion*) in five days; no Milesian shall be liable to taxes, except those who participate in offices and lawcourts in another city; in the same manner citizens of Olbia shall not be liable to tax in Miletos and in other regards citizens of Olbia shall be treated in Miletos as Milesians in Olbia.

105   Stiris (Phokis – Central Greece), Unification (*sympoliteia*) agreement between Stiris and Medeon

*Syll*³ *647*   *175 or 135 BC*

This agreement provides the conditions under which two *poleis* shall be unified. It includes sharing cities and countryside, ports and sanctuaries. Prominent is the guarantee of political equality to members of both communities; this is translated into access to magistratures of the new political unit as well as equality of magistrates of both cities. However, no one shall be forced to hold any office. The distinctiveness of the merging communities is not lost since the Medeonians retain the right to perform their own ancestral sacrifices.

A. Gods. Good fortune. When Zeuxios was *strategos* among the Phokians, on the seventh of the month, agreement between the *polis* of the Stirians and the *polis* of Medeonians;[64] the Stirians and the Medeonians have decided to unify, having sanctuaries, *polis*, countryside, ports, everything free of any burden, on the following conditions: all the Medeonians shall be equal and have similar treatment to the Stirians and they shall convene assemblies and elect magistrates together with the Stirians and those who reach the appropriate age shall judge cases in the *poleis*; one treasurer of the sacred (*hierotamias*) shall be elected from among the Medeonians who will perform their ancestral sacrifices, those incorporated in the constitution, together with the archons elected in Stiris; and the *hierotamias* shall take a share, half a minas, equal to the one the archons took, and from the libations what befits to a *hierotamias*; and the *hierotamias* will judge cases together with the archons, those cases the archons decide and he will allot lawcourts, those he has to, together with the archons; no Medeonian is going to be coerced to exercise office in Stiris, those Medeonians who are archons, judges for foreigners (*xenodikai*), revenue-collectors (*prakteres*), *demiourgoi**, priests,

---

64 Stiris and Medeon (near modern Antikyra) were *poleis* in coastal Phokis and members of the Phokian League. Collection of evidence in J.M. Fossey (1986) *The ancient topography of Eastern Phokis*, 26–9 and 32–4, Amsterdam. The witnesses mentioned at the end of the agreement come from *poleis* (Elate, Tithorea, Lilaion) situated in the mountainous, inland Phokis.

hierarchai in Medeon and of the women those who exercised priestly duties, unless anyone voluntarily submits. Archons should be elected from among those Stirians and Medeonians without any function to exercise. Administration of the temples in Stiris will proceed as the constitution sanctions. And the countryside of the Medeonians will belong to the Stirians and that of the Stirians will belong to the Medeonians, being all common. Medeonians shall take part in all the sacrifices performed in Stiris and Stirians in all the sacrifices performed in Medeon; it shall not be allowed to the Medeonians to dissolve the union with the Stirians nor to the Stirians to dissolve the union with the Medeonians; people who do not conform with the written agreement, shall pay ten silver talents to those who conform.

B. [. . .] they do; the agreement shall be written on a *stele* and it shall be set up in the temple of Athena; and the agreement shall be sealed and deposited with an individual. The agreement was deposited with Thrason from Lilaion. Witnesses: Thrason, son of Demetrios from Elate, Eupolidas, son of Thrason from Lilaion, Timokrates, son of Epinikos from Tithorea. And the Stirians shall give to the *phratry* of Medeonians within four years, five silver minas and a place called Damatreia.

106 Stymphalos (Arkadia – Peloponnese), Bilateral judicial agreement with Sikyon-Demetrias (Korinthia – Peloponnese)

IPArk 17   *303–300 BC*

Judicial agreements (called *symbola*) were concluded between two, usually neighbouring, *poleis*. They are an attempt to regulate the process of adjudicating disputes between the citizens and one of these *poleis*. Quite often a third *polis* is named to act as an appeal judge. The agreement between Stymphalos and Sikyon (refounded by Demetrios Poliorcetes in 306 BC and called Demetrias) includes clauses on judicial procedures, theft, arresting fugitive slaves, arbitration, responsibility for damage caused by animals, redress to justice by resident foreigners and the process of reforming the agreement.

[. . .] the members of the court (*sunlutai*) [. . .] in front of the court for foreigners on the charge of giving false testimony; and if anyone prosecutes someone else for false testimony, he shall bring first the person who gave the false testimony to court according to the agreement. And if the person who gave the false testimony is defeated in court, he shall owe half of the penalty. As far as the suit on the basis of this agreement is concerned, if the false witness was testifying for the plaintiff, the plaintiff shall lose the case; and if the false witness testified for the defendant, the defendant shall owe the penalty and no vote will take place. But if the plaintiff in a case of false testimony does not get one-third of the votes, he shall owe one-third of the penalty to the defendant and the two secretaries (*katakooi*) shall give the money to the magistrates as in other cases. And if anyone is summoned to testify but he does not appear, having sworn an oath in front of the judicial authorities that he does not know what he is summoned to testify, he shall be released from the obligation to testify. If he does not swear the above oath, he shall pay the penalty to the injured party, and the president shall register the suit as other suits for which there is dismissal. And each *polis* shall elect, from among the citizens not younger than forty years old, three members of the court and an arbitrator (*katalutes*) who will resolve the disputes in the month when petitions are submitted. And the elected members of the court will start mediating between the litigants on the first day of the following month. And the members of the courts on the tenth day after full moon (i.e. the 24th of the month) shall stop mediating; the members of the court (*synlytai*) shall continue for ten days and the court shall issue the decision. And the *polis* shall send the members of the court (*synlytai*) and the arbitrator and their secretary carrying the submitted suits. The arbitrator is allowed to resolve disputes in the *polis* as the judges do. And the magistrates shall send the suits submitted according to the agreement and the secretaries (*katakooi*) shall bring all the registered suits before the members of the court (*synlytai*) in the order in which the magistrates wrote them down. And if anyone has registered a suit to the court for foreigners, if he does not wish to wait there for the testimony to resolve the dispute, the secretaries (*katakooi*) shall be allowed to decide the case employing the procedure for civil litigation, as if it was registered to be decided by a regular court; in this court the plaintiff shall pay the fee (*epidekaton*) for the case according to this agreement, and the court shall decide instead of the court for foreigners with the use of the fee (*epidekaton*) and [. . .] no testimony [. . .] in front of the court for foreigners shall proceed [. . .] on the basis of (free) consideration shall be decided. And the fee (*epidekaton*) shall be paid to nobody else but the members of the court (*synlytai*). And they shall write the decision of the court on the writing tablet on which the dispute is recorded and the names of all the elected (conciliators?). And the registered (conciliators?) shall arbitrate before the court stops judging; and the plaintiff shall pay one-tenth of the penalty. And if the individuals registered do not arbitrate [. . .] in accordance with the judicial agreement they shall repay the charge to the plaintiff. And the magistrates shall vote for the conviction of the arbitrators who have not resolved, wholly or partly, a dispute. The elected men are allowed to examine the suit in its entirety or partly and not to leave anything in connection with the suit without scrutiny, which was not inserted in the suit. People involved in a dispute shall not pay the fee (*epidekaton*) to the treasurers of both *poleis*, but either to the arbitrator or to the members of the court (*synlytai*). For the court [. . .] the suit [. . .] shall pay. The people who paid the fee (*epidekaton*) to the members of the court (*synlytai*) [. . .] for the submitted suit and given a date they shall bring to the court the written testimonies and the written agreements and they shall deposit them in jars (?), till the court reaches a decision. And if anyone involved in a lawsuit does not bring to the members of the court (*synlytai*) the written testimonies, he shall not be allowed to use other testimonies in court but those brought forward to the members of the court (*synlytai*). [. . .] the lawcourt [. . .] the lawcourt [. . .] decided [. . .] allotted and written for the same lawcourt; and if [. . .] the lawcourt [. . .] to bring suits. And the authorities shall impose a fine of five Aiginetan drachmas to the absent [. . .] and to the members of the court who obey, the authorities shall provide [. . .] to the lawcourt [. . .] as [. . .] and if he (a judge?) swears that he is ill, he shall be released; if not, the presidents shall invite the litigants three times to join the court. If one of them does not appear in court while the other does, the arbitration shall not go through; the next day after both litigants being invited three times by heralds, they (the conciliators?) shall decide on the lawsuit; and the presidents shall follow the procedure for civil cases; when the process starts it shall be legal. Both litigants shall pay the fee (*epidekaton*) before the beginning of the trial, and the defeated litigant shall pay the fee (*epidekaton*) (to the winner); and if one litigant pays the fee (*epidekaton*) and the other does not, the one who has paid shall be the winner and he shall not be judged by the court for the charges that the court has already decided upon; it is permitted to pay the fee (*epidekaton*) after the court issues its decision. After the trial has been concluded, the voting and the counting is carried out, the lawcourt is not allowed to decide; and the absentee litigant shall pay to the person who obeyed the fee (*epidekaton*), if nobody else will pay it instead of him; if it is hindered and no additional payment (*epidosis*) for the trial took place, the presiding magistrates shall call citizens from the reserve lists [. . .] and when they pay the additional payment (*epidosis*) the trial shall continue. And if the defendant is not present at the trial or if he is present but does not pay, he similarly shall be fined as the absent [. . .] appear and is absent, the trial shall continue. Both secretaries (*katakooi*) [. . .] there are trials and do not want [. . .] written [. . .] by the magistrates who registered the lawsuits [. . .] witnesses; after [. . .] the witnesses and the laws [. . .] it is permitted to anyone to act as an advocate (*syndikos*). [. . .] The magistrates, in Demetrias the *strategoi**, in Stymphalos the *demiourgoi** shall send the decisions [. . .] in thirty days; those on [. . .] sending the (name of) the winner [. . .] advocate (*syndikos*) [. . .] it can be a trial; and if it is not sent [. . .] send, increased by fifty per cent. After the decision was issued, within ten days he shall be released from the obligation [. . .] if he is not released within ten days [. . .] thirty days pass [. . .] thirty days [. . .] written [. . .] he shall be responsible; both [. . .] magistrates are not allowed [. . .] it is allowed, shall pay [. . .] magistrates and allowed [. . .] according to the bilateral agreement. And if anyone reports someone from [. . .] citizens with property shall be registered with the authorities as guarantors [. . .]; and if he does not appoint guarantors, the authorities shall not be allowed to seize; and if the authorities are allowed [. . .] to seize, they shall be responsible for the fine [. . .]; and if later a trial is initiated, it is not going to be legal. Nobody is to seize any man, either a Demetrian to seize a Stymphalian or a Stymphalian to seize a Demetrian, [. . .] of both *poleis*, neither to remove property nor to take property [. . .] if they do not show the embassy to the authorities and the decision according to the bilateral agreement. And if anyone holds a man or removes or takes property, he shall pay [. . .] Aiginetan drachmas to [. . .] the authorities shall exact from the one who does not comply with the agreed; and if he does not appoint guarantors [. . .] the authorities [. . .] and if he agrees in the presence of three witnesses with property, it shall be valid; and if he agrees something more, an agreement (*syngraphon*) shall be drafted in the presence of three witnesses; and if he is making agreements or delays it in any other way, it shall be invalid. On account of securities and guarantees, if anyone defrauds a foreigner, he shall pay double the damage he caused. If anyone during the night steals from a house or breaks into it, he shall be slain without any legal redress (*atimos*) even if he breaks in during the day; and if he is arrested, the victim shall sue him for five hundred drachmas and double that amount if he causes any damage; and if he steals from a house during the day, he shall pay fifty drachmas and double the worth of the stolen property; and if he steals property worth more than fifty drachmas, he shall owe two hundred drachmas and double the worth of the stolen property; and if anyone else bought in the marketplace something stolen and has it, he is not going to be punished and he shall keep it, after he has given a good testimony. If the victim of theft finds the stolen property in someone else's house, he (the owner of the house?) shall pay damages; and if anyone is defending himself on the charge that he has taken or bought stolen property, in the *polis* an advocate (*syndikos*) of the defendant [. . .] the suit; in addition to double the worth of the stolen property he shall pay the fee for reporting, to the person who paid, as long as it does not exceed the fee (*epidekaton*). If a slave, man or woman, is found, their master shall be allowed [. . .] to keep the property? if he has paid; and the master shall pay the reward for bringing them back, in the case of a male slave a hundred drachmas and in the case of a female and of a child ten drachmas; the person who caught the fugitive shall register the name with the magistrates[65] [. . .] of the fugitive and of the master to whom the slave belongs and keep him for ten days [. . .] if he uses anyone, and if earlier the master did not get him; when the ten days pass, no court shall discuss the case of the litigants?; and the magistrates shall report to the magistrates of the *polis* where the fugitives are [. . .] writing down the names of the person who caught and of the fugitive; and the master shall refund the cost of feeding and guarding (the fugitive) but not more than two drachmas per day. With regard to four-footed animals and birds, and if the

---

65 What is meant under the title *archontes* is the *demiourgoi* in Stymphalos and the *strategoi* in Demetrias.

owner, who was wronged, wins the suit, the person who wronged him shall pay the damages; the claims of the injured party? [. . .] if the defendant is defeated, he shall pay the fee (*epidekaton*) for the amount claimed in the suit; and if anyone says to assess (the object of contention) differently, the judges again shall vote; the fifth part of the value [. . .] together with the plaintiff. And the resident-foreigners (*metoikoi*) when they bring a suit shall use citizens from Demetrias or Stymphalos as guarantors; and if any resident-foreigner does not provide a respectful guarantor, he shall be unharmed?; and if any resident-foreigner wishes to sue, he shall submit his suit in Demetrias to the *strategoi* and in Stymphalos to the *demiourgoi*; they shall submit them at the same time as the other suits. And if any clause in the bilateral judicial agreement seems, during application, to the *poleis* to be non-beneficial, they shall send ambassadors to the other *polis*, the *polis* which thinks so; and the *poleis* shall elect correctors (*diorthoteres*) for the agreement; and the elected correctors shall show to the council and to the people's assembly their proposals in each city; and those of the proposals which seem to be right? shall be written in the agreement, and no one of the *poleis* shall modify any other clause of the agreement; and if anyone [. . .]

Relevant texts

Bilateral judicial agreements: **Miletos** – Cretan cities, *Staatsvertrage* III 482 (after 260 BC); **Delphoi–Pellana (Central Greece)**, *Staatsvertrage* III 558 (early 3rd century BC); **Gortyn–Lato (Crete)**, *Staatsvertrage* III 569 (end 3rd century BC); treaty (*symbole*) between **Athens and Phaselis**, *IG* i^3 10 (*c.* 469–450 BC); **Athens**: officials for judging the cases on the basis of these agreements, *AthPol* 59.6; [And.] iv 18; arbitration, *AthPol* 53; cases of false testimony, And. i 17; Lys. xix 4; theft, Dem. xxiv 105 (above, no. 62). *Synoikismos* – agreements: collection of literary and epigraphical evidence until 338 BC, M. Moggi (ed.) (1976) *I sinecismi interstatali greci* I, Pisa; and the new edition of the agreement between **Orkhomenos–Euaimon (Arkadia – Peloponnese)**, *IPArk* 15 (360–350 BC). *Isopoliteia* – agreements: **Miletos–Phygela**, *Staatsvertrage* III 453 (end 4th century BC); **Miletos–Mylasa**, *Staatsvertrage* III 539 (*c.* 209/8 BC); **Miletos–Kyzikos**, *Staatsvertrage* III 409 (*c.* 330 BC); · **Hierapytna–Praisos (Crete)**, *Staatsvertrage* III 554 (early 3rd century BC); **Pergamos–Temnos**, *Staatsvertrage* III 555 (early 3rd century BC); **Axos–Tylissos (Crete)**, *Staatsvertrage* III 570 (end 3rd century BC); **Itanos–Hierapytna (Crete)**, *Staatsvertrage* III 579 (3rd century BC); **Aitolia–Trikka**, *Staatsvertrage* III 542 (*c.* 206 BC); **Naupaktos–Keos**, *Staatsvertrage* III 508 (223/2 BC); **Nagidos–Arsinoe (Cilicia – Asia Minor)**, *SEG* xxxix 1426 (after

238 BC); **Entella (Sicily)**, *SEG* xxx 1117–23 (3rd century BC); *isopoliteia* between two groups of Hierapytnians (Crete), *IC* iii III 5 (2nd century BC). *Sympoliteia* agreement: **Mantineia–Helisson (Arkadia – Peloponnese)**, *SEG* xxxvii 340 (early 4th century BC); **Teos–Kyrbissos (Ionia – Asia Minor)**, *SEG* xxvi 1306 (4th century BC); **Gomphoi–Thamia (Thessaly)**, *SEG* xxxvii 494 (230–200 BC); **Myania–Hypnia (Lokris – Central Greece)**, *IG* ix 1² (2) 748 (*c.* 190 BC).

Further reading

New edition and full commentary *IPArk* 17 pp. 200–51; bilateral judicial agreements, Gauthier (1972: 157–204, 285–346); S. Cataldi (1992) 'Statuto e capacita giuridica dello straniero nella stele di Stinfalo' in R. Lonis (ed.) *L'étranger dans le monde antique* II, 127–46, Nancy; W. Gawantka (1975) *Isopolitie. Ein Beitrag zur Geschichte der zwischenstaatlichen Beziehungen in der griechischen Antike*, München; H.H. Schmitt (1993) 'Überlegung zur Sympolitie', *Symposion 1993*, 35–44; political/historical reasons and not economic/commercial for relocation, N.H. Demand (1990) *Urban relocation in archaic and classical Greece. Flight and consolidation*, Bristol; relationship between Miletos and its colonies, N. Erhardt (1983) *Milet und seine Kolonien*, Frankfurt; S. Cataldi (1983) *Symbolai e relazioni tra le citta greche nel V sec. a.C.*, Pisa.

RELIGION AND *POLIS*

107   Priene (Ionia – Asia Minor), Law about the sale of the priesthood of Dionysos Phleos

LSAM 37   *2nd century BC*

Certain *poleis*, especially in west Asia Minor, were selling the right to be the priest of a particular deity to the highest bidder. This arrangement, unconventional for us, guaranteed certain privileges for the individual such as honour for exercising, most of the time, a life-long priesthood and bonuses such as exemptions from taxation or other forms of contribution to the *polis* finances. This regulation includes the definition of the sacral duties of the priest to be, his share of the offerings and immunities.

Sale of (the priesthood of) Dionysos Phleos.[66] Good fortune. We shall sell the priesthood of Dionysos Phleos under these conditions: the purchaser shall exercise the duties of the priest for life; he shall also exercise the duties of the priest of Dionysos Katagogios; he shall not be liable to taxation; he shall have the right to free meals for all the days in the *prytaneion** and in the *Panionion*;[67] he shall take, from what the *polis* sacrifices, limb, tongue, skin, and a portion from the altar; he shall provide the offerings, barleycorns, censer, cakes, a quarter of an ox, one-twelfth of a *medimnos* of sheep, two *choinikes*[68] of lamb; he shall be allowed to have a special place in the front row in the theatre and to have whatever costume he likes and a wreath of golden ivy leaves; he shall perform the sacrifices in the theatre to Dionysos Melpomenos and he shall burn incense and perform libation and pray for the *polis* of Priene; he shall wear whatever costume he likes and a golden wreath in the months of Lenaion and Anthesterion;[69] during the festival of Katagogia he shall lead those who bring Dionysos down wearing whatever dress he likes and a golden wreath; if the priesthood is purchased for more than six thousand drachmas the purchaser shall be exempt from the functions of organizing a torch-race, games, horse-breeding, providing for the *gymnasion*, leading a sacred embassy; if the priesthood is bought for more than twelve thousand drachmas, he shall be exempt from the functions of preparing a ship for war, being in charge of a temple, providing and paying tax in advance; and the purchaser shall pay ten per cent of the price, half in the month of Metageitnion[70] in the same year and the other half in the month of Anthesterion, when Kleomenes is *stephanephoros*. Athenopolis, son of Kydimos, has bought the priesthood for twelve thousand and two drachmas and the ten per cent was one thousand and two hundred drachmas and three obols.

---

66 It is worth noting that Dionysos is referred to with three different epithets. The epithet 'Phleos' connects the god with the vegetation cycle and its celebrations. 'Katagogios' qualifies the advent of Dionysos from the sea; the festival of Katagogia corresponds to this epithet. 'Melpomenos' associates Dionysos with singing and playing a musical instrument.

67 Temple of Poseidon Helikonios near Mykale in Asia Minor where the festival of Panionia was celebrated. The celebration provided an occasion for the meeting of the Ionians.

68 In classical Athens a *medimnos* was a dry measure equal to *c*. 52 litres. A *choinix* was 1/48th of a *medimnos* and was equal to approximately 1 litre.

69 The calendar of Priene was similar if not identical with the Milesian one. The months Lenaion and Anthesterion were the tenth and eleventh months respectively.

70 Metageitnion was the fifth month in the calendar of Priene.

Relevant texts

Sale of priesthood: **Herakleia on Latmos (Caria − Asia Minor)**, *SEG* xl 956 (1st century BC−1st century AD); **Miletos (Ionia − Asia Minor)**, *SEG* xxxvi 1048 (mid 2nd century BC); **Skepsis (Troas − Asia Minor)**, *SEG* xxvi 1334 (2nd century BC); **Theangela (Caria − Asia Minor)**, *SEG* xxix 1088 (3rd century BC); **Priene (Ionia − Asia Minor)**, *LSAM* 38 (2nd century BC); **Miletos (Ionia − Asia Minor)**, *LSAM* 52 (1st century AD); **Kalchedon (Bithynia − Asia Minor)**, *IKalchedon* 12 (1st century BC−1st century AD); **Andros (Cyclades)**, *LSCG* 47 (1st century BC); **Hyllarima (Caria − Asia Minor)**, *LSAM* 56 (188−166 BC); **Tomoi (Scythia Minor)**, *LSCG* 87 (3rd century BC); list of sales: **Erythrai (Ionia − Asia Minor)**, *IErythrai* 201 (early 3rd century BC); regulations about sale of priesthood: **Erythrai (Ionia − Asia Minor)**, *IErythrai* 206 (end 4th century BC); **Kalchedon (Bithynia − Asia Minor)**, *IKalchedon* 13 (3rd century BC); **Mylasa (Caria − Asia Minor)**, *IMyl* 302 (1st century BC); **Halikarnassos (Caria − Asia Minor)**, *LSAM* 73 (3rd century BC); **Kasossos (Caria − Asia Minor)**, *IMyl* 942 (Hellenistic); **Chios**, *LSCG* 77 (early 4th century BC) and 78 (2nd century BC); **Kos**, *LSCG* 162 (3rd century BC) and 166 (2nd−1st century BC) and 167; sale of priesthood accompanied by arrangement of ritual duties: **Kos**, *ICos* 62 (1st century BC), 145 (early 2nd century BC), 178 (end 3rd century BC), 180 (1st century BC), 215 (1st century BC), 216 (end 3rd century BC), 238 (3rd century BC); sale of office of an association: **Thasos**: *IG* xii Suppl. 365 (2nd century AD).

Further reading

Role of priests in antiquity, M. Beard and J. North (eds) (1990) *Pagan priests. Religion and power in the ancient world*, London; sale of priesthood, P. Debord (1982) *Aspects sociaux et économiques de la vie religieuse dans l'Anatolie gréco-romaine*, 63–8, Leiden.

108 Samos, Regulation on sacrifices

LSCG 122   *3rd century BC*

One of the most interesting and telling aspects of the interrelation between *polis* and religion appears in inscriptions preserving decisions of a *polis* sanctioning a particular sacrifice or other offering to a god or goddess. This regulation from Samos imposes the duty to perform sacrifices on individuals appointed by their *chiliastys** or their representative in case they are away.

The legislators (*nomographoi*) have suggested the following about the sacrifice in the Helikonion;[71] the people who will be appointed by the magistrates of a *chiliastys* as magistrates (*epimenioi*) responsible for the organization of the sacrifice and of the gathering which takes place in Helikonion; if they are in the *polis*, they shall exercise the magistracy (*epimenios*); if they are abroad, the person they leave behind shall take up the responsibility; and if some individuals appear of their own free will and convince the magistrates of their *chiliastys*, each of them shall exercise the magistracy (*epimenios*); and if the person elected, himself or his replacement, does not exercise the magistracy, the guardians of the laws (*nomophylakes*) and the magistrates (*epimenioi*) who were appointed at the same time shall exact two hundred drachmas.

Relevant texts

Athens: sacrifices to Hephaistos, *LSCG* 5 (*c.* 420 BC); sacrificial calendar of the *deme* of Erchia, *LSCG* 18 (early 4th century BC); dedication of first fruits, *LSCG* Suppl. 13 (353/2 BC); law regarding the Panathenaic festival, *IG* ii² 334 and *SEG* xviii 13 (335/4 BC); regulation about Eleusinia, *LSCG* 4 (early 4th century BC); **Mykonos (Cyclades)**: sacrificial calendar, *LSCG* 96 (*c.* 200 BC); **Eretria (Euboia)**: regulation of the Artemisia, *LSCG* 92 (4th century BC); **Aigiale (Amorgos – Cyclades)**: public banquet (*demothoinia*), *IG* xii (7) 515; **Akarnania**: decree accepting the cult of Leukophryene, *IG* ix 1² (2) 582 (207 BC); **Ialysos (Rhodes)**: decree on the cult of Alektrone, *LSCG* 136 (*c.* 300 BC); **Erythrai (Ionia – Asia Minor)**: sacrificial calendar, *IErythrai* 207 (2nd century BC).

Further reading

Summary account of sacrifice as ritual, its meaning and technique, L. Bruit-Zeidmann and P. Schmitt-Pantel (1992) *Religion in the ancient Greek city*, 28–39, English translation, Cambridge, and the survey of J.N. Bremmer (1994) *Greek religion*, Oxford (Greece and Rome. New surveys in the classics 24); organization of public sacrifices in Athens,

---

71 Sanctuary of Poseidon Helikonios, whose cult is attested in various other *poleis*. The Samian sanctuary was on a hill outside the *polis*.

V.J. Rosivach (1994) *The system of public sacrifice in fourth-century Athens*, Atlanta (American Classical Studies 34).

109   Ioulis (Keos – Cyclades), Funerary law

LSCG 97   *5th century BC*

Religion and politics being intertwined in ancient Greek society, religious ceremonies were venues for competition and the display of wealth and prestige. The death of a person in Greece was followed by the laying-out of the body (*prothesis*) and its transfer to the tomb (*ekphora*). Several cities had passed laws trying to regulate the funerary procession and the rites to be performed. In this law there are restrictions imposed on the procession, the amount and the quality of offerings, defilement and cleansing.

I. These are the laws concerning the deceased. Bury the dead according to the following instructions; the body shall be wrapped in three white clothes; these may be covered with a further wrapping worth no more than a hundred drachmas; the body is to be covered, except for the head, and be carried in procession on a bier with wedge-shaped legs; nobody is permitted to bring more than three *choes*[72] of wine and one *chous* of olive oil to the tomb; the (empty) containers of wine and olive oil are to be removed; the deceased is to be brought to the tomb covered, and in silence; the sacrificial food should follow the ancient customs; the bed and the bedding are to be brought back home; the next day a freeman shall clean the house, first with sea-water and then with ordinary water by sprinkling the earth; at the end the house is clean and it is permitted to sacrifice; women who attended the funeral have to return from the tomb before the menfolk; it is not permitted to celebrate the thirty-days anniversary of the death; it is not permitted to put a wine-cup under the bed, to pour out water or to bring any offerings to the tomb; women other than the defiled are not permitted to enter the place where the deceased died; as those considered as defiled are considered: the mother and the wife and the sisters and the daughters and on top of them no more than five women, children of daughters or cousins; the defiled have to wash all over to be clean.

II. The *Boule* and the people decided: those who commemorate the third day from the death and the one-year anniversary from the death shall be clean but they shall not be allowed to enter a sanctuary and the members of the household shall not be clean till they return from the grave.

72 *Chous, choes* was a measure of capacity for liquid equal to 3 litres.

110 Gambreion (Mysia – Asia Minor), Law on mourning

LSAM 16   *3rd century BC*

The law concerns funerals but from a different angle than the law from Ioulis (above, no. 109). It aims at controlling the public display of wealth on the occasion of funerals by defining in a restrictive way what is acceptable and what is not. The main concern of the regulation falls on the behaviour of women, especially the duration of mourning and their attire.

Good fortune. When Demetrios was *hieronomos*, on the second day of the month Thargelion, Alexon, son of Damon, moved: There shall be a law among the citizens of Gambreion that women in mourning shall wear clean grey clothes; and the men and the children in mourning shall wear grey clothing unless they prefer white. The ceremonies in memory of the deceased shall be performed within three months and the men will stop wearing mourning clothes on the fourth month and women on the fifth month. Women will cease mourning and they shall participate in the processions prescribed by law. And the *gynaikonomoi**, elected by the people to preside over the purification before the festival of Thargelia, will pray for the well-being of those who obey the law and the opposite to those women who do not conform with the law; and these women shall not be considered clean, because they have committed impiety, and they shall not sacrifice to any of the gods for ten years. And the treasurer, elected after the year when Demetrios was *stephanephoros*, will have this law inscribed on two *stelai* and place one in front of the doors of the Thesmophorion and the other one in front of the temple of Artemis Lochia; the treasurer shall bring forward the expenses in the first meeting of the accountants (*logistai*).

Relevant texts

Different laws restricting mourning and other manifestations of grief: **Athens**, Ruschenbusch F109, F72b, c, [Dem.] xliii 57–8 and 64, Cic. *Laws* ii 64, 66, Pl. *Laws* 958d, 960c; **Mytilene (Lesbos):** Cic. *Laws* ii 6.6; **Syrakousai (Sicily):** D.S. xi 38.2; **Sparta:** Hdt. vi 58.1, Plu. *Lyk.* xxvii 2–4, *Mor.* 238d; **Katane (Sicily):** Stob. *Florileg.* 44.40; **Gortyn (Crete):** *LSAG* 315 nos. 2.4, 8 (6th–5th century BC); controlling funerary ceremonies, *IC* iv 76b (*c.* 450 BC); **Nisyros:** *IG* xii (3) 87 (3rd century BC); **Delphoi (Phokis – Central Greece):** *LSCG* 77 col. C (5th century BC); gynaikonomoi: Aristot. *Pol.* iv 12, 9; **Thasos:** public funeral of war dead and restrictions on mourning, *LSCG* Suppl. 64 (above, no. 78).

Further reading

Summary account of the ritual of burial, Burkert (1978: 190–4); various aspects of practices, ritual and iconography of death, R. Garland (1985) *The Greek way of death*, London (with most of the earlier bibliography); comparison of dress code regulations in ancient Greece and Rome, P. Culham (1986) 'Again, what meaning lies in a colour!', *ZPE* 64, 235–45; a comprehensive review and discussion of motives behind such regulations, R. Garland (1989) 'The well-ordered corpse: An investigation into the motives behind Greek funerary legislation', *BICS* 36, 1–15 and R. Seaford (1994) *Reciprocity and ritual. Homer and tragedy in the developing city-state*, 74–105, Oxford; laws concerned with the public aspect of the funeral, designed to curb power and influence, M. Toher (1991) 'Greek funerary legislation and the two Spartan funerals' in M.A. Flower and M. Toher (eds) *Georgika: Greek studies in honour of George Cawkwell*, 159–75, London (*BICS* Suppl. 58); association of funerary legislation with funerary ideology, C. Sourvinou-Inwood (1995) *'Reading' Greek death to the end of the classical period*, 439–41, Oxford; testimony of Plutarch on war-dead in Sparta, N. Richer (1994) 'Aspects des funérailles à Sparte', *Cahiers Glotz* 5, 51–96; defilement caused by death, Parker (1983: 34–48); sumptuary legislation of Syracuse, A. Brugnone (1992) 'Le leggi suntuarie di Siracusa', *PdelP* 47, 5–24; archaeological and other comparative evidence on the sumptuary laws and social practices, D.B. Small (1995) 'Monuments, laws, and analysis: combining archaeology and text in ancient Athens' in D.B. Small (ed.) *Methods in the Mediterranean. Historical and archaeological views on texts and archaeology*, 143–76, Leiden (Mnemosyne Suppl 135).

111 Thessalonike (Makedonia), *Diagramma*[73] concerning the temple of Sarapis[74]

IG x (2) (1) 3   *186 BC*

This well-known decision, which was probably part of a longer *diagramma*, regulates the administration of the property of the Sarapeion. It decrees that the property of Sarapis cannot be alienated

---

73 See this chapter fn. 14.
74 The temple of Sarapis in the west part of the old Thessalonike was renowned in antiquity, and second only to the Delian one.

in any way, and if anyone does, the loss shall be replaced from his property. The treasuries shall be opened in the presence of the civic magistrates, and expenditure should have their agreement.

From Andronikos.[75] The ruling (*diagramma*) about the property of Sarapis, which I have sent to you, was sent to me by the king; have it inscribed on a stone *stele* and put it up in the sanctuary, so that the people in charge may know what the king decided on how things should be done. In the thirty-fifth year on the fifteenth of the month Daisios.[76] Ruling (*diagramma*) issued by the king Philip (the fifth). Nobody is allowed to alienate any of the property of Sarapis, by any means, or to mortgage anything of the other votive offerings or to propose any decree about these. And if anyone commits an act prohibited hereforth, he shall be guilty and the punishment shall be as in the case of theft and the alienated property shall be restored to the sanctuary, having been exacted from the property of the offender. Similarly, it is not allowed to open the treasuries of the god unless the *epistates** and the judges (*dikastai*) are present and to consume the money from the treasuries without good reason but only with their consent. Otherwise, anyone who acts in this way shall be liable to the same punishment.

Relevant texts

Military *diagramma*: **Amphipolis (Makedonia)**, Hatzopoulos (1996: ii no. 12) (*c.* 200 BC); **Chalkis (Euboia)**, *IG* xii Suppl. 644 (221–197 BC); *diagramma* concerning the *gymnasion*: **Amphipolis (Makedonia)**, Hatzopoulos (1996: ii no. 16) (182 BC); similar provisions in a decision of arbitrators over sacral property: **Athens**, *IG* ii² 1289 (260–240 BC); *prostagmata* of Ptolemies in Egypt collected by M.–Th. Lenger (ed.) (1964) *Corpus des Ordonnances des Ptolémées*, 2nd edn 1990, Brussels.

Further reading

Hatzopoulos (1996: 405–10).

---

75 Andronikos was a civic official, most probably an *epistates**.
76 The eighth month in the Makedonian calendar corresponding to May–June.

GLOSSARY

Agela, -ai (Gortyn): Young men in Gortyn, as in other Cretan *poleis*, were organized in age groups called *agelai* (lit. 'herds'). The minimum age for participation in such a group was the seventeenth year. The function of these groups can be paralleled to *ephebia*, an institution well known in Athens.

Agoranomos, -oi: *Agoranomoi* (lit. 'supervisors of the market') are widely attested in the Greek *poleis*. In Delos, there were three and their duty was to ensure respect for trading standards and to register the merchandise brought into the market. They had the authority to check the prices in the market, to receive complaints and to carry out the decisions of courts. In Erythrai, they had the responsibility of exacting the fines. In Thasos, they participated in the leasing of public property and were involved in the public funerals of those killed at war. In Athens, there were five allotted to supervise the market and five for the market in Peiraieus. Their duties included ensuring that the quality of the merchandise was acceptable and that no fraud could take place. Cf. *AthPol* 51.1 and Rhodes (1981: 575–6).

Aisymnetes, -ai (Teos): In Homeric times, *aisymnetai* were a kind of referee/judge while in classical times they were probably high-ranking officials in the *polis* administration.

Amphodarches, -ai (Pergamos): Their responsibility was the supervision of neighbourhoods, which involved keeping them clean, preventing anybody from digging ditches, making bricks, or installing uncovered pipes and receiving pledges when fines were not paid. They reported to the *astynomoi** to whom they were accountable. An official with a similar title and similar functions (*amphodogrammateus*) is attested in Graeco-Roman Egypt.

Andreion, -a (Gortyn): The gathering of men and the sharing of

146

meals was a common feature of almost all Dorian *poleis*. The Cretan *andreion* (lit. 'men's house') was, according to Aristotle, *Politics* 1272a, better organized than the Spartan because the Cretans contributed from all available sources of produce. Cf. M. Lavrencic (1988) 'Andreion', *Tyche* 3, 147–61.

Apetairos, -oi (Gortyn): People who did not belong to the Gortynian *etaireiai* were called *apetairoi*. They were free people without political rights and were of inferior status to that of full citizens. People expelled from the *etaireiai* were included in the class of *apetairoi* as, probably, were freed slaves. Cf. Willetts (1967: 12–13).

Apodektes, -ai: In Paros, an *apodektes* (lit. 'receiver') was involved in the maintenance of an archive in the sanctuary of Pythian Apollo. In Thasos, an *apodektes* dispensed portions of the sacrificed animal, equal to those for magistrates, to the relatives of war-dead. In Athens, there were ten *apodektai* allotted, one from each tribe. Their task was to keep track of the debts owed to the *polis*. If a citizen paid the debt, then his name was erased from the register; if he did not pay, he was registered as a state debtor and would have to pay double the amount or be jailed. Cf. *AthPol* 48.1–2, Rhodes (1981: 557–60) and Harrison (1971: 27–8).

Apodromos, -oi (Gortyn): *Apodromos* (lit. 'the one who has not the right to participate in a running competition') was a young man who had not reached his seventeenth year and was considered unable to act as a witness or to conclude transactions. Cf. Willetts (1967: 10–11).

Apologos, -oi (Thasos): They were involved in the settlement of commercial disputes and disputes arising in maritime transport, as well as policing the harbour. Cf. Velissaropoulou (1980: 260–3).

Archons, nine (Athens): A term designating the total of the allotted authorities in Athens. The nine archons were: a *polemarchos**, a *basileus**, an (*eponymous*) *archon* and the six *thesmothetai**. Cf. *AthPol* 55ff.

Areiopagos (Athens): The oldest and most venerated council in Athens. Its members were persons who had served as archons*. The political powers of the council were curtailed by Ephialtes in the 460s. It remained a lawcourt for cases of intentional homicide and treason. In the 4th century BC the council could investigate any affair concerning the *polis'* security and recommend a course of action. Cf. *AthPol* 3.6; 4.4; 8.2, 4; 16.8;

23.1; 25; 26; 27.1; 35.2; 41.2; 57.3, 4; 59.6; 60.2; of Rhodes (1981) and R.W. Wallace (1989) *The Areopagos Council to 307 BC*, Baltimore.

Astynomos, -oi (Pergamos): Magistrates responsible for overseeing the application of regulations on building and hygiene. They were accountable to *strategoi**. In Athens, they were responsible for supervising the hiring prices for certain categories of entertainers and for the upkeep of the building regulations and cleanliness in the *polis*. Cf. *AthPol* 50.1 and Rhodes (1981: 573–5).

Basileus, -eis: In Mytilene, officials attested as helping the return of the exiles and performing sacrifices on behalf of the *polis*. In Paros, suits against anyone abusing the archive were lodged with the *basileus* (lit. 'king'). In Athens, he was one of the nine archons. The *basileus* took care of religious celebrations, indictments for impiety were brought before him, and he conducted preliminary hearings and presided in homicide cases. Cf. *AthPol* 3.2–3, 5; 47.4; 55.1; 56.1; 57; and Rhodes (1981).

Chiliastys, -ai (Samos): Samians were divided into two tribes (*phylai*) and into *chiliastai* (lit. 'thousands'). The latter was probably the most functional subdivision, since *chiliastai* participated in the setting up and administration of the grain fund (see no. 45), as well as overseeing the administration of certain religious ceremonies (see no. 108). Cf. N.F. Jones (1987) *Public organization in ancient Greece. A documentary study*, 198–202, Philadelphia.

Demiourgos, -oi: In Thasos, officials with this title were responsible for prosecuting the officers from the mainland if they did not prosecute transgressors of the law on wine trade. According to Pouilloux (1954: 389) they were introduced during the reorganization of the *polis* after the political upheavals of the late 5th century BC. In Stymphalos, as in many other Doric *poleis*, the *demiourgos* was the eponymous archon. Cf. Ch. Veligianni-Terzi (1977) *Damiurgen. Zur Entwickelung einer Magistrature*, Heidelberg.

Demos, -oi (Athens): This was the major subdivision of the citizen body. In the whole of Attica there were 139 *demoi*. Kleisthenes, in his reforms in 508/7 BC, organized demes into ten tribes. *Demoi* had corporate existence and were administering their own affairs; membership of demes was hereditary and a (rather irregular) register of members was kept. Cf. *AthPol* 21.4, and Whitehead (1986).

Dikaskopos, -oi (Kyme, Mytilene): Officials appearing exclusively, so far, in Kyme and Mytilene. Their title, as well as the scraps of information about their function, implies that their job was connected with the administration of justice. In Kyme, they were expected to prosecute certain categories of offenders and keep half the fine, while in Mytilene they were not allowed to introduce any suits after the 'restoration' of democracy.

Dromeus, -eis (Gortyn): A man over 17 years of age and therefore having full legal rights to participate in transactions and to act as a witness. Cf. Willetts (1967: 11).

Eisagogeus, -eis (Arkesine – Amorgos): *Eisagogeis* (lit. 'introducers') were magistrates to whom suits were submitted and they, in turn, introduced them to the court. In Athens, there were five *eisagogeis*. Their responsibility was to introduce the 'monthly' cases to court. Cf. *AthPol* 52.2, Rhodes (1981: 582–3) and Harrison (1971: 21–3).

Eleven (Athens): The council selected by lot eleven members to act as caretakers for those imprisoned. Thieves, people enslaving free persons, and thieves arrested in the act were immediately put to death by them, if they admitted their crime; if they did not, each case was to be introduced in court. If the court decided that the defendant had committed the crime he was accused of, the Eleven were responsible for his execution. The Eleven also introduced cases of disputed property to court before confiscation. Cf. *AthPol* 7.3 and 52.1, Rhodes (1981: 579–82) and Harrison (1971: 17–18).

Emporion (Peiraieus): *Emporion* (lit. 'trading place') can mean either (i) the trading place, the market in a *polis*, supervised by officials of that *polis*, or (ii) a trading post, usually founded by the Greeks in remote areas of the Mediterranean coast and the Balkan inland. Cf. Velissaropoulou (1980: 29–34), and for the regulation of an *emporion* in sense (ii) in Pistyros (Thrace), of the second half of the 4th century BC, *BCH* 118 (1994) 1–15, and in Pizos (Thrace), *IGB* 1690 (AD 202).

Ephetai (Athens): Jurors older than 50, possibly allotted from the members of the *Areiopagos** sitting in cases of justifiable homicide (in the *Delphinion*), of unintentional homicide (in the Palladion), and of a defendant exiled for another killing (in the Phreatto). See D.M. MacDowell (1963) *Athenian homicide law in the age of the orators*, 48–58, Manchester, and commentary in no 63.

Epiballon, -tes (Gortyn): A category of people called to inherit when there were no children, brothers or sisters (or their children) of the deceased. Unfortunately, we do not know what kind of nearest relatives were included in the term *epiballontes*. Cf. Willetts (1967: 18–22).

Epimeletes, -ai: *Epimeletai* (lit. 'caretakers') are widely attested in ancient Greek *poleis*. Their duties varied according to *polis* and time. In Keos, an *epimeletes* was involved in the maintenance of the fountains. In Athens, there were several officials called *epimeletai*. Some of them were responsible for the fountains, others for supervising trade, and others for religious festivals. Cf. *AthPol* 43.1, 51.4, 56.4, 57.1, and Rhodes (1981: 516, 579, 627, 636).

Epistates, -ai: *Epistatai* (lit. 'supervisors') are attested at different times in several *poleis*. They may be members of the *polis* administration or officers of associations. In Samos, an *epistates* was not allowed to propose any decree or law against the grain law; in the decree from the phrygian Zelea an *epistates* seems to act as an eponymous archon. In Thasos, *epistatai* were responsible for the cleaning of the streets and for exacting fines. In Athens, there was an *epistates* for each day and night for the councillors of the presiding tribe. He kept the keys to the treasury, to the archive, and the seal of the *polis*. When there was a meeting of the Council and assembly, the *epistates* allotted nine presiding councillors from the non-presiding tribes and from them selected by lot an *epistates* to be responsible for the business of the day. Cf. *AthPol* 44.1–2, and Rhodes (1981: 531–4).

Etaireia, -ai (Gortyn): Male citizens in Gortyn were organized in *etaireiai*. Participation in them guaranteed political rights, and exclusion from *etaireiai* meant loss of these rights. The assembly of an *etaireia* was the venue for the performance of adoptions. Cf. Willetts (1967: 11).

Exetastes, -ai (Athens, Beroia): In Athens the title does not denote a particular official but *ad hoc* appointed officials to investigate. In Beroia, *exetastai* received and probably examined the accounts of the *gymnasion*. In other *poleis*, they were responsible for inscribing the decisions of the Council and of the assembly. See S. Gelato (1983) 'La magistratura degli exetastai' in A. Kalogeropoulou (ed.) *Acts of the 8th Congress of Greek and Latin Epigraphy*, vol. 2, 123–5, Athens.

Gynaikonomos, -oi (Thasos, Gambreion): *Gynaikonomoi* (lit. 'regulators of women') are attested in several *poleis*, including Athens and Sparta of the Imperial era; their duty was mainly to apply the laws about luxury in periods of mourning and to supervise women's behaviour during ceremonies or festivals. Cf. Pouilloux (1954: 407–10) and C. Wehrli (1962) 'Les gynéconomes', *MH* 19, 33–8.

Hieropoios, -oi: Magistrates widely attested in antiquity, not only in *poleis* but in cult associations and other groups. In Thasos, *hieropoioi* were responsible for the inscription of a decree in the sanctuary of Herakles. In Beroia, they were responsible for the organization of the sacrifice and the ensuing feast for the young men during the festival of Hermes. In Athens, the Council elected ten *hieropoioi* for the sacrifices and ten others for performing sacrifices and celebrating festivals. Cf. *La loi gymnasiarchique*, 110–13, *AthPol* 54.6, and Rhodes (1981: 605–10).

Hippeus, -eis (Athens): In the Solonian classification, *hippeis* (lit. 'cavalrymen' or 'knights') were the second property class. They were so called because in case of war they could provide a horse. Cf. *AthPol* 7.3, and Rhodes (1981: 137–8).

Kadestas, -ai (Gortyn): Their responsibility included the guardianship of an heiress and action on her behalf in cases of seduction and marriage. For R.F. Willetts (1965) *Ancient Crete. A social history from early times until the Roman occupation*, London, *kadestai* were an exogamous grouping with ties created by marriage. Cf. Morris (1990).

Klaros (Gortyn): A group of people called to inherit if there were no children, brothers, sisters (or their children) and *epiballontes*. Who was included in this group is not clear. Willetts (1967: 10–12) claims that the serfs attached to the property composed the *klaros*.

Kolakretes, -tai (Athens): Officials similar to treasurers, originating possibly in the pre-Solonian era. They were abolished *c.* 411 BC. Cf. *AthPol* 7.3, and Rhodes (1981: 139).

Kosmos, -oi (Gortyn): The chief officials in Gortyn were called *kosmoi*. They were ten in number and were elected from certain tribes only. Among their duties were included leading in war, religious duties, adjudicating cases where foreigners were involved, adoption, caring for an heiress, and introducing laws for approval to the assembly of the citizens.

Lebes, -tes (Gortyn): Used in Crete in the early 5th century BC for payments in kind instead of coins.

Meledonos, -oi (Samos): A *meledonos* (lit. 'manager') was responsible for the administration of the grain fund. He was elected by the assembly and scrutinized for his property qualification.

Mna: Unit of the Athenian coinage system. One mna was equal to one-sixtieth of a talent, or to 100 drachmas or 600 hundred obols*. It weighed *c.* 433 grams.

Mnemon, -es: *Mnemones* (lit. 'memorizers') were officials entrusted with the administration of archives (Paros), or acted as registrars (Halikarnassos). In some cases they were the main authority in the *polis* (Gazoros). Cf. Aristot. *Pol.* 1321 b39.

Neopoios, -oi (Samos and Halikarnassos): In Samos, officials responsible for the administration (supervision of the space allotted to retailers, for the imposition and exacting of fines) of the temple of Hera. In Halikarnassos, the *naopoios* was, together with the *prytanis**, the highest ranking official. Cf. the tables of *naopoioi* from Delphoi *Syll*[3] 244–8 (349–340 BC).

Neotas, -ai (Gortyn): A council of youth. Appears in two inscriptions, one of which is the coin decree (see no. 51). It seems that this council counterbalanced the council of Elders (*Gerousia*).

Nomothetes, -ai (Athens): A panel of eligible members of the popular court (*Heliaia*) who were appointed to hear proposed legislation, at the request of the assembly of the people, and make a final decision. This procedure was set up after 403 BC.

Obol, -oi: The basic unit in Athenian coinage. Six obols equalled one drachma, and one mna* was equal to 600 obols. The jury pay in Athens in the late 5th and 4th centuries was three obols. In Gortyn, six obols were equal to one drachma and twelve obols equalled one stater.

Oikeus, -eis (Gortyn): The term describes household slaves and distinguishes them from common chattel slaves. These household slaves were the property of the house owner. *Oikeis* had a few rights, such as the right to marry and to divorce and to own animals (see nos. 16 and 3). Cf. Willetts (1967: 13–17).

Pentakosiomedimnos, -oi (Athens): Members of the highest property class in the Solonian classification. Cf. *AthPol* 7.3 and Rhodes (1981: 137–8).

Pentekostologos, -oi: Officials attested in several *poleis* (Athens, Delos, Kyparissia). Their main duty was to exact the 2 per cent duty (hence their name) on imported and/or exported goods. For the different taxes on imports, see Velissaropoulou (1980: 208–15).

Polemarchos, -oi: In Thasos, a *polemarchos* was involved in maintaining ritual purity before funerals of the war-dead. In Athens, he was one of the nine archons. He was responsible for cases brought against foreigners, resident foreigners (*metoikoi*) and representatives of foreigners (*proxenoi*), as well as suits submitted by them. He introduced cases against resident foreigners in inheritance disputes. Cf. *AthPol* 58 and Rhodes (1981: 650–7).

Poletes, -tai (Athens): There were ten *poletai* (lit. 'sellers') allotted, one from each tribe. Their duties included the leasing of public property, the selling of the right to collect taxes, the right to exploit mines, the auctioning of property belonging to exiled or banned Athenians. Cf. *AthPol* 47, Rhodes (1981: 549–57), Kl. Hallof (1990) 'Der Verkauf konfiszierten Vermögens vor den Poleten in Athen', *Klio* 72, 402–26, and the remarks of M. Langdon (1994) 'Public auctions in ancient Athens' in R. Osborne and S. Hornblower (eds) *Ritual, finance, politics. Athenian democratic accounts presented to D. Lewis*, 253–65, Oxford.

Politarches, -ai (Beroia): A distinctively Makedonian institution attested, outside Beroia, in Amphipolis, Philippopolis, Thessalonike and *poleis* under Makedonian influence. Introduced in the late 3rd or early 2nd century BC, there were, initially, two, but in Roman times their number was increased to five. They had executive power, they could introduce laws, convene and preside in the assembly and the Council. Recent discussion in Hatzopoulos (1996).

Prostates, -tai (Thasos): Officials introduced for a short period of time into the political structure of the Thasian *polis* at the beginning the 4th century BC. Their remit included most probably the reconciliation of the factions in the *polis* and the protection of the returning exiles. Cf. Pouilloux (1954: 388).

Prytanis, -eis (Erythrai, Athens, Halikarnassos, Arkesine – Amorgos): In Samos, they convened the assembly of the citizens. They put down names of guarantors and scrutinized property. In Athens, fifty members of each tribe were elected as members of the Council and each tribe presided for a month in the workings of the Council. Then the representatives of each tribe assumed the title of *prytaneis*. Cf. *AthPol* 43.2 and Rhodes (1981: 517–22).

Sitones, -ai (Samos): A citizen elected by the assembly, whose responsibility was to buy grain. The only qualification he was required to have was property worth two talents or more.

Sitophylax, -kes (Athens): Officials responsible for the supervision of the grain trade in the market, the price of flour, and the price and weight of loaves of bread. Five were allotted for Athens and five for Peiraieus, but later in the 4th century BC their number increased to twenty in Athens and fifteen in Peiraieus. Cf. *AthPol* 51.3 and Rhodes (1981: 577–9).

Stephanephoros: (lit. 'the crown-bearer'). Official equal to the (eponymous) archon in Athens, widely attested in Asia Minor (Gambreion, Priene) during Roman times.

Strategos, -oi (Mytilene, Pergamos, Sikyon): *Strategos* (lit. 'general') usually denotes the military commander of the *polis*. However, in some *poleis* he might have been the most important official. In Hellenistic times, *strategoi* were appointed by the monarchs as administrators of regions.

Syllogeus, -eis tou demou (Athens): Officers appearing at the beginning of the 4th century BC. Their task was to punish truancy from the assembly and supervise the payment of the fee for attending the assembly. In the inscription included (see no. 50) they are charged with punishing the tester, who was a slave. Cf. *IG* ii² 1257 (324/3 BC) and *IG* ii² 1425.129 and 224 (368/7 BC).

Symposion (Thasos, Gortyn): *Symposion* in archaic Greece denoted the drinking parties and banquets usually attended by the aristocracy. Cf. O. Murray (1990) *Sympotica. A symposium on symposion*, Oxford, and for a wider discussion of banqueting, P. Schmitt-Pantell (1992) *La cité au banquet. Histoire des répas publics dans les cités grecques*, Rome (Bibliothèque de l'École Française à Rome). However, *symposion* in Thasos clearly denotes a location in the *polis*, while the Gortynian reference implies an institutionalized gathering, synonymous with *agela** and *andreion**.

Thesmothetes, -ai (Athens): The original responsibility of the *thesmothetai* in pre-Drakonian Athens (7th century BC) was the preservation of the decisions of the archons which had the force of law. They were elected for one year. In 4th-century Athens, they were appointed by lot from among the citizens. They were responsible for the allocation of courts on each day and for the presiding magistrate. They introduced denunciations (*eisaggeliai*), suits against the president of *prytaneis**, against the *epistates** and the generals, suits for proposing an illegal decree or a law in conflict with an existing one, suits for usurpation of civic rights, corruption to avoid prosecution for usurping civic rights, sycophancy, false inscription of debtors, and adultery. They introduced the procedure of scrutiny of magistrates, cases of people rejected by their demes and people condemned by the Council. They introduced cases concerning trade, mines, and slaves who had insulted citizens and given false testimony. They ratified the judicial agreements with other *poleis* and they introduced cases regulated by these agreements in the Areiopagos. They participated in allotting the judges. Cf. *AthPol* 3.4; 55.1; 59, Rhodes (1981: 657–68) and Harrison (1971: 15–16).

Thes, -tes (Athens): The lowest property class in the Solonian classification. In the beginning they could only participate in the assembly and in the courts. Cf. *AthPol* 7.3 and Rhodes (1981: 136–41).

Timouchos, -oi (Teos): Title used to denote *polis* officials, usually the highest in rank. Originated in the aristocracies of *poleis* in Asia Minor. Cf. G. Gottlieb (1967) *Timuchen. Ein Beitrag zum griechischen Staatsrecht*, Heidelberg (Sitzungsberichte der Heidelberger Akademie der Wissenschaften, Philos.-Hist. Klasse).

Titas, -ai (Gortyn): Officials appearing in several inscriptions from Gortyn. Their responsibility seems to have been the exaction of fines. Cf. *IC* iv 165 (3rd century BC).

Trierarchos, -oi (Athens): The obligation of wealthy Athenians to undertake certain public functions was called *leitourgia*. One of the most burdensome was *trierarchia* (lit. 'leading of a *trieres*'). It involved not only commanding a ship but also bearing all the expenses for the running of that ship for one year. The Athenians tried several systems of sharing this expensive public function.

Zeugites, -ai (Athens): The third property class in fourfold Solonian classification. Their name was once thought to be connected with the ability to provide two oxen; however, it seems now that their name may have come from their participation as armed citizens (*hoplitai*) in the wars. They could be elected as one of the *nine archons** after the middle of the 5th century BC. Cf. *AthPol* 4.3; 7.3; 26.2 and Rhodes (1981: 136–41, 330).

REFERENCES

Asheri, D. (1969) *Leggi greche sul problema dei debiti*, Pisa.

Biscardi, A. (1982) *Diritto greco antico*, Milan.

Boegehold, A.L. and A.C. Scafuro (eds) (1994) *Athenian identity and civic ideology*, Princeton.

Burkert, W. (1985) *Greek religion. Archaic and classical*, English translation 1985, Oxford.

Carey, C. (1995) 'Rape and adultery in Athenian law', *CQ* 45, 407–17.

Cohen, D. (1983) *Theft in Athenian law*, Münich (Münchener Beiträge zur Papyrusforschung und antiken Rechtsgeschichte 74).

—— (1991) *Law, sexuality and society*, Cambridge.

—— (1995) *Law, violence, and community in classical Athens*, Cambridge.

Cohen, E.E. (1973) *Athenian maritime courts*, Princeton.

—— (1993) *Athenian society and banking*, Princeton.

Dimakis, P.D. (1959) *O thesmos tes proikos kata to archaion ellenikon dikaion*, Athens.

Dover, K.J. (1974) *Greek popular morality in the time of Plato & Aristotle*, London.

van Effenterre, H. and F. Ruze (eds) (1994) *Nomima. Recueil d'inscriptions politiques et juridiques de l'archaisme grec* 2 vols, Roma (Collection de l'École Française de Rome 188).

Finley, M.I. (1951) *Studies in land and credit in ancient Athens, 500–250 B.C.*, with a new Introduction by P. Millett, 1985, New Haven.

Fisher, N.R.E. (1992) *Hybris*, London.

Foxhall, L. and A.D.E. Lewis (eds) (1996) *Greek law in its political setting. Justifications not justice*, Oxford.

Gagarin, M. (1985) 'The function of witnesses at Gortyn', *Symposion 1985*, 29–54.

Gauthier, Ph. (1972) *Symbola. Les étrangers et la justice dans les cités grecques*, Nancy.

Gehrke, H.-J. (1985) *Stasis. Untersuchungen zu den inneren Kriegen in den griechischen Staaten des 5. und 4. Jahrhunderts v. Chr.*, München (Vestigia. Beiträge zur alten Geschichte 35).

Graham, A.J. (1983) *Colony and mother city in ancient Greece*, 2nd edn, Manchester.

Hansen, M.H. (1976) *Apagoge, endeixis and ephegesis against kakourgoi, atimoi, and pheugontes. A study in the Athenian administration of justice in the fourth century BC*, Copenhagen (Odense University Classical Studies 8).

Harrison, A.R.W. (1968) *The law of Athens*, vol. 1, Oxford.

—— (1971) *The law of Athens*, vol. 2, Oxford.

Hatzopoulos, M.B. (1996) *Macedonian institutions under the kings. A historical and epigraphical study*, 2 vols, Athens (Meletemata 22).

Isaac, B. (1986) *The Greek settlements in Thrace until the Macedonian conquest*, Amsterdam.

Karabelias, E. (1982) 'La succession ab intestat en droit attique', *Symposion 1982*, 41–63.

—— (1992) 'L'acte a cause de mort (diathéke) dans le droit attique' in *Actes à cause de mort* I, 47–121, Brussels (Recueils de la société Jean Bodin pour l'histoire comparative des institutions 59).

Klingenberg, E. (1974) 'La legge platonica sulle fontane pubbliche', *Symposion 1974*, 283–303.

—— (1976) *Platons Nomoi Georgikoi und das positive griechische Recht*, Berlin (Abhandlungen zur Rechtswissenschaftlichen Grundlagenforschung 17).

Laiou, A.E. (1993) (ed.) *Consent and coercion to sex and marriage in ancient and medieval societies*, Washington.

Lambert, S.D. (1993) *The phratries of Attica*, Oxford.

Lonis, R. (1991) 'La réintégration des exiles politiques en Grèce. Le problème des biens' in P. Goukowsky and C. Brixhe (eds) *Hellenika Symmikta. Histoire, Archeologie, Epigraphie*, 91–109, Nancy (Études d'archeologie classique 7).

MacDowell, D.M. (1978) *The law in classical Athens*, London.

—— (1986) *Spartan law*, Edinburgh.

—— (1990) *Demosthenes. Against Meidias*, Oxford.

Maffi, A. (1983) *Studi di epigrafia giuridica greca*, Milano.

Martin, R. (1974) *L'urbanisation dans la Grèce antique*, 2nd edn, Paris.

Metzger, R.R. (1973) *Untersuchungen zum Haftungs- und Vermögens- Recht von Gortyn*, Basel (Schweizerische Beiträge zur Altertumswissenschaft 13).

Millett, P.C. (1991) *Lending and borrowing in classical Athens*, Cambridge.

Morris, I. (1990) 'The Gortyn code and Greek kinship', *GRBS* 31, 233–54.

Parke, H.W. (1977) *Festivals of the Athenians*, London.

Parker, R.C.T. (1983) *Miasma. Pollution and purification in early Greek religion*, Oxford.

—— (1996) *Athenian religion. A history*, Oxford.

REFERENCES

Pouilloux, J. (1954) *Recherches sur l'histoire et les cultes de Thasos. De la fondation de la cité à 196 avant J.-C.*, Paris (Études Thasiennes 3).

Rhodes, P.J. (1981) *A commentary on the Aristotelian Athenaion Politeia*, Oxford.

Schaps, D.M. (1979) *The economic rights of women in ancient Greece*, Edinburgh.

Sealey, R. (1990) *Women and law in classical Greece*, Princeton.

Shipley, G. (1987) *A history of Samos. 800–188 B.C.*, Oxford.

Todd, S.C. (1993) *The shape of Athenian law*, Oxford.

Travlos, J. (1970) *Pictorial dictionary of Athens*, Princeton.

Vatin, Cl. (1976) 'Jardins et services de voirie', *BCH* 100, 555–64.

Velissaropoulou, J. (1980) *Les nauclères grecs: recherches sur les institutions maritimes en Grèce et dans l'Orient Hellénisé*, Genève.

Whitehead, D. (1986) *The demes of Attica, 508/7–c. 250 BC: A political and social study*, Princeton.

Willetts, R.F. (1967) *The law code of Gortyn*, Berlin (Kadmos Suppl).

INDEX OF SOURCES

INDEX

19213985R00113

Made in the USA
Middletown, DE
10 April 2015